# EXPERIMENTS IN MUSICAL INTELLIGENCE

**THE COMPUTER MUSIC AND DIGITAL AUDIO SERIES**
John Strawn, Founding Editor
Christopher Yavelow, Series Editor

DIGITAL AUDIO SIGNAL PROCESSING
Edited by John Strawn

COMPOSERS AND THE COMPUTER
Edited by Curtis Roads

DIGITAL AUDIO ENGINEERING
Edited by John Strawn

COMPUTER APPLICATIONS IN MUSIC: A BIBLIOGRAPHY
Deta S. Davis

THE COMPACT DISC HANDBOOK
Ken C. Pohlmann

COMPUTERS AND MUSICAL STYLE
David Cope

MIDI: A COMPREHENSIVE INTRODUCTION
Joseph Rothstein
William Eldridge, *Volume Editor*

SYNTHESIZER PERFORMANCE AND REAL-TIME TECHNIQUES
Jeff Pressing
Chris Meyer, *Volume Editor*

MUSIC PROCESSING
Edited by Goffredo Haus

COMPUTER APPLICATIONS IN MUSIC:
A BIBLIOGRAPHY, SUPPLEMENT I
Deta S. Davis
Garrett Bowles, *Volume Editor*

GENERAL MIDI
Stanley Jungleib

EXPERIMENTS IN MUSICAL INTELLIGENCE
David Cope

■

Volume 12 • THE COMPUTER MUSIC AND DIGITAL AUDIO SERIES

# EXPERIMENTS IN MUSICAL INTELLIGENCE

David Cope

■

 A-R Editions, Inc.

Madison, Wisconsin

Library of Congress Cataloging-in-Publication Data

Cope, David.
    Experiments in musical intelligence / David Cope.
        p.    cm. — (The computer music and digital audio series ; v. 12)
    Includes bibliographical references and index.
    "The accompanying CD-ROM and its contents require an Apple Macintosh computer that runs system 7.0 or later with at least four megabytes (eight or more megabytes suggested) of RAM. The code requires Apple Computer's Macintosh Common LISP software and MIDI Manager"—p.
    ISBN 0-89579-314-8
    1. Composition (Music) — Computer programs.  2. Cope, David.  EMI.  I. Cope, David.  SARA.  II. Title.  III. Series.
MT56.C67    1995
781.3'453—dc20                                    95-6042
                                                            CIP
                                                            MN

A-R Editions, Inc., Madison, Wisconsin 53717–1903
   © 1996 by A-R Editions, Inc.
   All rights reserved.
   Printed in the United States of America.

10 9 8 7 6 5 4 3 2 1

# Contents

**Preface**     vii
     Description of CD-ROM   xi

■ **Chapter One    Background and Overview**     1
     Challenges   23
     General Algorithm   25
     Approaches to Analysis   27
     Approaches to Pattern Matching   33
     Augmented Transition Networks   40

■ **Chapter Two    The Analysis Component**     53
     Databases   54
     Analytical Techniques   64
     Analysis Program   73

■ **Chapter Three    The Pattern-Matching Component**     79
     Testing the Signature Theory   81
     Pattern-Matching Techniques   83
     Pattern-Matching Program   118

■ **Chapter Four    The Object System**     123
     Object Orientation   124
     Classes and Superclasses   131

Slots   131
Methods   139
Object Program   140

## ■ Chapter Five   The ATN Component   151
ATN Basics in LISP   154
ATN Basics in Music   162
ATN Program   183

## ■ Chapter Six   An Application-Level Program and Sample Output   189
Putting It All Together   189
Application-Level Program   193
Interface   196
Variations   199
Sample Output and Extensions   201

## ■ Chapter Seven   Conclusions and the Future   217
Expanding the Parameters   218
Beyond MIDI   234
Conclusions   236
The Future   244

## Bibliography   251

## Index   257

# Preface

I began *Experiments in Musical Intelligence* (EMI) in the early 1980s as the result of a composing block (Cope 1988). Issues of musical style surfaced immediately as it became clear that I wanted to create programs that could produce music in my style. Using musical recombinancy, pattern matching, augmented transition networks (ATNs), and object orientation, the EMI program eventually created new examples of music in, arguably, the styles of classical composers such as Mozart and Bach as well as the more contemporary Cope.

As a result of this research, I completed my book *Computers and Musical Style* (1991a), which presents a history of automated music (chapter 1), relationships between music and language (chapter 2), an introduction to the computer language LISP (chapter 3), a small composing program (chapter 4), examples of the output of EMI (chapter 5), and a look at the future of musical automata via interactive composition (chapter 6). Although seemingly all-inclusive, *Computers and Musical Style* does leave out important material:

> The functions presented in Chapter 4 did not create the EMI inventions shown at the beginning of this chapter. They did, however, present enough of the theory and principles for readers to extend the code and compose similar works. The music that follows requires a more substantial leap of faith. The functions responsible for its creation are far too elaborate and lengthy to present here in their entirety. (Cope 1991a, p. 147)

*Experiments in Musical Intelligence* is intended to address this required leap of faith and present the code for more elaborate replications. Those familiar with *Computers and Musical Style* will be able to continue developing LISP skills begun with that book. They will also be able to observe the basic principles introduced in *Computers and Musical Style* that are elaborated on and extended in the present book. Readers unfamiliar with *Computers and Musical Style* should read that volume, although such referencing is not absolutely necessary for reading *Experiments in Musical Intelligence*.

Chapter 1 of this book describes the computational problems posed for creating music in the styles of encoded music. This chapter includes a number of important historical precedents for algorithmic composition, including *Musikalisches Würfelspiel* (a "musical dice game") and other less formal examples, and provides a basic overview of EMI through example algorithms, giving the reader a broader sense of the program and its various components. Chapter 2 covers the ways in which EMI stores and accesses data, including details on the EMI database format, the weightings used for harmonic analysis, and the principles of clarification. This chapter also covers the basic techniques for melodic, harmonic, and structural analysis. Chapter 3 presents basic pattern-matching principles, the use of global variables (controllers) in the matching process, and the techniques of pitch and interval matching. It also describes how pattern matching more than one work can lead to signature recognition and culminates with a sample pattern-matching session, in which a Mozart signature is revealed.

Chapter 4 acquaints the reader with the basic principles of object orientation and the advantages of using such approaches. The Common LISP Object System (CLOS) as outlined by Steele (1990), is broadly described in this section. The nature of classes and superclasses, instances, and inheritance are discussed. This chapter also discusses the concepts of standard and user-created methods and why the EMI approach follows the CLOS standard. Chapter 5 presents natural language processing (NLP) finite state, recursive, and augmented transition network (ATN) musical examples. It also describes the symbiotic relationship between objects and ATN in EMI and ATN information stored in slots in objects that can then be musically recombined. Finally, it describes linear and nonlinear transition network subtypes as well as the techniques of micro-ATN (MATN).

Chapter 6 outlines how the various programs (analysis, pattern matching, objects, and ATN) combine at the application level to produce large, robust programs in EMI. This chapter also covers the techniques that EMI uses for such components as counterpoint, form, and melodic variations. Chapter 7 discusses program expansions—including dynamics, articulations, timbre, tempo, and non-pitch/duration pattern matching for stylistic signatures—and self-referencing program techniques, and non-MIDI output. It presents examples from an EMI opera based on texts by Mozart as well as examples from a collection of five thousand machine-composed works. This chapter also discusses the prospects for algorithmic composition in the future.

Although EMI is the subject of this book, most of the code presented here and on the accompanying CD-ROM is a subset of EMI called SARA (Simple Analytic Recombinancy Algorithm). EMI and SARA have many things in common, but they also differ in many ways. I have attempted, whenever possible, to distinguish these differences and to articulate their similarities. In chapter 3, for example, there are separate subsections on EMI and SARA pattern-matching controllers. Also, the musical examples throughout the book clearly differentiate between EMI and SARA output. In contrast, the sections on analysis (chapter 2), object orientation (chapter 4), and ATNs (chapter 5) underscore the similarities between EMI and SARA.

The code of SARA presented in this book and on the accompanying CD-ROM will produce output in the form shown in many of the examples. Both source and object code for SARA are included on this CD-ROM, as are fast-loading (.fasl) database files. The CD-ROM contains manuals in a variety of formats for operating and understanding this code. Thus, you may rewrite or add to the code to fulfill more specialized needs. Musicologists may require only pattern matching in attempting, for example, to verify the authenticity of musical signatures. Composers might want a more interactive top level. Analysts may be interested only in those aspects of the program that could corroborate certain functional or hierarchical models of analysis.

The accompanying CD-ROM also contains a number of useful adjunct programs. The program *Würfelspiel* contains *Musikalisches Würfelspiel* by a number of eighteenth-century composers including Johann Philipp Kirnberger, Carl Philipp Emanuel Bach, Wolfgang Amadeus Mozart, Joseph Haydn, and others discussed in chapter 1 of this book. The *Is It Mozart* program was demonstrated at the American Association of Artificial Intelligence (AAAI) conference in San Jose, California, in the summer of 1992. Hypercard versions of *Is It Mozart* as well as *Chopin* and *Bach Chorales*, both of which involve recombinance in a non-LISP environment, are also included. All these programs demonstrate aspects of the EMI program, and compositions are playable through the Macintosh speakers using sampled piano sounds. I have included the code contained in *Computers and Musical Style* as well as that code from a number of my published articles about EMI on the CD-ROM.

The accompanying CD-ROM requires an Apple Macintosh computer running system 7.0 or later with at least four megabytes (eight or more megabytes suggested) of RAM. The code requires Apple Computer's *Macintosh Common LISP* software and *MIDI Manager*. Many of the programs (especially SARA) also require a MIDI interface, a sampler, proper cables, and playback equipment. Users of the CD-ROM are expected to have a working knowledge of how Macintoshes work (pull-down menus, windows, etc.) and how to connect MIDI devices. More advanced musical skills are highly recommended but not required. You need no knowledge of programming. Most of the operations of SARA can be accomplished using the point-and-click operation of the Macintosh mouse. However, skill with Common LISP at the level of that presented in chapter 3 of *Computers and Musical Style* and chapter 4 of this book would be helpful.

It should be noted that SARA, although modeled on EMI, can only rarely be expected to equal the quality of EMI's output and then, only in small forms. The reasons for not including the full EMI program here are numerous. Suffice it to say that the reader of this book is best served by a small, fast, easily learned program rather than the opposite.

I wish to thank Scot Gresham-Lancaster for all his important contributions over the years as well as Fred Cohen, Randall Wong, Fredric Lieberman, Eleanor Selfridge-Field, and Walter Hewlett, who have worked so tirelessly to promote EMI's works as well as for the use of CCARH (Center for Computer Assisted Research in the Humanities) databases, and Joseph Chung, Jon Hallstrom and Dale Skrien (along with Gunnar Proppe, Zhongwei Wu, Steve Lilley and Zachary Geisz) for much of the MIDI code on the accompanying CD-ROM. I would also like to thank Victor Sachse, whose faith in EMI fostered the first CD of EMI-composed works (CRC-2184) on Centaur Records (8867 Highland Rd., Suite 206, Baton Rouge, La. 70808). Continued thanks go to those I have mentioned already in *Computers and Musical Style*. Without the moral support and advice from colleagues such as these, work such as EMI could not take place.

## ■ DESCRIPTION OF CD-ROM

The EMI CD-ROM that accompanies *Experiments in Musical Intelligence* contains almost 650 megabytes of machine composing and performing programs as well as musical examples in a variety of formats.

**Requirements**

Macintosh 680xx series computer or Power Macintosh
8 megabytes of RAM minimum
4 megabytes of free disk space
System 7.0 or later

*CD-Browser*
Requires Sound Manager 3.0 or later for audio playback
Requires QuickTime and QuickTime Musical Instruments extensions for MIDI
Requires QuickTime PowerPlug extension when used with a Power Macintosh
(All extensions should be in the Extensions folder in your System folder)

*Apple's HyperCard or HyperCard Player*
To use the documents found in the HyperCard folder

*Apple's Macintosh Common LISP version 3.0 or later*
To use the documents found in the LISP folder

**Contents**

The EMI CD-ROM contains a Read Me First! document, the CD-Browser application, and five folders at the uppermost level.

*CD-Browser*
This CD-Browser program lets you quickly examine the entire contents of the CD-ROM. With a single mouse-click you can read all the text documents; audition any of the digital audio files; play back any of the MIDI files (without an external synthesizer); view all the program code, databases, and manuals found in the LISP folder; print any of the documents; and even launch the HyperCard Composing programs (provided you have enough memory for both the Browser and the HyperCard). Click on the tabs at the top of the main window to navigate between data types. Next, choose items to view or audi-

tion from the scrolling list by clicking on the items with the mouse pointer. Alternatively, you can use the Right and Left arrow-keys to navigate the top-level tabs and the Up and Down arrow-keys to navigate the scrolling list, in which case you must initiate playback with the Enter key. For both digital audio playback and MIDI playback you can press Command-Period to stop playback at any time. Most of the data types offer several additional controls. For example, Audio and MIDI data present a volume slider, whereas the Code area provides an optional external viewing window. A few additional self-explanatory options are found in the menus.

Note that the CD-Browser does not open any of the Microsoft Word format files on the CD-ROM. However, there are text-only copies of all these files to which the Browser does provide access. In several cases, the original Microsoft Word documents contain embedded graphics, which are not found in the text-only versions of the files. In most cases, when viewing a text-only version of one of these files, you will notice a reference to a missing graphic or a little white box to indicate that there is a graphic in the Microsoft Word version of the same file (always found in the same folder).

Alternatively, rather than use the Browser, you may wish to navigate the entire CD-ROM as if it were another hard disk connected to your system. In this case, you can audition the digital audio and MIDI examples with your favorite audio or MIDI software (all the MIDI files are SMFs). To use the files in the LISP folder, you need to read the instructions found in the document cd-rom cross ref, which is located in the This CD-ROM folder inside the Read folder. You will also need to copy some files to your local disk.

### *Read*

The Read folder contains text files in two versions: (1) those created by Microsoft Word version 5 and (2) those created as text-only files that can be read by any text-editing or page-layout program. Such files explain how to use the various programs on this disk. Because these files often contain information without which a program will not run or may crash during operation, it is highly advisable that users take the time to read them before attempting to use any of the programs in that folder.

### *Hypercard*

There are three types of Hypercard documents on this CD-ROM: (1) Is It Mozart, a program used for the first time at the 1992 American Association of Artificial Intelligence conference in San Jose, California; (2) composing programs such as Bach Chorales and Chopin

Mazurkas, which demonstrate various principles described in *Experiments in Musical Intelligence*; and (3) performance files, which play back various EMI-composed works. You may also audition these performance files directly from the CD-Browser.

Hypercard requires that you have a Macintosh with a minimum of 8 megabytes of RAM. It may be necessary to increase the HyperCard's memory allocation using the Finder's Get Info option (Command i), which displays a window in which you can set HyperCard's preferred size. It would also be useful, but not necessary, to listen to the examples using speakers of a higher quality than those built into your Macintosh; for example, plug a component system into the phone jack at the rear of the Mac or on the side of your monitor.

### LISP

The LISP files on this CD-ROM require that you install the Apple MIDI Manager extensions and that you have Apple's Macintosh Common LISP version 3.0 or later. This latter program should be placed, along with its Examples and Library folders, in the LISP folder (see the various manuals in the LISP folder of this CD-ROM). Also, you will need a MIDI interface, a synthesizer or sampler, a playback system, and the connections between these various pieces of equipment. Most of these are standard equipment for composers. The one item that is not, Macintosh Common LISP, will provide the means to understand and implement a number of the programs discussed in *Experiments in Musical Intelligence* as well as in *Computers and Musical Style* (see the Bibliography file in this folder).

Each of the LISP programs on the CD-ROM comes with a manual that describes in detail how to initiate and use the program. Because these manuals often contain information without which a program will not run or may crash during operation, it is highly advisable that users take the time to read them before attempting to use the program in that folder.

### MIDI

We have provided a CD-Browser program that plays all the example MIDI files without requiring any external MIDI devices. Alternatively, you can use an internal (virtual) synthesizer such as the commercial Cyber-Synth (available from CyberSound) or the built-in synthesizer that came with your Macintosh or Macintosh System Update—this uses the sounds in the QuickTime Musical Instruments extension. If you want to send MIDI output to an external device, you will need a hardware MIDI interface, which should be connected to a MIDI device of your preference. A high-quality sampler with a selection of traditional musical instrument samples is recommended, because timbral quality contributes to the overall aesthetic response to the output of this software. Your MIDI device should have a range of at least five octaves.

### Audio

The CD-Browser program also allows you to audition many of the examples referred to in the text. Alternatively, you could use a separate sound playback program to listen to these files. You will find three subfolders in the Audio folder: (1) Examples, (2) emi mac AIFs, and (3) emi ppc AIFs. The soundfiles in the Examples folder are numbered to correspond to musical examples in the text. They are in CD-quality format: 16-bit stereo 44.1 kHz AIFF files. The remaining two folders contain 8-bit mono AIFF files that are identical to the sounds referenced by the documents in the EMI HyperCard folder with the exception of their sample rates. The AIFF files in the emi mac AIFs folder use a sample rate of 22.254 kHz, which is optimal for playback on non-PPC Macintoshes, whereas the AIFF files in the emi ppc AIFs folder use a sample rate of 22.050 kHz, which is optimal for playback on non-PPC Macintoshes. If you use the CD-Browser to audition these files, the program will automatically select the appropriate soundfile for your Macintosh.

**Credits** Figures 3.22, 3.24, and 3.27 of EMI-Rachmaninoff for two pianos is performed here by Anatole Leikin and Maria Ezerova. Figures 7.4 and 7.7 are performed by David Cope conducting the University of California at Santa Cruz Symphony Orchestra. Randy Wong, sopranist, and Linda Burman-Hall, fortepiano, perform figures 7.5 and 7.6 from the opera Mozart by EMI.

Feel free to send comments to any of the following e-mail addresses:
howell@cats.ucsc.edu
yavelow@xs4all.nl
Bytehoven@aol.com
ARJLZ@aol.com

Use the following e-mail address for CD-ROM technical support questions:
yavelow@xs4all.nl

Check the Computer Music and Digital Audio Series home page on the World Wide Web for additional information:
http://www.xs4all.nl/~yavelow/ARE/CompMus.html

# ONE

## Background and Overview

*Computers and Musical Style* (Cope 1991a) argues that computers can be of significant help in finding musical *signatures*, or often used patterns that signal a composer's style. *Experiments in Musical Intelligence* argues that composers create music by mixing such signatures and using *recombinancy*, or the recombination of elements found in other of their works and in the music of other composers. The program that is described in this book and on the accompanying CD-ROM uses signatures and recombinancy to create music. This program thus parallels what I believe takes place at some level in composers' minds, whether consciously or subconsciously. The genius of great composers, I believe, lies not in inventing previously unimagined music but in their ability to effectively reorder and refine what already exists.

Deryck Cooke, in *The Language of Music*, states that "inspiration is an unconscious re-shaping of already existing material" (Cooke 1959, p. 171). For centuries, composers have experimented with ways of consciously "re-shaping" existing music to create new but stylistically convincing works. For example, Athanasius Kircher (1650) and Wolfgang Printz (1696) wrote extensively about melodic and harmonic permutations called *ars combinatoria* (Ratner 1970). Kircher's lengthy Book VIII of his *Musurgia Universalis* (1650) is dedicated to *ars combinatoria*. Kircher begins with a mathematical exploration of the possibilities of combining melodic elements, complete with charts listing the number of permutations of available notes given certain numbers of repetitions. Unlike later treatises, Kircher devotes little discussion either to histories of music *combinatoriae* (of which there were few in his time anyway) or to compositional and aesthetic processes involved in making or choosing particular sets of *combinatoriae*. Rather, he delights in large numbers as if he were an astronomer extolling the virtues of a night sky resplendent with stars. *Musurgia Universalis* is important for its time, and it is significant in that such a major section of this work is devoted to the nascent concept of combinatorial possibilities in music.

Printz's *Phrynis Mytilenaeus oder der Satyrischer Componist* (Printz 1696), although not as devoted to mathematical extrapolations as Kircher's *Musurgia Universalis*, demonstrates its author's interest in the extensive combinatorial possibilities of the variety of melodic lines possible above a given bass. He notates these melodic alternatives thoroughly and in a way not inconsistent with more formal *ars combinatoria* of the century to come.

One of the first formal types of music to incorporate combinatorial possibilities was the eighteenth-century *Musikalisches Würfelspiel*, or musical dice game. The idea of these musically sophisticated games was to compose a series of measures of music that could be reassembled in many different ways and still be stylistically viable. Thus, even a very simple piece becomes a source of innumerable new works (a typical *Würfelspiel* of sixteen measures yields $11^{16}$, or roughly forty-six quadrillion, works), and each, although varying in aesthetic quality, is stylistically correct. The music of a *Musikalisches Würfelspiel* is typically arranged randomly to obscure the fact (particularly to the musically uninitiated) that all the choices for a first measure, for example, are of the same general musical function. These arrangements no doubt made such games seem all the more fantastic in the eighteenth-century parlor, where they were often played. However, matching the numbers in the pool of choices with their respective measures demonstrates that the music of each measure is in fact functionally specific and note-similar, with each measure often a simple variation of, and interchangeable with, others of the same function.

Acknowledged to be the first such *Musikalisches Würfelspiel*, the polonaise from Johann Philipp Kirnberger's *Der allezeit fertige Polonoisen- und Menuettenkomponist* (Kirnberger 1757) is organized in phrases of six- and eight-measure lengths. The combinatorial possibilities here equal $11^{14}$, which, including the minuet and trio (with $11^{32}$ possibilities), results in a number so large that the "entire population of eighteenth-century Europe, working a lifetime on these games could not exhaust the combinations that lie within Kirnberger's minuets and polonaises" (Ratner 1970, p. 344). Figure 1.1 provides an example of a matrix for a first phrase and a polonaise drawn from this prototype *Musikalisches Würfelspiel*. The numbers

**CD-ROM**

The *Musikalisches Würfelspiel* shown in figures 1.1 to 1.4 can be heard via MIDI playback by launching the *Würfelspiel* program on the accompanying CD-ROM and selecting the composer desired. Timbre suggestions, which appear in the windows accompanying each selection, are based on the composer's own instrumentation given in the original publications. Listening to these *Musikalisches Würfelspiel*, rather than just studying their layout, provides clues to their musical logic, aesthetic basis, and effectiveness of conveying elements of musical style. ❖

---

to the left of the matrix in figure 1.1a represent all possible results of the toss of two dice (2–12). Each vertical column of the matrix to the right of these numbers indicates successive measure choices (six in this case because it is the first phrase of a polonaise). Each number in these columns is keyed to a measure of music. To get a first measure of music, one tosses the dice, locates the resulting number to the left of the matrix, and then notates the measure of music corresponding to the number in the square directly to the right of the number tossed. Subsequent tosses complete an initial phrase, and subsequent phrases are produced in the same way (see one resulting polonaise in figure 1.1b). Interestingly, Kirnberger includes a separate guide for the polonaise so that one die or two dice can be used to give six or eleven choices, depending on one's situation.

C. P. E. Bach's *Einfall einen doppelten Contrapunct in der Octave von sechs Tacten zu machen ohne die Regeln davon zu wissen* (Bach 1757) differs from Kirnberger's *Musikalisches Würfelspiel* by combining individual notes rather than measures from tables. Figure 1.2 gives both a sample from his tables and an invention as output. The arcane process used to create this invention involves choosing six random numbers from the numbers 1 to 9 (inclusive) for each of two voices. Numbers may be repeated as desired. These numbers then represent entry points into the six respective tables, each representing one measure of music for one of the voices. Once the initial note is found, one continues to select successive ninth members of the table until an "X," signaling a barline, is found. Eventually, six complete measures of music are produced in this manner.

**Figure 1.1** Excerpt from Kirnberger's *Der allezeit fertige Polonoisen- und Mennuettenkomponist* (1757): a) Matrix for a first phrase.

| Measure:<br>Dice: | 1 | 2 | 3 | 4 | 5 | 6 |
|---|---|---|---|---|---|---|
| 2 | 70 | 34 | 68 | 18 | 32 | 58 |
| 3 | 10 | 24 | 50 | 46 | 14 | 26 |
| 4 | 42 | 6 | 60 | 2 | 52 | 66 |
| 5 | 62 | 8 | 36 | 12 | 16 | 38 |
| 6 | 44 | 56 | 40 | 79 | 48 | 54 |
| 7 | 72 | 30 | 4 | 28 | 22 | 64 |
| 8 | 114 | 112 | 126 | 87 | 89 | 88 |
| 9 | 123 | 116 | 137 | 110 | 91 | 98 |
| 10 | 131 | 147 | 143 | 113 | 101 | 115 |
| 11 | 138 | 151 | 118 | 124 | 141 | 127 |
| 12 | 144 | 153 | 146 | 128 | 150 | 154 |

Thus, a selection of 1 for the first table yields the quarter note E followed by the quarter note G, nine elements to its right. Then E and C quarter notes complete the first measure for the upper (descant) voice. The bass voice is constructed in the same manner from a separate set of tables. The resulting six-measure, two-voice coun-

*Figure 1.1* b) A resulting polonaise.

terpoint may then be successfully inverted by transposing either the top voice down one octave or the bottom voice up one octave. Eugene Helm (1966) computes the possible number of works from Bach's tables to be more than 282 billion, with inversions giving an identical amount.

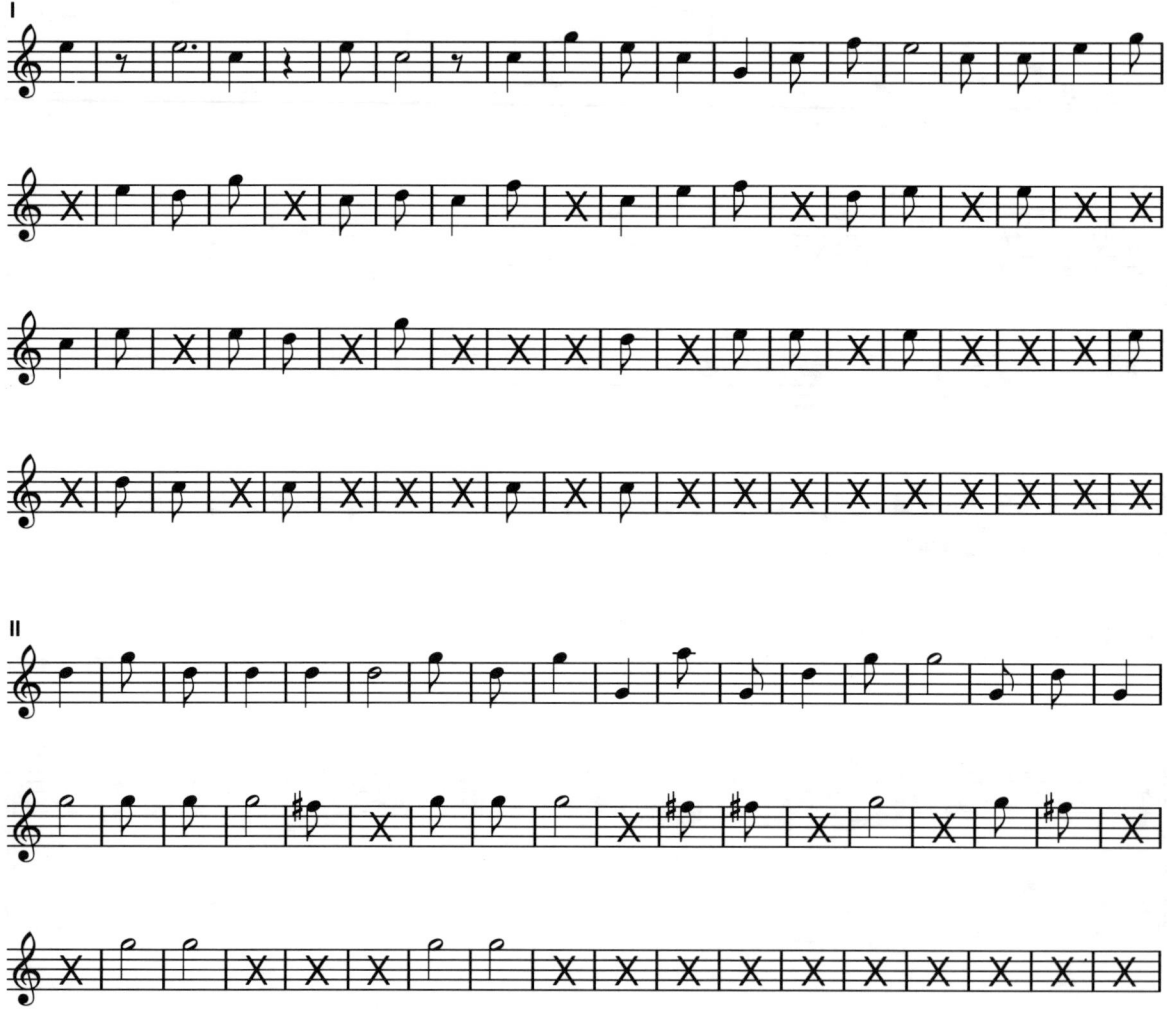

**Figure 1.2**  a) Tables 1 and 2 from *Einfall einen doppelten Contrapunct in der Octave von sechs Tacten zu machen ohne die Regeln davon zu wissen* by C. P. E. Bach.

C. P. E. Bach's original description and tables first appeared in volume 3 of Marpurg's critical/historical survey of music (Bach 1757) as the only foldout tables of music in the lengthy five-volume set. Helm refers to Bach's work in this genre as "the trivialization of music's ancient and honorable relation to number" (Helm 1966, p. 150). On the other hand, Ratner states that although these works

**Figure 1.2** b) A resultant *Invention:* upper voice (descant): 2-5-6-3-4-1; lower voice (bass): 6-8-2-1-9-3.

"are not superb musical compositions, they possess coherence and validity of style because their harmonic, rhythmic, and melodic components are built of useful musical stuff" (Ratner 1970, p. 344). Regardless of import, Bach's method stands as a precursor of the *micro augmented transition network* (MATN), one of the cornerstones of EMI and SARA (see chapter 5).

Another particularly good example of a *Musikalisches Würfelspiel* from this period is shown in figure 1.3. Attributed to Mozart (K. 516f) but not authenticated, it consists of two 8-by-11 matrices containing the numbers 1 to 176 ($2 \times 8 \times 11$) and the corresponding keyed measures of music in the same way as the previously discussed *Würfelspiel* by Kirnberger. According to the formula $N = D^r$, where D = vertical dimension and r = rank, these two matrices allow for $11^{16}$ combinations, or 45,949,729,863,572,161 possible new works.

Figure 1.4 shows the musical results of a *Musikalisches Würfelspiel* attributed to Haydn (1793; see also the anonymous attribution in Taubert 1988). This full-scale *Würfelspiel* contains four matrices: two $11 \times 8$ matrices for a two-phrase minuet and two $6 \times 8$ matrices (a die version) for a two-phrase trio. The music is extensive and highly varied, and although it remains a dice game, the amount of effort taken to complete the work suggests that the composer saw it as a significant achievement.

**Figure 1.3** Mozart, *Musikalisches Würfelspiel* (K. 516f).

Other composers who created *Würfelspiel* include Maximilian Stadler (1780), Antonio Callegari (1802), and Pasquale Ricci (n.d.). Pierre Hoegi, whose *A Tabular System Whereby the Art of Composing Minuets Is made so Easy that any Person, without the least knowledge of Musick, may compose ten thousand, all different, and in the most Pleasing and Correct Manner* (1770) uses number choices from 8 to 48 for composing two eight-bar phrases, and E. F. Delange (n.d.), who employs a nine-sided top for chance selection, also contributed combinatorial compositions similar to the *Würfelspiel*. Obviously, the composers involved with these games knew the style of their period intimately and coupled that knowledge with their own ingenuity to compose musical fragments that could be assembled in various ways and still work effectively.

**Figure 1.4** Haydn, *Musikalisches Würfelspiel*.

**Figure 1.4** continued.

Arnold Feil (1955) postulates that the *Musikalisches Würfelspiel* demonstrates the harmonic and melodic thinking of its musical time. Feil points out that Joseph Riepel and Heinrich Christoph Koch, two influential theorist-composers of eighteenth-century Germany, used Kirnberger's dice music for instructional purposes in composition. Both Riepel (1757) and Koch (1782–93) also included *Würfelspiel* exercises in their respective treatises on composition (see the bibliography at the end of the book). Francesco Galeazzi (1791–96) employed similar *Würfelspiel* techniques for teaching composition, though his approach more resembled the permutations of Kircher of 150 years earlier in that he used only rearrangements of melodic groupings rather than harmonically interchangeable measures. Interestingly, both of these approaches seem to be oriented toward the defeat of composer's block—to unleash the imagination—an aim not dissimilar from that used for the creation of EMI itself.

William S. Newman states that Kirnberger's *Musikalisches Würfelspiel* and other writings about combinative and modeling musical processes "were done in dead earnest" (Newman 1961, p. 517). Newman further notes that these comments regard the relation between Kirnberger's "Ever-Ready Polonaise- and Minuett-Composer" and his later "method for tossing off sonatas" that "were formerly regarded as intentional jests if not deliberate pieces of satire." Ratner adds that

> the process by which the games were put together reflects a substantial view of musical construction, one that permeates the seventeenth and eighteenth centuries. In this view, the play of musical elements is controlled so as to achieve a coherent and persuasive flow of rhetoric. At this time in musical history it was possible to codify the mechanical elements of musical composition more clearly than at any other time. (Ratner 1970, p. 345)

Many composers and theoreticians did not stop at employing the *Würfelspiel* and paraphrasing techniques for small forms. For example, Riepel (1755) proposed the creation of major works using combinatorial procedures: "Riepel proceeds along these lines as he works out melodic combinations in the construction of minuets, concertos, and symphonies. Within a given model he seeks to achieve optimum effects by substituting figures, phrases, and cadences" (Ratner 1970, p. 351). If one were to substitute the words "signatures" and "measures" for "figures" and "phrases" in Ratner's comment, the quotation could just as easily be applied to EMI as Riepel's work of 230 years earlier. Riepel also calculated permutations for other elements of music, such as bowings and rhythms, and became one of the eighteenth century's most serious advocates of recombinancy: "The unique art of permutations, by which one can uncover in a single day far more than 99 themes, is at least 99 times healthier for composition than the calculation of ratios" (Lester 1992, p. 226, as quoted from Riepel 1755, p. 25).

These thoughts again underline the seriousness with which composers and authors of the eighteenth century took these supposed diversions. In many cases, such as that of Galeazzi (1791–96), the techniques of combination were used as vehicles for teaching music theory and composition:

> We find many who can proceed with a given figure with little effort but who have insuperable difficulties when they have to create new material. Here is something that can assist in composition with which one can discover a hundred, a thousand in the twinkling of an eye: it may appear puerile but first experiment with it and then judge. (Galeazzi 1791–96, vol. 2, p. 248)

Again, the similarity to EMI is unmistakable, including the references to the number and speed of discoveries, which read like a description of a computer program.

Aside from more formal *Musikalisches Würfelspiel*, many composers devised and developed techniques for musical invention on the basis of similar principles. For example, Kirnberger's *Methode Sonaten aus'm Ermel zu schüddeln* (1783) describes the composer-theorist's method for creating new sonatas by borrowing and then varying melodies and thorough basses of other composers. Described by Newman as "a panacea for the would-be composer devoid of inspiration," it

> suggests that such a person, or anyone else, should borrow a thorough bass from some existing source, contrive a new melody to go over it, then contrive a new bass to go under that melody. In other words, by changing first the roof, then the foundation, he can have an entirely new house! (Newman 1961, p. 519)

In his method Kirnberger creates a partial list of rules that provide an interesting vehicle for the creation of variations: (1) know how to compose in a thorough bass style, (2) frequently invert the counterpoint, (3) change the meter, and (4) change the key. Figure 1.5 gives the first few bars of Kirnberger's example, which illustrates his text. As can be seen (if not by his rules then by his example), the new music is an embellished version of the older Bach gigue, with notes being added usually in the form of anticipations, delays, scales, and arpeggiation of implied and actual harmonies. Interestingly, Kirnberger's techniques are not dissimilar to those found in EMI's and SARA's composing programs (see chapter 6).

Kirnberger's variation techniques introduce yet another, more flexible approach to Cooke's musical "re-shaping": the borrowing or lifting of previously composed music. Such borrowing necessarily suggests recomposition in the manner of the *Würfelspiel* even though the recomposer is the only one playing the game. Composers have been borrowing motives and themes, consciously or subconsciously, for centuries. Whether this is plagiarism or the sincerest form of flattery is perhaps best determined by the one being imitated. Such piecemealing of other composers' ideas with one's own music certainly falls into the category of musical pastiche if not *Würfelspiel*. For example, Clementi documented his Piano Sonata, op. 24, no. 2 (1781), with a note indicating that Mozart was present ("Mozart étant présent" [Plantinga 1977]) when he performed this piece for Emperor Joseph II (Barlow 1948, p. xii). Figure 1.6 compares the first theme of the first movement of Clementi's work with the main theme of the overture to Mozart's *Magic Flute* (K. 620), which appeared ten

**Figure 1.5** Excerpt from Kirnberger's *Methode Sonaten aus'm Ermel zu schüddeln*, demonstrating how he embellished the gigue from J. S. Bach's French Suite no. 6.

years later (1791). Clearly this is more than influence: it is an example of the plagiarism or flattery that lends some credence to the notion that classical composers often feasted on one another's music. At the very least, classical composers borrowed stylistic signatures and, more likely, actual musical fragments that they liked too much to leave unappreciated in their own works.

**Figure 1.6**  a) Clementi theme from Piano Sonata, op. 24, no. 2, first movement, mm. 1–3.
b) Mozart, theme from *The Magic Flute* (K. 620), overture.

Another example of this type of borrowing is Beethoven's use of a Mozart fragment in the second movement of his *Pathétique* Sonata (figure 1.7). Although only three melodic notes (C–B♭–E♭) exist in common between these two themes, Beethoven's use of the identical key (A♭ major) and nearly identical harmonization reveals the Mozartean origins. Leonard Meyer (1989) points out even subtler refinements of these kinds of borrowing techniques by Handel, Bach, and Mahler as well as further examples from Haydn and Mozart.

A number of classical composers employed variants of the "Mannheim rocket," so named because the ascending arpeggiated figure was popular with eighteenth-century composers in Mannheim. Rockets are another example of simple but reasonably elegant borrowing, though the source is not as clear as in the previous examples. Figure 1.8 shows six examples of the well-known figure spanning over fifty years of the eighteenth and nineteenth centuries. Each of these examples occurs in exposed and primary sections of their respective works, and each is yet another example of how classical composers grafted known musical fragments together to create what I call recombinancy. What is even more fascinating about the Mannheim rocket, however, is the way in which composers varied the recognizable motive beyond the simple transpositions and rhythms shown in figure 1.8. Figure 1.9 presents three examples of such a variant used by composers with quite different compositional styles. Here, scale degree $\hat{5}$ is anticipated with a chromatic lower-neighbor tone combining the Mannheim rocket with another classical signature (see figure 1.17). Thus, even borrowed fragments fall prey to further, more subtle recombinancy.

**Figure 1.7** a) Beethoven, Piano Sonata, op. 13 (*Pathétique*), second movement, mm. 1–8. b) Mozart, Piano Sonata (K. 457), second movement, m. 24.

Many theorists (notably Cooke 1959) believe that certain figures, used by many classical composers over hundreds of years, have quasi-definable meanings. Cooke presents exhaustive charts of compositional resemblances and suggests associations to support his thesis that music is a quantifiable language. Such a language can be thought of, at least in part, as a compilation of various known intervallic or pitch sets borrowed not from the themes of individual composers but from a larger musical-cultural frame of reference. Figure 1.10 presents eleven highly similar melodies from over ten centuries of Western traditional music. Each of these examples follows the $\hat{1}-\hat{5}-\hat{6}-\hat{5}$ (scale degrees) pattern, though many have interpolated notes as well as different rhythms and modes (major or minor). A discussion of whether these themes are just coincidentally similar or whether they belong to a cognitive vocabulary of identifiable gestures within a larger linguistic composite belongs in a larger volume than the present one. However, as with thematic borrowing, such theorizing suggests that a musical semiotics might exist wherein

**Figure 1.8**  a) Mozart, String Quartet, K. 465 ("Dissonance"), third movement (1785). b) Mozart, Symphony no. 40 in G minor, K. 550, fourth movement (1788). c) Beethoven, Piano Sonata, op. 2, no. 1, first movement (1795). d) Beethoven, Symphony no. 5, op. 67, third movement (1808). e) Mendelssohn, String Quartet, op. 44, no. 2, first movement (1837). f) Schumann, String Quartet, op. 41, no. 2, third movement (1842).

***Figure 1.9*** a) Haydn, Symphony no. 103, second movement (1795). b) Schubert, Symphony no. 4, fourth movement (1816). c) Saint-Saëns, *Le rouet d'Omphale*, op. 31 (1870).

***Figure 1.10*** a) The plainsong *Puer natus est* (ninth century). b) Brulé, *Cil qui d'Amors* (twelfth century). c) Ockeghem, *Malheur* (1480). d) Josquin des Prez, *Qui velatus est* (1510).

**Figure 1.10** e) Byrd, *O Lord my God* (1611). f) Bach, Cantata no. 67 (1725). g) Bach, *St. Mathew Passion* (1729) using chorale tune *O Lamm Gottes unschuldig*. h) Mozart, Piano Sonata K. 545 (1788. i) Mendelssohn, "Then shall the righteous" from *Elijah* (1846). j) Verdi, "Presago il core" from *Aida* (1870). k) Vaughan-Williams, "So shalt thou enter in" from *Pilgrim's Progress* (1949).

signs and signals have definite meanings for initiated listeners. This use of semiotics again hints at a recombinant approach to composition where, intentional or not, music is not simply through-composed but rather an intricate mosaic of potentially recognizable gestures and subgestures. Interestingly, semiotic organization very much resembles natural language analytic processes such as ATN, so integral to EMI and SARA (discussed in the relevant sections of this chapter and in chapter 5).

Figure 1.11 presents yet another example of quasi-quotation that includes elements of each of the previous examples. The music here

**Figure 1.11** a) Henry Purcell, *Dido's Lament* from *Dido and Aeneas* (1689). b) Beethoven, Piano Sonata, op. 13 (*Pathétique*), first movement (1798). c) Tchaikovsky, Symphony no. 6 (*Pathétique*), first movement, mm. 20–21 (1893).

was composed over a two-century period. However, the mutual influence appears to be more than random. Subtitles aside (because not all were given by their respective composers), all three works show clear similarities in tempo, mode choice, and general use of dissonance. The rising $\hat{1}$–$\hat{2}$–$\hat{3}$–$\hat{2}$ scale degree figure is predominant in all three cases, though the Beethoven example extends the foreground iterations of the Purcell, and the Tchaikovsky further varies the initial motive by extended repetition. The harmonic accompaniments to the minor-key figures include embellishing secondary dominants (Beethoven and Tchaikovsky) as well as differing metric emphasis, though all three examples include placement of scale degree $\hat{3}$ on a strong beat. Harmony, then, as well as melody participates in the recombinancy of the imitations that continue in quite diverse ways beyond the music shown.

On an even more sophisticated level, Meyer (1989, p. 54) demonstrates how the foreground notes of a Mahler theme follow the background structures of "and He shall reign for ever and ever" from Handel's *Messiah*. In a similar manner, he argues convincingly that the *Adeste Fidelis* theme, so often heard in baroque and classical music, occurs infrequently in romantic music, suggesting unconscious but nonetheless purposeful avoidance of the vocabulary of previous centuries. Again, the notion of music created from fragments of previous compositions is foremost.

Figure 1.12a shows a recombinant example created using various segments of music from Mozart and Beethoven. Note that this phrase is quite similar in sound to the beginning of the second movement of Beethoven's *Pathétique* Sonata, op. 13, though none of the music emanates from that source. Figure 1.12b shows the music of figure 1.12a transposed to the proper key so that the melody and harmony generally follow that of Beethoven's original Adagio Cantabile of op. 13 (shown in figure 1.12c). None of this cutting and pasting is presented to indicate that these derivations were the actual source of Beethoven's inspiration for the theme of the *Pathétique*. This example, however, indicates one possible process by which music can be created—the process of recombinancy.

***Figure 1.12***   a) A recombinant example from (1) Mozart, Piano Sonata (K. 457), second movement, m. 24; (2) Beethoven, Piano Sonata, op. 10, no. 2, first movement, mm. 19–20; (3) Beethoven, Piano Sonata, op. 10, no. 2, first movement, m. 28; (4) Beethoven, Piano Sonata, op. 2, no. 3, second movement, m. 9; (5) Beethoven, Piano Sonata, op. 2, no. 1, second movement, mm. 15–16.

# BACKGROUND AND OVERVIEW 21

**Figure 1.12** b) Example a with transpositions to the same key. c) Beginning of Beethoven, Piano Sonata, op. 13, no. 2, second movement.

A clear, common link among all these examples is that the *process* of composition, at least in many cases, involves combining elements of previously heard music. This process includes everything from stylistic signatures of a composer's period to actual paraphrases of certain works. These techniques, in combination with possibly more innovative ideas, are then used to create new works. This combination, or recombinancy, is not simply a game or superficial technique but rather a deep manifestation of the creative process. Thus, the concept of *Würfelspiel* becomes less a digression and more an insight. In fact, it becomes a significant part of the fabric of all music. Whether such techniques are discernible and translatable as language (as Cooke would have it) or whether they present a route to recognize sources and influences is beside the point. If these techniques are integral to the compositional process, then they are logical rationale for the basis of computer programs such as EMI and SARA, which are themselves far more than *Würfelspiel* and far more than simple digressions from more traditional composing rhetorics.

Thus, quotation, paraphrase, and semiotics contribute to a sense that composers of Western concert music at least, acquire techniques that allow them to formulate their music as subtle *Musikalisches Würfelspiel*. If this is true, even to a superficial degree, it leads one to a proposition that computers, with the same wealth of potential quotations, paraphrasing abilities, and semiotic information, might effectively mimic such compositional strategies. One can certainly imagine a computer program that is modeled on these techniques producing examples like those found in the variations of all the previous figures.

# ■ CHALLENGES

The challenges for computer composition are numerous (Hiller 1970; Hiller and Isaacson 1959; Lidov and Gabura 1973; Winograd 1968). Computers have been used in automated music (Ames 1987; Rowe 1993; Winsor 1987), in algorithmic composition (Fry 1984; Janzen 1992), and as stochastic probability generators (Xenakis 1971), to name a few examples. Also, artificial intelligence systems have created serious interest for music analysis (Buxton 1978; Roads 1984) and composition (Cope 1987). However, the problems posed by computer composition are more profound than just computers creating interesting, even aesthetically engaging, new music.

The concept that music can be quantified into categories and then analyzed, replicated, and/or performed by digital means continues to be one of the greatest challenges facing computer composition today. Just the thought of describing complex analog phenomena in supposedly equivalent digital terms leads some to believe that computers will never be able to adequately compose or perform nontrivial music. The use of MIDI by many computer programs compounds these problems by allowing a complex phenomenon such as timbre to be assigned to tracks and channels rather than being linked to the compositional process, as they often are in real life. At the same time, advances made in the computational world in just the past twenty years gives one optimism for future potential. It is possible that the sophistication of computers and programming will be able to surmount any such obstacles in the not-so-distant future.

Another challenge facing music composition by computers is overcoming human bias toward machines (or, more subtly, against programmers of machines). As I have said on many occasions, "Machines don't compose" (Duisberg 1993, p. 87), and computers "do not possess any choice capabilities other than those that have been composer programmed or those derived from random selection" (Cope 1977, p. 210). Humans write programs that compose *by* machines. The machine follows the dictates of the programmer. Somehow in the perceived magic of computer composition, machines are often seen to create from a vacuum and as such are often perceived as aliens competing for activities previously held sacrosanct for humans. Computers, however, are not our rivals—they are our slaves.

Critics of computer composition can point to the many works composed by computer programs that have been destined to obscurity by their experimental nature or their necessary reliance upon almost immediately out-of-date machines. There are also many examples of very bad computer music (not unlike similar bad acoustic music) that can (and do) fuel arguments against successful work emanating from this technology. It is my hope that this book, along with *Computers and Musical Style* (Cope 1991a), will contribute to the notion that composers who create notes on paper and composers who write computer composition programs are of the same cloth. As in all artistic matters, it should be aesthetics and not ideology that separates the wheat from the chaff.

Computers offer extraordinary opportunities for creating recombinant music through their arbitrary decision making, speed, and accuracy. As previously noted, computers are controlled by programs, and programs that create new output are often called *algorithms*. A musical algorithm is a sequence or set of rules for solving (accomplishing) a particular problem in a finite number of steps that combines musical parts into a whole composition (see Cope 1992, p. 24). Thus, algorithms offer composers and musicologists great opportunities to create and study music from the standpoint of recombinancy. Ultimately, the levels and degrees of recombinancy lead one to musical style and its inheritance and development as well as to a better understanding of the processes involved in composing itself.

EMI and SARA create new examples of music by analyzing, disassembling, and recombining music that was not written to be analyzed, disassembled, and recombined. EMI and SARA separate and analyze musical gestures and then mix and recombine the patterns of those gestures in such a way that each new resultant composition, although different, is nonetheless substantially correct. New works generally inherit aspects of the style of the analyzed and disassembled music and, to a lesser degree, the style of the composer of that music. This process is not just a parlor game but a serious attempt to understand how listeners recognize the style of a composer or period, one of the more elusive and difficult-to-describe musical phenomena. It is also an attempt to model a computer program on recombinant musical processes.

Although music naturally includes timbre (Slawson 1985) and other performance complexities (Anderson and Kuivila 1991), research with EMI and SARA focuses exclusively on pitch, duration, and to some extent dynamics. This is not meant to denigrate other areas of possible study. However, this limitation confines the research to a reasonable frame of endeavor.

## ■ GENERAL ALGORITHM

EMI began in 1981 as an attempt to create new instances of music in my style. With a lack of quantifiable definitions of style (especially my own style), I concentrated on pattern matching the works of certain composers. This resulted in the identification of what I call *signatures*. By 1987 EMI had produced works (arguably) in the styles of Bach and Mozart (among others) using such signatures. Further experimentation with pattern matching, the use of certain natural language processes, and the employment of object orientation allowed for more extensive output in terms of work length, complexity, and stylistic diversity. EMI subsequently produced new works in the styles of composers as different as Stravinsky, Palestrina, and Scott Joplin. These works have been discussed and partly reproduced in my book *Computers and Musical Style* (Cope 1991a).

As previously mentioned, EMI and SARA attempt to make *Musikalisches Würfelspiel* out of music not designed to be such by using pattern matching to avoid deconstructing elements integral to the style of the works being recombined. Although this simple abstraction belies both the intricate analysis required during deconstruction and the complicated networking necessary during recombination, it does present the basic plan of the EMI and SARA processes. Figure 1.13 gives a more specific general algorithm for the program presented in this book. Each of the six stages presented is an integral function of the system as a whole. In stage 1, music enters the algorithm in the form of events (see chapter 2) that describe the note attributes of pitch, timing, duration, dynamic, and channel. In stage 2, this music is analyzed according to the SPEAC system of identifiers (for definitions, see chapter 2 of both this book and *Computers and Musical Style* [Cope 1991a]). In stage 3, pattern matching protects signatures from recombinancy by a special process described further in chapters 3 and 4. In stage 4, deconstruction places each musical segment in an appropriate lexicon according to its SPEAC meaning. These musical segments are then reconstructed in stage 5 according to a musical augmented transition network, or ATN (described further in chapter 5), producing new music in stage 6.

The analysis in stage 2 of figure 1.13 is not unlike that of creating music for a *Musikalisches Würfelspiel*. Likewise, the ATN of stage 5 is similar to the rolling of the dice of a *Musikalisches Würfelspiel*, although the ATN provides a much more intelligent approach than random selection. The intervening stages of pattern matching, which determine which fragments may *not* be deconstructed, and deconstruction itself roughly parallel the creation of the music and the matrices of a *Musikalisches Würfelspiel*. If the input music is analyzed properly, retains its stylistic signatures through pattern matching, and is deftly reconstructed through the ATN, then the new connections in stage 5 will create musically interesting and stylistically believable new music output. Elements of revision, similar to Kirnberger's *Methode Sonaten aus'm Ermel zu schüddeln* (1783) and C. P. E. Bach's note-by-note processes, occur in stage 5 of this algorithm. Databases, signatures, and new works can be found in stages 1, 3, and 6, respectively.

Note that the algorithm shown in figure 1.13 is devoid of any interface descriptions such as MIDI playback, database storage, file types, and so on. These are described in the manual on the accompanying CD-ROM. This algorithm could therefore be implemented on any platform. However, it should be noted that LISP is the language used here for programming, and CLOS (the Common LISP Object System) is the object system of choice.

*Figure 1.13* A general algorithm for EMI.

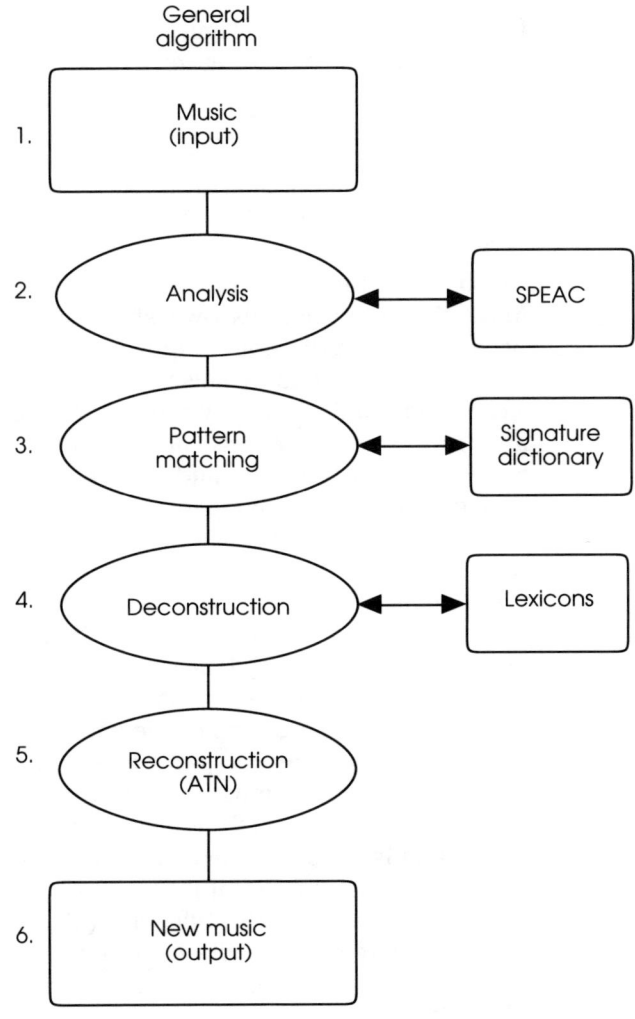

# ■ APPROACHES TO ANALYSIS

Some of the fundamental problems of building a program to produce effective recombinant music include determining (1) the length of the elements of the original music to be deconstructed, (2) the method to be used to analyze these elements, and (3) how these elements should be recombined to make musical sense. After all, random recombination produces chaotic results (compare the music in figures 1.14 and 1.15). Figure 1.14 presents two examples of music from Mozart's sonatas. Figure 1.15 is a random recombination of the quarter-note beats of figure 1.14 and shows the source of each reorganized beat. Here, "A" refers to figure 1.14a and "B" to figure 1.14b, with the numbers representing the location by measure number and then by beat number. (Another random recombinant example is given in figure 5.14b.)

The new composition shown in figure 1.15 is musical gibberish, as can be seen (and heard if played). Neither the common practice of Mozart's period nor his own style has survived the recombination because Mozart did not compose these phrases to be deconstructed and recombined and because the deconstruction and recombination were done unintelligently and unmusically. Important questions about the size of the musical elements (one beat in figure 1.15) and about whether harmony and melody should be considered together or separately have been ignored, as has the repetition of the first two measures in both originals in figure 1.14 (in both cases with variation). Nor has attention been paid to the manner in which the reorganized material has been reconnected. For example, the harmonic progressions of both figure 1.14a and figure 1.14b have been mutilated and no longer fit the stylistic constraints of Mozart or his period.

Obviously, great care must be taken in deconstructing the original works, analyzing each of the various constituent parts, and then recombining the various parts in a new but musically viable order. Recombinant music must assume the musical logic inherent in the original works on which it bases its new composition. In EMI and SARA, this is accomplished by (1) analyzing each component for its deep hierarchical musical function, (2) pattern matching for signals of a certain composer's style, and (3) reassembling the parts sensitively, using techniques drawn from natural language processing.

The first stage of this process is a critical element of the program. There are a number of ways to analyze musical groupings for hierarchical functions. One way is to employ traditional reductions of harmonic function using what theorists call *tonic*, *dominant*, and so on, or I (C triad in the key of C), V (G triad in the key of G), and so on. Then, when recombinancy takes place, it could follow the form of a fixed sequence of functions and freely substitute the actual music that the functions represent. Thereby, functions would remain intact in the new work (and be in the same order as they were in the original work) but could exchange music with other analyzed music of that same

**Figure 1.14** Music from Mozart sonatas clarified according to the principles presented in chapter 2: a) K. 283, second movement, mm. 1–4. b) K. 330, third movement, mm. 9–16.

**Figure 1.15** Random recombinant music and its analysis. "A" here refers to figure 1.14A and "B" to figure 1.14B; the numbers represent the location of the measure number and the beat number, respectively.

function. The hierarchical analysis of such a process could be quite deep. That is, fragments could be keyed by strata of information, such as *cadence-tonic* or *tonic-6-incipient* and so on, that would indicate their original location and nuance of function. With a large number of works for analysis, the program could have hundreds of different categories, each with numerous musical subphrases to choose from such that successive parts of the new work could be musically tied to the next grouping and not just randomly chosen. One such subprogram of EMI operates in just this manner (see Cope 1991b).

As an alternative to traditional harmonic analysis, however, I developed the SPEAC system in 1985 (a variation of which appears in Cope 1987), which provides methods for the abstraction of musical notes and harmonies on the basis of ideas derived from the work of Heinrich Schenker (1935). SPEAC is an acronym for *statement* (S), *preparation* (P), *extension* (E), *antecedent* (A), and *consequent* (C), each term roughly equaling its standard dictionary definition. SPEAC analysis allows notes and chords to vary in meaning depending on context.

Although the standard function of a C–E–G chord changes depending on key (in C major this chord is tonic and in F major is dominant), in SPEAC analysis the C–E–G chord may have different meanings within the *same* key. For example, at the beginning of a phrase in C major, C–E–G can be a statement, S, whereas in a cadence it can be a consequent, C. Thus, whereas traditional functions provide information about surface detail, the SPEAC system provides insight into the deeper meaning of music. (For further information, see chapter 2 of *Computers and Musical Style* [Cope 1991a] and chapter 2 of this book.)

Analysis for proper connectivity must also occur before the elements of the music are fragmented and mixed. This analysis can fall into many categories, including melody, accompaniment, and harmony. Melodies that rise, for example, can be followed by falling ones for balance. Accompaniments, otherwise a kind of pastiche of various motives, can be made consistent so that they flow regularly with the melodic line. Harmonies can have real voice leading in the tonal common-practice sense, which includes measuring the strength of chord functions so that stronger cadences can be saved for the last chords of new works.

An example of such connectiveness can be found by making a more intelligent analysis of the various beats of figures 1.14a and 1.14b as shown in figures 1.16a and 1.16b. Both of the Mozart sonata examples shown in figure 1.14 begin on a *tonic* chord, or S (statement), which can be interchanged successfully with the application of musical transposition to the left hand of B1.1 (i.e. moving it up one octave). A1.4 is *dominant*, or A (antecedent), in function and can be substituted for the dominant, or A-function chord, of B2.2 with no ill effects and no transposition necessary. Likewise, the first half of measure 1 of figure 1.16a could be interchanged with the first full measure of figure 1.16b with no substantive damage. On the other hand, taking the second measure of figure 1.16b and interchanging it with the first half of measure 1 of figure 1.16a would cause serious problems. Not only do the functions not match, but beginning the work on an unprepared dissonance is stylistically uncharacteristic.

As previously noted, certain harmonic functions can have different SPEAC analyses depending on their location in a phrase and thus their context. Here, the tonic chord in the first half of measure 1 of figure 1.16a is analyzed as an S (an initial statement), whereas the tonic chord in the second half of measure 4 of figure 1.16a is analyzed as a C (the consequent of the harmonic motion of the entire phrase). Note also that the program can separate harmony and accompaniment from melody (see the discussion of MATN in chapter 5). However,

**Figure 1.16** A SPEAC analysis of: a) Mozart, Piano Sonata (K. 283), second movement, mm. 1–4. b) Mozart, Piano Sonata (K. 330), third movement, mm. 9–16.

*Figure 1.16* continued.

such separation occurs *after* the hierarchical function analysis so that melodic groupings retain their harmonic implications. This order is very important for the recombination process. Because music often contains structural repetitions at various levels (i.e., within and between measures, etc.), EMI also analyzes the substructural repeats in the original music. This analysis involves a pattern matcher not unlike the one about to be described for discovering signatures but having a different function. This analysis pattern matcher informs the recombination part of the program where internal (to the phrase) repeats take place so that similar repeats can take place in the final output. Once all the elements of the music have been analyzed, harmonic functions of the same type are stored together in lexicons.

## ■ APPROACHES TO PATTERN MATCHING

Pattern matching (also known as pattern recognition) has long been held as one of the premiere disciplines of artificial intelligence. In fact, it is

> tempting to assert that the basic aim of all science is the recognition of patterns. Scientists study observed groups of variables, trying to isolate and identify functional relationships—qualitative and quantitative. These associations provide mathematical models which are in turn used to infer objective properties of the process being modeled. (Bezdek 1981, p. vii)

Pattern matching is used in fields as disparate as graphics imaging, biology, DNA research, psychology, mathematics and statistics, and linguistics (particularly in word and character recognition).

Therefore, a history of pattern matching would have to encompass each of these fields (and others as well) to be accurate and complete. Obviously, such a history is not possible within the space of this volume. However, the various approaches from discipline to discipline have many similarities that present a good point of departure for defining pattern matching for researchers in music and for EMI:

> The term "pattern recognition" embraces such a vast and diversified literature that a definition of it always invites debate. Nonetheless, it is pedagogically useful for us to begin by attempting to describe what pattern recognition entails. I think one can successfully defend a literal approach: quite simply, pattern recognition is a search for structure in data. (Bezdek 1981, p. 1)

Pattern matchers have existed for years in a variety of useful forms. For example, the *grep* command in UNIX (an acronym that stands for "Get the Regular Expression and Print it") is a very useful and powerful pattern-matching function that finds text in a file or group of files. Standard grep-type commands often feature wildcard symbols such as "?" for characters or "*" for folder names or file names in path descriptions. These, along with searching for partial words, combine to form a powerful word search pattern matcher. The Search Files command in Macintosh Common LISP (the language used to create the program on the CD-ROM accompanying this book) is a grep-type pattern matcher that searches through the indicated (by path name) text-only files for words or parts of words.

The notion that two patterns can be considered similar enough to match, even though they are different, is complex and nontrivial. For example, one must determine which similarities are necessary for a match. Conversely, the allowable differences making two patterns not match must be clearly defined. To create pattern matchers capable of discerning which similarities and differences between patterns are critical and which are unimportant or less important requires programs that can approximate rather than simply differentiate. The capability that computers add to pattern recognition

> has stirred a concomitant interest in the notion of precision: precision in nature, in the data we gather from nature, in our machine representation of the data, in the models we construct from the data, in the inferences we draw from the models, and, ultimately, in our philosophical perception of the idea itself. (Bezdek 1981, p. vii)

Pattern matching has also been a serious subject of study in music (Simon and Kotovsky 1963; Simon and Sumner 1968). In a summary statement to their ground-breaking work with patterns in music, Simon and Sumner state that

> The pattern description language we have described may prove useful both in psychology and in music theory. As a tool in psychology, it can be used to try to arrive at an understanding of the cognitive activity of the music listener. As a tool of music theory, it may be used to provide rigorous descriptions of musical pattern as a prerequisite for the characterization and comparison of style. In the more distant future, it may provide an interesting basis, different from those employed heretofore, for experiments in musical composition by computer. (Simon and Sumner 1968, p. 250)

Thus, in one brief paragraph they foreshadow work with pattern matching in both musical style and composition.

Simon and Sumner were also among the first to describe a musical pattern matcher based on pattern induction, patterns of patterns (compound patterns), and multidimensionality (melody, harmony, and counterpoint). Their work covers the field from psychological and perceptual concepts of musical patterns to algebraic formulas of pattern frequencies and their representations. They also introduced a pattern language that is an extension of a formalism previously used to describe patterns in aptitude tests. For example, the Thurstone nonmusically related Letter Series Completion Test calls for the completion of sequences such as ABM CDM ———. These investigations led to concepts of pattern periodicity, which seem as applicable to music as they are to letter or number sequences.

The Humdrum Toolkit program (Huron 1993) uses a UNIX-based grep-like program for pattern matching music. It finds patterns of various types, including melodic patterns, metric positions of dissonances, harmonic patterns, and key profiles in tonal music. The program also conducts searches for specific or generalized pitch contours and arbitrary combinations of parameters such as rhythm, melody, and harmony. Unlike EMI and SARA, however, the Humdrum Toolkit does not search for patterns independently of user input; rather, one must know in advance what patterns, however vague, are being searched for.

Robert Rowe's Cypher (Rowe 1993) is a composing tool that incorporates a string-matching algorithm. Based on the object-oriented MAX programming environment, Cypher finds both melodic and harmonic patterns. Pattern matching in Cypher involves two phrases: the current phrase and the one immediately preceding it. Pattern matches exceeding four (considered a successful local match) are then matched against a larger, more global list of known patterns. If the matched patterns again exceed four, the pattern successfully meets the criteria of the program. The pattern strength is then increased, and the program continues to compose.

Compass (Mahling 1991), created at the Institut für Informatik in Stuttgart, Germany, is built on Smalltalk-80, an object-oriented language that originated at the Palo Alto Research Center. Compass uses *constant matching*, an abstract pattern matcher. Found patterns are used directly in the composition process. Abstract patterns represent diverse musical concepts such as voice leading, intervallic pattern matching, and other useful musical techniques.

Metamuse (Iverson 1990) is a program that analyzes music by breaking it into its constituent patterns and then reassembling these patterns using hierarchical self-similarity. Metamuse uses autocatalytic theory, a chemical process of enzyme reproduction that, in its musical form, creates chain reactions of similarly patterned music into strings of patterns biased toward similar structures on various levels and sublevels. The results, although limited to melodic lines, are good examples of numerous current attempts to base computer composition on natural phenomenon such as fractals. Unfortunately, in Metamuse the style of the original music does not generally survive the process.

As noted earlier, most traditional pattern-matching programs require that those using them know in advance what patterns are to be matched. In contrast, EMI and SARA seek patterns without any preconceived notion of their content. Also, pattern matching in EMI and SARA must recognize not only when two patterns are exactly the same (which is fairly trivial) but also when they are *almost* the same. This *almost* must also be *musical*, for some patterns in music can sound similar yet appear very different. Scientific pattern matching often relies on probability and statistics, which are excellent approaches for complex systems to accomplish such tasks. By contrast, EMI employs a limited set of variables called *controllers*, which affix musical parameters to vague outlines within which patterns are accepted as viably recognizable. This notion of vagueness, described further in chapter 3, enables EMI and SARA to compile patterns that look numerically dissimilar but sound similar.

Controllers act like the widths of a grid through which patterns are passed or not passed. If these controllers are resolved too narrowly, the patterns that are one aspect of a composer's style will not pass. If these controllers are resolved too broadly, elements that are not patterns identifying a composer's style will be allowed to pass. If these controllers are set correctly, only signatures will pass. Such pattern matching allows us to detect previously heard patterns even though the music may be new to our ears.

Figure 1.17 shows an example of how the presence of signatures can aid in style recognition. This example demonstrates Mozart's typical use of the Alberti bass, the repeated four-note structure in the left hand. The right hand in this example demonstrates a more subtle Mozart trait, namely, the leap to the lower chromatic nonharmonic tones C♯ and D♯ from the second to the third beats of the first and the second measures, respectively. The musical logic of the signatures in figure 1.17 along with the harmonic progression and the melodic sequence (the second measure being a transposed repetition of the first, with one subtle variation) combine to create an elegant passage of recognizable Mozartean craftsmanship. The constraints of his period and the signatures of his personal style are both evident and abundant.

Imagine that these two measures of music have been found in different works of Mozart rather than in the same work and that a pattern-matching program is attempting to determine whether they constitute a signature. As it stands, it is improbable that a nonmusical pattern matcher would find the two measures of figure 1.17 very similar except in rhythm. They have less than half their pitches in common (i.e., [C C B C E C♯ D] [D C♯ D F D♯ E]), and none of these fall in the same location. The second measure has less notes than the first, but, to our trained ears, these are easily identifiable as simple variations of the same pattern.

What is needed is a musical pattern matcher that can make the patterns appear more similar. One way EMI and SARA accomplish this is by reducing pitch representations to intervals. This means calculating the distances between notes in the patterns in half steps. This gives *[0 -1 1 4 -3 1]* for the first measure and *[-1 1 3 -2 1]* for the second measure. Note how the interval sets now show the similarity of the two patterns in both direction and amount of motion.

*Figure 1.17* Mozart, Piano Sonata (K. 279), first movement, mm. 5–6.

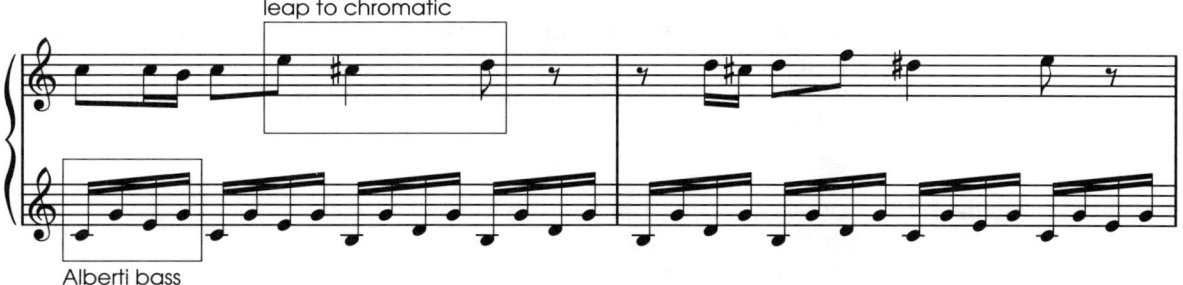

Discounting unisons and using a single controller (one that determines accuracy) proves the patterns to be musically similar enough to be a signature. Allowing, for example, any interval to be off by just a half step in either direction indicates the musical similarity of the patterns. This is very common in tonal music, where composers, to remain within a diatonic framework when sequencing, often substitute whole steps for half steps and vice versa. Thus, an allowance for these variations helps the pattern matcher find the musical similarities.

Defining a logical sample size is also an important matter. In Mozart's and Haydn's *Musikalisches Würfelspiel* (discussed earlier in this chapter), each "sample" is usually a measure in length and begins and ends in ways that allow for successful connectivity with other measures in a newly created work. Discovering the proper length for "samples" in the more complex recombinant process undertaken by EMI and SARA is more difficult. One way of determining sample size involves pattern matching as described in *Computers and Musical Style* (Cope 1991a; see particularly chapter 2, p. 46).

Figure 1.18 shows the same two phrases from Mozart sonatas given in figure 1.14 with signatures shown in boxes. The harmonic signature is indicated by S, AM stands for accompaniment motives and MM for melodic motives. These latter two matching elements comprise a pattern-matching subprogram that provides information about the dominating melodic and accompaniment models to the analysis portion of the program. The cadential signature in figure 1.18b will be discussed further in chapter 3 (see figure 3.1 and the section "A Sample Pattern-Matching Session").

The two musical examples in figure 1.18 have very much in common. This is critical to the pattern-matching process just described. The music chosen for EMI and SARA *must* be reasonably similar. This includes meter, key, and especially the predominant duration, which is particularly important. For example, imagine a work written first in quarter notes with the metronome set to 60 (one quarter note per second) and then rewritten in eighth notes with the metronome at 30 (one quarter note per two seconds or one eighth note per second). Performances of both versions would sound basically the same yet the scores would look and analyze very differently, particularly if the program being used assumes that certain beat constraints are in effect. Thus, entered music must be coerced to look the same in both

***Figure 1.18*** Some characteristics of: a) Mozart, Piano Sonata (K. 283), second movement, 1–4. b) Mozart, Piano Sonata (K. 330), third movement, mm. 9–16.

# BACKGROUND AND OVERVIEW

musical and numerical notations (for more information, see "Clarifying the Data" in chapter 2).

Ultimately, if a recombinant compositional process is to be successful, it must ensure that signatures survive the recombinative process in some recognizable form and in an appropriate context. This requires that the program controlling the deconstruction of, for example, the original Mozart determine the appropriate size of the signatures as well as recognize the signatures themselves. The recombination of signatures with nonsignatures must also be contextually sensitive. Signatures are location-dependent and must be immutable to the extent that all intervallic relationships remain intact. However, they must also be transposable so that they reconnect in a variety of logical and musical ways and in various different keys.

Once EMI and SARA discover signatures, these signatures are frozen to their location and then protected from recomposition. Without this protection, signatures would get lost in a Pandora's box of confused musical ideas. Once signatures are frozen, the remainder of the music can be fragmented fairly freely in terms of size as, at this stage, the idea is to create a *new* instance of the composer's style, that cannot be recognized as one of the individual works used for recombination.

## ■ AUGMENTED TRANSITION NETWORKS

Augmented transition networks (ATNs) offer excellent advantages for the sophisticated analysis and generation of natural languages and subsequently (as in the case of EMI and SARA) of music, particularly for the logic required for the reassembly of recombinant music. These networks were first formulated by researchers in natural language processing (NLP), a branch of both linguistics and computer science.

Natural languages are the spoken and written languages (e.g., English, French, and Chinese) that humans have used for thousands of years. Natural languages are rich and complex, the result of countless negotiations within and between cultures over those same thousands of years. Researchers in NLP attempt to study and reproduce such natural languages on computers. Natural language processing is important because it can provide insights into natural language origins, uses, and variations and because it will eventually allow humans to converse more naturally with computers.

Natural language communication with computers continues to develop as computers become more sophisticated, faster, and more user-friendly. Joseph Weizenbaum's ELIZA (1966), one of the first attempts to create dialogue-capable programs, responds to input with often credible statements and questions. Figure 1.19 shows a sample session with ELIZA, a simple program mimicking the conversational abilities of a nondirective psychologist. ELIZA keys on certain words that it finds in its database. These key words then initiate responses such as those shown in figure 1.19. Initial sessions with ELIZA give the impression that one is conversing with a conscious entity. However, protracted use quickly dispels such a notion as responses become predictable and, eventually, even irritating. Nonetheless, ELIZA's simplicity and conversational approach provide a useful introduction to the goals of NLP. Thus, implementations in LISP and other artificial intelligence–linked languages are often packaged with ELIZA modules.

**Figure 1.19** A sample session with the computer program ELIZA.

**Eliza:** May I help you?

**User:** Yes.

**Eliza:** How may I help you?

**User:** Answer a few questions for me.

**Eliza:** Are we talking about you?

**User:** No we are talking about questions.

**Eliza:** What questions do you wish to ask?

**User:** Who are you?

**Eliza:** Does that question really interest you?

**User:** No.

**Eliza:** Are you just saying no to be negative?

**User:** Must you always answer questions with questions?

**Eliza:** Does that question really interest you?

Another important landmark of NLP was SHRDLU (Winograd 1972). This program, written in LISP, demonstrated that computer programs were capable of understanding natural languages. However simplistically SHRDLU accomplished its tasks, it was able to interpret questions, statements, and commands; draw inferences; explain its actions; and, more importantly, learn new words. SHRDLU, a robot as well as a program, was capable of picking up and stacking blocks of various colors and responding to queries about their presence and location. The following is a brief conversation between a user (boldface) and SHRDLU:

> **put the blue pyramid on the block in the box.** ok. **is there anything which is bigger than every pyramid but is not as wide as the thing that supports it?** yes, the blue block. **does a steeple** sorry, I don't know the word "steeple." **a "steeple" is a stack which contains two green cubes and a pyramid.** I understand. **are there steeples now?** no. **build one.** ok. (Winograd 1972, pp. 14–15)

Finite state transition networks (FSTNs) represent another critical evolutionary step in NLP. These networks can best be diagramed through a series of arcs, with arrows representing program flow. Figure 1.20 is a simple FSTN. Here, Gertrude Stein's "A rose is a rose is a rose" is defined with flow moving left to right, except when an arc doubles back to initiate a recursive call to an earlier node. This flow could be described with the following text:

***Figure 1.20***  A finite state transition network (FSTN).

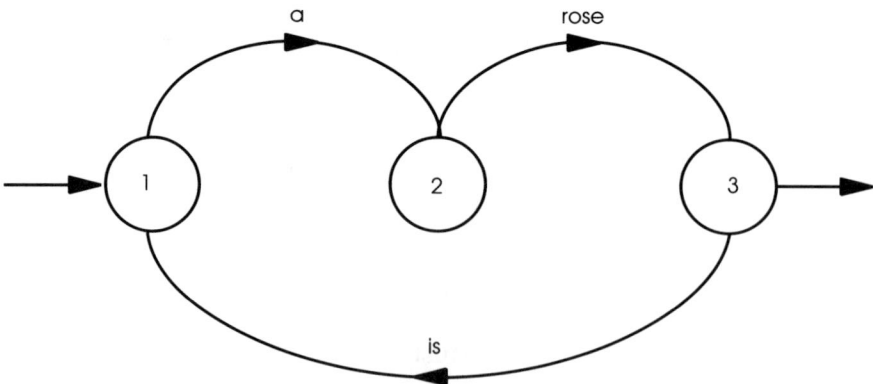

initial 1
final 3
from 1 to 2 by a
from 2 to 3 by rose
from 3 to 1 by is

with 3 to 1 referring to a backtracking directional arc. Thus, "A rose is a rose," "A rose is a rose is a rose," and so on are legitimate realizations of this figure. Representing such diagrams with explicit textual descriptions like the one above is useful for translating them into code. An FSTN could also be diagrammed with word types (e.g., nouns and verbs) so that "A car is a car" could be recognized or generated. This produces a more abstract network applicable to a wider variety of sentences. Such a net is similar to the ground plan of a *Musikalisches Würfelspiel*: word types substitute for harmonic function and the musical repeat sign parallels the role of 3 to 1. Thus, we can see that, even from the limited perspective of an FSTN, networks can have useful musical applications.

Finite state transition networks are one of the simplest computing programs for NLP, and their code can be small, fast, and effective. Therefore, FSTNs are powerful tools that should be used whenever they can adequately solve a given problem. Such use includes the recognition of finite languages and the simple translation of one language into another. Unfortunately, FSTNs fail when these languages allow an unlimited number of embedded structures. Such languages are called *nonfinite languages*. For example, a single FSTN could not recognize sentences that differ in terms of subphrases such as "The cup is full" and "The cup is full of water." A separate network would have to be built for each sentence, an extravagant price to pay for the analysis of relatively simple sentence constructions.

Nonfinite languages require the use of recursive transition networks (RTNs). Both FSTNs and RTNs are examples of transition networks (TNs). Recursive transition networks allow for embedded structures so that arcs may move between self-contained subnetworks. Thus, sentence subphrases may replace individual words. Figure 1.21 shows an example of an RTN with its subnetwork separated from the main structure. Note that this RTN is context free; it contains no actual words but rather representations for words, such as verbs (V), noun phrases (NP), verb phrases (VP), proper nouns (PN), and WH words like "who," "what," "where," and so on. The RTN shown in figure 1.21 could recognize the following sentences: "George eats cheese" (1–2–3–4) or "George, who eats cheese, is a mouse" (1–2–1–2–3–4–2–3–4) or "Who is George, when George eats

**Figure 1.21** A recursive transition network (RTN).

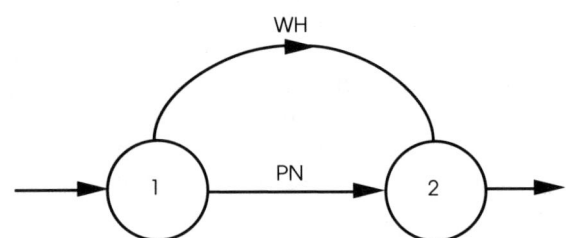

NP network

cheese" (1–2–3–1–2–1–2–1–2–3–4) and so on. However, neither an FSTN nor an RTN could recognize "The cheese was eaten by George" because this requires a transformational process. To accomplish such recognition, researchers in NLP use ATNs (augmented transition networks) which represent a transformational variation of RTNs. Augmented transition networks allow for output language to occur correctly but differently. Registers, or nodes where text, gender, and so on are stored, provide an opportunity to test elements in complex circumstances with the results being "built in a flexible order" (Gazdar and Mellish 1989, p. 108). William Woods adds that an ATN is a "recursive transition network which is capable of performing the equivalent of transformational recognition without the need for a separate transformational component and which meets some of the objections that have been raised against the traditional model of transformational grammar" (Woods 1970, p. 592).

Augmented transition networks were originally designed by natural language researchers to create computer interfaces that communicated easily and without redundancy. The ability of ATNs to recognize sentences such as "Jacob told Mary" as well as "Mary was told by Jacob" with the same parsing algorithm greatly enhances NLP programs. Augmented transition networks are similar to FSTNs in that they can be diagrammed using arcs and nodes and are often recursive. They differ from FSTNs in that they have registers associated with arcs and nodes that determine routes on the basis of conditions of those registers (ATNs will be discussed more fully in chapter 5).

In EMI and SARA, ATNs initially take the form of measure organizers. They first take a set of functions from the analysis of one of the works or phrases being used. For example, one possible analysis of figure 1.14a could be S-alberti-60-major-duple, S-6-alberti-60-major-duple, and so on. EMI then uses this progression or other extrapolated progressions as templates for creating new works by substituting applicable measures of music from collections of similar measures stored previously by the analysis portion of the program. For example, the same S-alberti-60-major-duple given above could logically be chosen as the first measure of a new work. This might be followed by another version of an S-6-alberti-60-major-duple second measure based on connectivity allowed by the local register of the ATN. EMI could even choose the same S-60-alberti-6-major-duple as the one that originally followed the first choice. Of course, the chance of that happening depends on the amount of analyzed music available (i.e., the larger the amount, the greater the chance for variety).

Resultant phrases may also be embellished in ways similar to those described in Kirnberger's *Methode Sonaten aus'm Ermel zu schüddeln* (1783) as well as having inner repeats of motives. As will be seen, EMI is also capable of projecting ATNs through the larger processes of phrase and form building. The creation of simple forms stems from a combination of analysis of music stored in databases and coded rules. Larger forms—such as multiphrased binary and ternary song forms and even more sophisticated forms such as sonata allegro, rondo, and fugue—result principally from coded rules.

Combining the concepts of hierarchical analysis, pattern matching, and ATN yields a process that can create new examples of music in a given style. Figure 1.22 shows an actual machine replication and one possible analysis that led to this replication (based on figure 1.16). The program itself is sufficiently complicated to make the determination of the actual sources difficult at best. Note here how the results are logical and, to a degree, even musical. The opening, first-measure melody seems balanced in direction with the two

**Figure 1.22** An EMI recombination with signature and a suggested analysis. The superscript "t" refers to transposition.

two-beat groupings acting in typical Classical-era antecedent/consequent motion. The cadential signature in the final measure is particularly effective and, as mentioned earlier, is a legitimate signal of the composer's style. In typical fashion, this signature is just over two beats in length. Transposition here is fairly routine. Note how the repetition of bar 1 in bar 3 helps contribute to stylistic recognition. In EMI this kind of repetition is based on the previously discussed analysis of repetitions found in the original music.

The signature presented in figure 1.17, that of the lower chromatic neighboring tone, appears in the recombinant example shown in figure 1.23, measures 2 and 4, an EMI-composed theme in the style of Mozart. This beginning of a sonata movement is sparse (mostly two voices) and simple (mostly scales), yet it has many Mozartean traits. For example, the harmonic functions follow the straightforward orders typical of Mozart's time. Also, the harmonic rhythm moves mostly by measure (typical of Mozart's style in third movement rondo form, the music used in the database for the creation of this example). This music is the result of hierarchical analysis, pattern matching, and ATN recombination of *all* the third movements of

*Figure 1.23* The beginning of an EMI-Mozart sonata movement.

his sonatas and demonstrates his subtle implied harmonies and voicing. By the time all the computational processes have taken place, it is almost impossible, save for the obvious signatures, to identify the origin of each element. The form (i.e., the amount and location of phrase repetition and contrast) was prescribed by the code and the key choice was chosen by random processes. However, the important ideas, signatures, and harmonic protocol were formed completely by the recombinant processes thus far described.

Figure 1.24 provides a good example of EMI output for complete works and directly relates to the code for creating inventions presented in chapter 4 of *Computers and Musical Style* (Cope 1991a). This invention, arguably in the style of Bach, represents an example of the imitative style of inventions and demonstrates how EMI uses an interlocking approach to inheritance (from databases) and rules for creating new works in given styles. Inheritance is clearly from Bach's Invention 9 (see figure 1.25) in both key, the first six notes of the melody, and two notes of the left-hand counterpoint. Interestingly, Bach's Invention 9 is a variation of his own Invention 7, shown in figure 1.26, though the keys are different and the rhythm and metric placement have changed. The invention rules in EMI circumvent exact inheritance (in this case of Invention 9) by requiring immediate imitation in the lower-voice counterpoint, an imitation not found so exactly in the Bach example (figure 1.25).

Inventions (and contrapuntal forms in general) seem aptly suited to computer generation. These kind of local formalisms do not typically demand the larger structural attention that, say, sonata allegro and other homophonic forms require. The variations created by the program, such as ignoring the tied note initially and then centering on it (see measures 5 through 10 and later of the EMI imitation in figure 1.24), are welcome aberrations that infuse EMI output with a kind of nonimitative vigor similar to that which seems to have sparked the originals. As we will see in the ensuing chapters, successful computer composition and imitation of style require an interplay between the various components of large programs and their databases. This interplay performs best when imitating the very process used by the composer whose works reside in the databases EMI uses as models.

**Figure 1.24** An EMI-Bach Invention.

**Figure 1.24** continued.

**Figure 1.24** continued.

***Figure 1.25*** The beginning of Bach Invention no. 9.

***Figure 1.26*** The beginning of Bach Invention no. 7.

# TWO

## The Analysis Component

The EMI and SARA analysis components constitute the first program element that entered music encounters. The analysis component prepares music for composition and, indirectly, for pattern matching. Such analysis stores segments of music as objects in the database in the various lexicons necessary for attaching incipient (pickup figures) and cadential gestures to newly composed music. Although the analysis component is not a formal element of the compositional process, it is a crucial part of the overall compositional system. In fact, in early versions of EMI, music was analyzed during the compositional process. However, the redundancy of reanalyzing music for each compositional run proved restrictive and time consuming. Reading through a typical database (e.g., figure 4.11) will quickly convince you of the importance of analysis in EMI's and SARA's composition strategy.

The EMI and SARA analysis programs determine the boundaries and identities of potentially independent segments of music. Such analysis is critical to the success of a program that attempts to construct *Musikalisches Würfelspiel* from works that were not intended to be such. If segmenting occurs at too large an increment, one may recognize elements of the originating databases in the output. If segmenting occurs at too small an increment, output can sound disheveled and pastiche-like.

Analysis in EMI and SARA takes place on many levels and in a variety of areas. First, the analysis program is responsible for segmenting the music into measure-sized lengths (automatic in EMI, user-controlled in SARA). This involves resetting onset times as if each segment were the beginning of a work, which may ultimately be the case. It also involves determining which notes fall on which side of a segment demarcation. Such decisions must be made intelligently, or output may contain two notes of fractional durations rather than a single note as in the original music. Second, EMI and SARA analyze the objects in the database using beat-to-beat `SPEAC` functions (see "Harmonic Analysis" below) as well as aspects of melody, form, and ATN (see chapter 5) connectivity. Third, EMI and SARA analyze and store incipient and cadential measures for special storage in lexicons and treatment during recomposition. Finally, EMI and SARA create appropriate lexicons for storing music of similar function. Although this aspect of the program does not constitute analysis per se, it ultimately makes composing possible.

## ■ DATABASES

Selecting, entering, and editing databases are among the most critical elements of creating viable new music in EMI and SARA. Almost all unsuccessful attempts at machine composition with these programs can be traced to poor databases rather than poor code. Expertly created and honed databases become wellsprings for a nearly endless supply of new, interesting works. Poorly created databases can make the results of even the very best code sound amateurish and even comical.

Selecting music with a perceived commonality of style is paramount to creating a viable database. This is often quite difficult. In some cases, one can misconstrue style as familiarity with often-heard works. In other words, specific themes and harmonic progressions are recognized rather than an actual style. In other cases, a style can be so broad that it identifies dozens of composers rather than a single composer. Choosing works which share a common and distinct style ensures at least a successful beginning to the replicating process.

One way to determine whether a certain composer's music has a perceivable style is to imagine recognizing a yet unheard work in that style. If such recognition depends on pitch and rhythm signatures, then EMI and SARA will probably be good at re-creating new works in that style. If only full-melody recognition or performance qualities (the sound of a particular ensemble) indicate style, then EMI and SARA probably will not be able to successfully imitate that style. Style often resides in orchestration (timbre), texture, lyrics, and so on, which are now only partially utilized by EMI and SARA. Choosing the appropriate timbral output can greatly enhance the perceived success of EMI and SARA. However, the use of certain lyrics or the familiarity of a performer's personal style is beyond the capabilities of either program.

Entering music into a database requires three separate but related steps. First, one must ensure that the data is mistake free. Playing and replaying databases as they are entered and cross-checking such performances against the original music is necessary to guarantee such correctness. Second, databases must be properly channelized; that is, data destined for separate timbres must be assigned separate MIDI channels for correct playback and pattern matching. One must often be able to accurately discern several channels per staff and several staves per work to accomplish this translation. Finally, metrical equivalencies must be observed. This means that duple meters such as $\frac{2}{4}$, $\frac{4}{4}$, $\frac{6}{8}$, and so on must be carefully assigned to the same duple meter. This is a skill that must be developed. A further explanation follows.

In figure 2.1a, the movement is by eighth note. In figure 2.1b, the music moves by sixteenth note. It is imperative that one of the two examples be altered to account for this difference. Otherwise, the output will exaggerate the apparent discrepancies between the two examples. Figure 2.2 demonstrates how the different rhythmic notations of the left-hand figurations of figure 2.1 might conflict during recombinancy. The examples here have been transposed to C major and follow a typical implied harmonic pattern. Note, however, how the speed of the Alberti-style bass appears to shift dramatically and without regard to style. In fact, such a simple conflict can cause immediate style contradictions even when, as in this case, only one voice (left-hand accompaniment) is involved. Without great care being taken by both the user when inputting music and the program when analyzing music, compositional output becomes trivial. Finding a common rhythmic dimension for databases containing music from different movements and works is a critical element in creating successful recombinant examples.

Figure 2.3 shows the two ways in which equivalency can be obtained. In figure 2.3a, the measures of figure 2.1a have been halved in duration to match the tactus of figure 2.1b. Figure 2.3b shows the reverse. Either case can effectively accomplish metric equivalency. This kind of alteration must be consistently adhered to for all the music of a given database. Note that this procedure is the first step toward clarifying the data, a subject that will receive a more detailed explanation shortly.

***Figure 2.1*** Mozart's sonatas: a) K. 545, first movement, mm. 1–2. b) K. 332, second movement, m. 1.

***Figure 2.2*** Conflicting rhythmic notations of figure 2.1 during recombinancy.

***Figure 2.3*** The music of figure 2.1 clarified rhythmically in two different ways.

Databases must also have a common key and mode: for simplicity, the key of C major. This is as true of phrases that conform to the key signature of a work as it is of those that have modulated to another key without altering the key signature. EMI and SARA can make such changes automatically but not without some risk, as even the most intelligent code occasionally loses its place, especially in highly chromatic music. Indicating the key of entered music makes database creation much more error free.

Nontonal music may be entered without regard to key. However, it should be noted that nontonal music sometimes requires redefinition of SPEAC symbols and other program variables. However, I have successfully entered and replicated Cope-style music on numerous occasions without making a single alteration to the program other than those normally associated with database entry and pattern matching.

## Database Format

Choice of method of storing music in a database depends on how such databases will be used for composition and for performance. Optimally, databases need to respond reliably to the requirements of a program and not require unnecessary translation to different formats. This means, at least for the applications described here, that data should respond to analysis, pattern matching, composition, and MIDI performance. EMI and SARA use what I call *events* for this purpose. Events describe the various attributes of each note with a single list of parameters of five separate but related elements. Figure 2.4 shows an example event as it would appear in an EMI or a SARA database.

The first element of the event list (or zero in figure 2.4) is the on-time. It is listed first because it is the most often referenced piece of data in the list. On-times of notes must constantly be refigured because the very nature of the recombinant approach requires that measures be reordered and the resulting on-times recalculated for performance. On-times are computed at 1,000 ticks per second, usually equated to a quarter note's duration. Relative values of half notes (2,000 ticks), eighth notes (500 ticks), and so on are computed from this standard. Triplet eighth notes are figured at 333 ticks with one of the three notes listed at 334 ticks to total 1,000 or with all three at 333 ticks; the loss of 1 tick per 1,000 is considered unimportant. On-times can reach quite large numbers. However, dividing by 1,000 makes computations fairly simple. On-times are relative, not absolute. As with printed music, the actual on-time of a pitch is

***Figure 2.4*** An event in EMI or SARA.

```
(0 72 1000 1 100)
```

determined by a combination of on-time (location in the score) and tempo. For example, an on-time of 1,000 could begin (1) one second after zero with a tempo of M.M. 60, (2) two seconds after zero with a tempo of M.M. 30, (3) half a second after zero witha tempo of M.M. 120, and so on.

The second entry of the event list (or 72 in figure 2.4) represents pitch. It is figured from the MIDI standard with middle C equal to MIDI note number 60; additions and subtractions of 12 produce C in various octaves, and additions and subtractions of 1 create half steps. Thus, 60–62–64–65–67–69–71–72 is the C major scale with intervening numbers producing chromaticism to that key. The accompanying CD-ROM has a note equivalency chart that is useful for converting MIDI note numbers to their note names. Events describe only *notes* (note ons and note offs) and not *rests*, relieving databases of vast amounts of unnecessary data. Rests occur naturally as the result of a lack of events. Not all systems function in this manner. Systems that use standard musical notation, for example, must signify rests because all measures must be complete. Other systems require rests to signal channel presence for internal clocks or other timing devices. For nearly a decade, EMI had such a channel/clock structure, which required that all channels have a continuous data stream whether notes were present or not (an approach that seems logical to a performing musician). Events, on the other hand, simply signify the presence of notes, and rests are implied by the absence of events. Events therefore provide an optimum means for data storage and retrieval.

The third entry of the event list (or 1,000 in figure 2.4) represents duration. Duration, as with on-time, is calculated with a quarter note equaling 1,000 ticks; relative durations are figured from that standard. The duration of an event contains the MIDI note off-time, which can be determined by the addition of the on-time plus the duration. Thus, an event with an on-time of 6,000 and a duration of 1,000 has an off-time of 7,000. Such information can be important to the EMI and SARA analysis systems when events straddle proposed measure subdivisions. Duration information can also be contradicted by choice of timbre in the MIDI output device. For example, performing a note of long duration with a sound of short duration (or vice versa) can nullify much of the durational aspects of the program's output. Duration, as with on-times, is relative, being a factor of its value within the current tempo.

The fourth entry of the event list (or 1 in figure 2.4) represents channel number (1 to 16). Channel numbers indicate the MIDI channel on which events are scheduled for performance. Ultimately, channels provide access to synthesizer and sampler timbre selections via MIDI interfaces. Channels may be assigned various roles in the MIDI instrument that is chosen for performance. The channel numbers stored in the database are intended to indicate the original voice separation of the music entered into that database.

The fifth entry of the event list (or 100 in figure 2.4) represents dynamics. Dynamics are based on 0 equaling silence and 127 equaling fortissimo, with the numbers between these values being relative to these extremes. Aftertouch, tremolo, filter shaping, and so on are considered post-MIDI controls in SARA and therefore are left to hardware/software combinations in the synthesizer/sampler stage of performance. Dynamics in EMI and SARA are relative in that they can be enhanced or contradicted by gain controls in amplifiers in the various playback hardware connected to the MIDI interface.

It should be noted that events are open ended; that is, one may add any desired parameter to the end of event lists with no ill effects on the first five elements. For example, a sixth position in some events may be occupied by an asterisk indicating that the event has been transposed during composition. This asterisk creates transposed sections and plays no other role in performance.

Events occur in larger phrase/work lists and do not occur independently in databases. Thus, because works can often be quite long, finding a given event may be difficult. The best method for locating events is by searching for on-times. Events are typically ordered sequentially to save time and make reading the event list easier.

## Clarifying the Data

EMI provides options to clarify data manually or automatically. SARA, however, requires users to manually clarify data to ensure that they have absolute control over the input music used for composition. SARA requires varying degrees of clarification for music to be properly stored as databases for composition. This clarification demands aural and computational skills beyond those of style detection and data entry.

Clarifying databases results in consistent output otherwise rendered haphazard by the vagaries of musical texture and notation. Figures 2.1 and 2.3 showed two versions of phrases by Mozart and how important it is that databases use the same tactus. This is a form of data clarification. It is also important to group phrases of the same meter type (i.e., triple, duple, etc.) together. In fact, EMI and SARA require that phrases of a particular metric type be placed in databases of that particular metric type (see chapter 4). As previously mentioned, such consistency also applies to key and mode, with C major being the preferred choice.

Ornaments such as trills, mordents, grace notes, and turns provide immediate indicators of certain musical styles and, as such, seem critical to the composing process. Unfortunately, leaving such details in coded music causes more problems than their retention enhances. This is similar to the problems that nonharmonic tones cause for harmonic analysis. The areas where ornaments create problems include (1) pattern matching, where the multitude of often extraneous notes can cause serious signature misinterpretations; (2) database recognition, where such distinguishing figures directly indicate their origins; and (3) functional analysis where such extra notes can cause problems. In some cases, such as pattern matching and analysis, special software filters can restrict program recognition to notes at or above a certain duration. Also, large databases can sometimes prevent ornaments from potential recognition because it is presumed that such a database would contain many instances of ornaments, some being subtle variants of others. Regardless, most of the databases coded for SARA do not contain ornaments. When output does require such figures, they can be added according to the performance practice of the period in which the composer lived.

The fact that EMI and SARA do not use ornamental figuration during composition remains one of their most controversial limitations. Whereas I favor a few tastefully added ornaments to the computer-finished product, some view this as tampering or insist that the original ornaments provide grist for interesting musicological and theoretical study. Regardless of the pros and cons of their inclusion, ornaments may be added to extant databases and/or included in user-created databases with duration subtracted from a previous or succeeding note.

Clarifying data also enhances the program's ability to compose effectively by ensuring that deconstructed musical fragments will create a multitude of choices for musical recombinancy. Data left unclarified will often have such unique characteristics as to almost guarantee that only the music that previously preceded and/or followed a particular fragment will do so again during recombination. Thus, unclarified databases often create instances of their former selves rather than new examples of music in their former styles.

Figures 2.5a and 2.5b show the opening measures of two of Mozart's piano sonatas. These phrases have different keys, modes (major or minor), rhythms (triplets in one and ties in the other), textures (3 to 5 notes in one and 3 in the other), and ranges. Maintaining the difference between these two phrases contributes to chaos in the resulting process of recombination or creates a repetition of one of the phrases as output. However, clarifying the data during the coding process will enhance the possibilities that the resulting output will be consistent, logical, and new.

Although some steadfastly maintain that the choice of key and mode are serious elements of composition, both EMI and SARA treat these attributes as superficial aspects of composition, leaving them to user choice in the output stage of the programs. Although key choice certainly has significant performance implications (e.g., one key being easier to perform than another on a given instrument) and thus can be a factor in composition, especially for composers who write through improvisation or in similarly tactile ways, such consideration is currently beyond the scope of SARA. Mode choice, on the other hand, can easily be considered integral to the composing process, and although SARA does not currently invoke special code for major versus minor keys (EMI does), the object system used (as will be seen in chapter 4) allows for storage and reapplication of such information during composition.

Rhythms are unique to the ideas expressed in composition and thus are difficult to alter or clarify without damaging the integrity of, among other things, the style of the composer. Ties, however, especially when they cross bar lines and thus fall out of the data of a single object in the database, must be altered. Ties become repeated notes in these circumstances. Ties internal to defined measures can remain intact and continue to provide essential information about style, such as syncopation. Ties that have been factored out of the stored databases may be returned at appropriate junctures in the final output by a user-controlled variable in the performance section of the user interface.

Tonal music often requires only three or four notes for defining function, so the doublings of notes can be removed to clarify texture. Conversely, notes may be doubled at the octave for the same reason. Such additions usually fulfill certain implied textural conditions of the original music. Added notes often maintain consistent textures at times when composers extracted notes because of fingering problems or other performance conflicts. Such additions give the stored music more opportunities for recombination during composition because textures of similar density find more suitable connections than those

**Figure 2.5** The first measures of the first movements of Mozart's sonatas: a) K. 281 and b) K. 282.

of dissimilar density. However, the practice of adding too many notes is discouraged in that the potential problems (notably that texture manipulation can obscure style) far outweigh the advantages.

Figures 2.6a and 2.6b show the two Mozart phrases of figures 2.5a and 2.5b after clarification. Note that the keys have been transposed to C major (the modes were already the same). The ties between duple beats have been changed to repeated notes, which is typically necessary only between metric divisions (see figure 2.5b, measure 1, beats 2 to 3 right hand). The textures have been clarified by removing the doubling (compare figure 2.5a, measures 3 and 4 left hand, and figure 2.6a, measure 2). Texture need not be altered if the music is generally of the same texture and/or if loading time and memory are not factors (thick textures represent more notes and require longer load times and more random access memory). A few of the embellishments have been removed for the previously discussed reasons (see figure 2.5a, measure 4 right hand, and figure 2.5b, measure 3 right-hand trill), and the grace note of measure 2 of figure 2.5b has been factored into the rhythm of the beat. The results demonstrate the effectiveness of the process: you can easily see that the potential for logical recombination has increased signifi-

***Figure 2.6*** Clarified versions of Mozart's sonatas from figure 2.5: a) K. 281 and b) K. 282.

cantly. Although this process might be seen as unscholarly by some, it is necessary for even the most simple pattern-matching and ATN processes.

Two other areas of data clarification need to be mentioned here. First, all database files in SARA require that input phrases have cadences. The program relies on user-defined phrase endings rather than on finding and defining cadences on its own. The program does analyze cadences for their basic structures and types (particularly half and full cadences) and stores them accordingly in cadence lexicons. However, SARA expects these cadences to be at the end of stored database phrases. The reasons for this user dependency should be clear to anyone attempting to locate cadences in complicated music: the task is not just onerous, but in some music it is often a matter of personal aesthetics rather than quantifiable judgment.

Clarification also includes identifying incipient gestures. Incipient gestures are considered special cases in SARA and are placed in lexicons designed for appropriate reuse (for definitions of lexicon objects, see chapter 4). Incipient gestures, usually a measure in length but containing mostly silence, are endemic to certain musical forms, optional in other forms, and a rarity in still others.

Such initial figures, because they often constitute single notes and chords, can disrupt normal recombinant composition by causing sudden silences and texture drop-out. Databases constructed prior to the current object system definitions avoided the inclusion of incipient gestures for this very reason. Incipient gestures are often difficult to define. Therefore, like cadences, SARA requires users to determine whether first notes are special (i.e., an incipient gesture) or ordinary (the first downbeat of music). The program is then able to (1) use the gestures in every instance of output (when the number of incipient gestures matches the number of phrases in a database), (2) use such gestures randomly (when there is a mismatch between the number of incipient gestures and number of phrases in a database), or (3) never use incipient measures (when the incipient lexicon is empty; for further definition, see chapter 4).

Critics of EMI and SARA databases often confuse data accuracy and data representation with the goal of output. The foremost goal when coding programs and data should be the potential for creating aesthetically pleasing and meaningful composition, not the accurate rendering of composer intent in a specific work. One should be concerned about musical style (and certainly a massaging of data can obscure style when practiced in the extreme). However, it is also important that the origins of the program's output not be detectable. When one can accurately perceive the music of derivation, the output becomes a superficial pastiche. Ultimately, those intent on absolute accuracy in translating data from score to coded database can still create their own unclarified databases.

## ■ ANALYTICAL TECHNIQUES

In general, SARA's analytical techniques fall into two distinct categories: pattern matching and SPEAC analysis. Pattern matching attempts to discover groupings of notes and rhythms, called *signatures* (discussed in chapter 3). SPEAC analysis attempts to determine the function or character of a bounded (in time, in simultaneity, or both) group of pitches. SPEAC analysis and pattern matching in EMI require that information be available in two forms: pitch and interval. Pitch information is important for recombination and inheritance by newly composed works. Interval information is important for comparing melodies, moving in similar directions, that occur in various transpositions and that, without interval comparisons, would not resemble one another. SPEAC analysis in SARA uses only pitch information, whereas pattern matching uses only interval information.

## Melodic Analysis

"Music is generally divided into harmony and melody, but we shall show in the following that the latter is merely a part of the former and that a knowledge of harmony is sufficient for a complete understanding of all the properties of music" (Rameau 1722, p. 3). I do not agree with this assessment by one of history's most renowned theorists of tonal harmony. Although most contemporary theory texts and courses at the university level seem to conveniently place melody and harmony together, melody and harmony have always seemed to be related but separate entities to me. I have therefore coded programs in both EMI and SARA according to this premise.

Melodic analysis in SARA requires figuring the contiguous notes of a melody across the seams of a proposed deconstruction. Thus, melodic analysis is determined by terminal-point destinations. These destinations are integral to the ATN portion of both the EMI and the SARA programs and are discussed at length in chapters 4 and 5.

Melodic analysis in both EMI and SARA follows the deeper structure of music described by Heinrich Schenker (1935). Figure 2.7a shows the melody of the opening four phrases from Mozart's Symphony no. 40. Looking at the first two phrases from a structural perspective reveals that repeated notes, upper neighbor notes, and scales all tend to embellish the straightforward dominant-to-subdominant motion of this music. This structure is shown in the first measure of figure 2.7b. The harmonic motion of tonic to supertonic, a member of the subdominant family, substantiates this simple motion. Performance by a conductor versed in structural analysis would tend to establish rather than contradict this middleground analysis, with dynamic emphasis on the downbeats of measures 3 and 5 of figure 2.7a. Furthermore, following Schenker's belief that a fundamental line (*Urlinie*) tends to move stepwise downward from significant scale degrees of the tonic triad (tonic, mediant, and dominant notes), one can almost predict that the next phrase(s) of this melody will emphasize the mediant note of the key (B♭). Figure 2.7a proves this to be true (as is often the case in tonal music). The third and fourth phrases of Mozart's symphony complement the first two phrases with a downward movement of the fifth to the third scale degree, as shown in the

**Figure 2.7** a) The melody of Mozart's Symphony no. 40 in G minor (K. 550). b) A reduction.

middleground layer analysis in figure 2.7b. This kind of structural analysis often reveals more about the tonal motion of a work than does a strictly functional analysis. Also, such middleground analyses complement functional analyses, providing indications of true structural motion (i.e., the real subdominant nature of the supertonic at the end of the second phrase of figure 2.7a).

Structural analyses such as the one just outlined provide clues to the underlying direction and form of tonal works. They provide performance grids indicating important notes for dynamic emphasis that otherwise might get lost amid foreground detail. These structural analyses also provide an understanding of how tonal composers successfully complete sections and movements and fulfill expectations on a large scale.

EMI analyzes databases for *Urlinie* notes and ensures that such scale degrees survive the recombination process by providing large-scale unity at a background level. Such analysis is based on a correlation between logical melodic notes and corresponding harmonic motions, just as in figure 2.7. This analysis depends, of course, on the logical ordering of phrases in the database (i.e., a phrase-numbering scheme that reflects that of the original work). Because SARA (the program included on the CD-ROM with this book) is small in comparison with EMI and composes with databases sufficient for interesting new compositions but not for compositions in larger forms, it does not contain the code for such analysis. However, it does contain structural projection code (see chapter 5, particularly figures 5.22 and 5.23 and relevant discussions) capable of large-scale structural control similar to that of EMI. For further information on how EMI analyzes databases for recreating structural middlegrounds and backgrounds in new compositions, see *Computers and Musical Style* (Cope 1991a, especially chapter 2).

Structural reductions, thought by many to be uniquely suited to tonal music (possibly because Schenker himself worked exclusively in that realm), have useful applications in nontonal music as well. Allen Forte (1955), for example, has analyzed elements of foreground, middleground, and background in Stravinsky's *Petrouchka* (1911), Arnold Schoenberg's Phantasy for Violin with Piano Accompaniment, op. 47 (1951), and Béla Bartók's Fourth String Quartet (1928), among others. My own work with the structural analysis of Balinese *gamelan gong kebyar* has produced interesting results in terms of analytical comparisons with both Western composition and EMI composition (Cope 1991a). In all these instances, however, it is the concept of layer reduction, not the rule, that has been applied.

## Harmonic Analysis

Harmonic analysis in EMI and SARA is a composite of the current definitions of harmonic rhythm (or segmenting) and harmonic vocabulary. These definitions are bound to special variables. The special form `defvar` (for "define variable") is the standard way of declaring global variables in a LISP program. Defining variables in a program in this way makes them available to all the functions in that program. Unlike `setq` (for "set quote"; see Cope 1991a, chapter 3), `defvar` allows for quoted documentation in its definition, making such variables easily understood during programming without having to glean their definition from their names or possibly opaque lists of data. Most variables of the special type `defvar` are stored in a special file in SARA (see the file sara-defvar on the accompanying CD-ROM). It should be noted, however, that to alter a variable originally set with the special form `defvar` requires the use of `setq` (which does not alter the documentation originally incorporated with the `defvar`). Successive calls to `defvar` using the same variable name will cause no alteration of the original definition. Also, variables defined by the special type `defvar` are often surrounded by two asterisks to denote their global status. This distinguishes these variables from temporary or local types, such as those defined by `setq` and the various forms of the macro `let` occuring in the body of function definitions.

**Figure 2.8** The default SPEAC settings for SARA.

```
(defvar *analysis-lexicon* '
  (((24 36 48 60 72 84 96 108 28 40 52 64 76 88 100 31
     43 55 67 79 91 103) c1)
   ((29 41 53 65 77 89 101 33 93 105 81 45 57 69 24 36
     48 60 72 84 96 108) p1)
   ((31 43 55 67 79 91 103 35 47 59 71 83 95 107 26 38
     50 62 74 86 98 29 41 53 65 77 89 101) a1)
   ((35 47 59 71 83 95 107 26 38 50 62 74 86 98 29 41
     53 65 77 89 101) a2)
   ((28 40 52 64 76 88 100 31 43 55 67 79 91 103 35 47
     59 71 83 95 107) c4)
   ((26 38 50 62 74 86 98 89 101 77 65 29 41 53 93 105
     81 69 33 45 57) p2)
   ((33 45 57 69 81 93 105 24 36 48 60 72 84 96 108 28
     40 52 64 76 88 100) c2)
   ((26 38 50 62 74 86 98 30 33 42 54 66 78 90 102 45
     57 69 81 93 105) s1)
   ((28 40 52 64 76 88 100 32 35 44 56 68 80 92 104
     47 59 71 83 95 107) s3)
   ((33 45 57 69 81 93 105 25 37 49 61 73 85 97 28 40
     52 64 76 88 100) e1)
   ((35 47 59 71 83 95 107 27 39 51 63 75 87 99 30 42
     54 66 78 90 102) e3)
   ((24 36 48 60 72 84 96 108 28 31 34 40 52 64 76 88
     100 43 55 67 79 91 103 46 58 70 82 94 106) c3)
   ((25 37 49 61 73 85 97 28 31 34 40 52 64 76 88 100
     43 55 67 79 91 103 46 58 70 82 94 106) e2)
   ((27 39 51 63 75 87 99 24 30 33 36 48 60 72 84 96
     108 42 54 66 78 90 102 45 57 69 81 93 105) e4)
   ((32 44 56 68 80 92 104 26 29 35 38 50 62 74 86 98
     41 53 65 77 89 101 47 59 71 83 95 107) a3)
   ((32 44 56 68 80 92 104 24 30 36 48 60 72 84 96 108
     42 54 66 78 90 102) p3)
   ((25 37 49 61 73 85 97 29 32 41 53 65 77 89 101 44
     56 68 80 92 104) p4)
   ((30 42 54 66 78 90 102 25 37 49 61 73 85 97 34 46
     58 70 82 94 106) s4)
   ((27 39 51 63 75 87 99 31 43 55 67 79 91 103 34 46
     58 70 82 94 106) a4)
   ((34 46 58 70 82 94 106 26 38 50 62 74 86 98 29 41
     53 65 77 89 101) s2)))
```

The analysis of harmonic function in SARA is relegated to SPEAC representations via reference to the defvar'ed definitions in figure 2.8 (see also Cope 1991a, chapter 3). Here, pitches, projected through various octaves, are catalogued according to function. The program then consults these definitions with groups of pitches in a given beat. The consultation that reveals the most corresponding matched pitches succeeds as a definition. Although simple, this process works and, given that any definitions may be substituted for those currently in the program, can provide analytical models for any music whose fundamental style attributes reside in the domain of pitch.

It should be noted that each SPEAC symbol belongs to a family of similarly named symbols (S1, S2, etc.). To some extent, the numbers represent Shenkerian "grounds," with lower numbers indicating deeper structural levels. Therefore, S1 represents a statement at a background level, whereas S3 represents a statement at the foreground level. In SARA these harmonic levels are then computed in counterpoint to the *Urlinie* to achieve an *Ursatz* (or fundamental statement; see Schenker 1935) of the music being analyzed.

Figures 2.9a–c shows how the SARA analytical process operates. In figure 2.9a, the program captures a beat of pitches. In figure 2.9b, these pitches are referenced to the SPEAC definitions. In figure 2.9c, C1 is returned as the symbol representing the definition because its comparison to the various definition lists produces the highest number of common elements. It should be noted again that this analysis is part of the database program and not part of the composition program. This saves repeating the process for each composition run. It should also be noted that in EMI (not SARA) the SPEAC lookup process is dynamic; that is, the definitions for SPEAC symbols change as context changes. Thus, a C1 (as in figure 2.9c) may result from one context (here C–E–G in a cadence), an S1 may result from another context (e.g., an initial chord in a phrase), and so on.

Figure 2.10 shows two analysis functions, the first of many functions presented in this text. These functions are written in the computer language LISP, which requires a brief introduction at this point. LISP (short for "list processing") requires that function names occur first and follow left parentheses and that arguments (data) be followed by right parentheses (for more information on LISP and descriptions of some basic LISP primitives, see Cope 1991a, chapter 3). Therefore, the addition represented by "2 + 2" in standard notation would be represented by "(+ 2 2)" in LISP, with "+" being the function and both "2"s being data. Function definitions in LISP include the function defun (for "define function"), followed by a list

**Figure 2.9** The analytical lookup process.

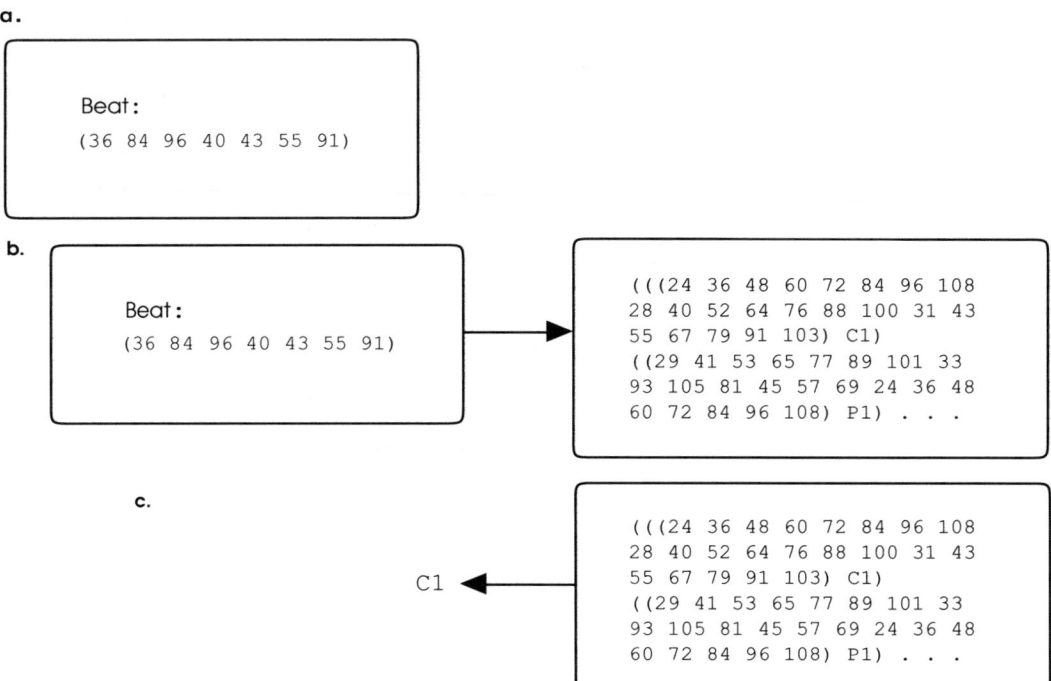

of arguments, followed in turn by the body of the function itself. It should be noted that the word *function* here does not mean the same thing as function in music. In computer languages, a function is an operator that alters data in ways described by the function's definition. In music, function is a manifestation of hierarchy. So that the two meanings can be distinguished here, reference words regarding musical and programming code will accompany the initial appearance of the particular use of the word *function* with the understanding that these meanings do not change until another reference is established.

Wherever possible in this book, I have used LISP functions whose name describes their action. Thus, the function `first` returns the first element of its argument. I have also attempted to create new function names with similar goals. The same is true with variable names for arguments and declared variables that represent data defined by using `defvar` or `setq`. Thus, the intent of the following code should be

***Figure 2.10*** The functions `get-function` and `compare`.

**a.**
```
1. (defun get-function (chord-notes)
2.    (second (compare chord-notes *analysis-lexicon*)))
```

**b.**
```
1. (defun compare (harmonic-notes harmonic-functions)
2.    (let* ((counts (count-harmonic-notes harmonic-notes
3.                                          harmonic-functions))
4.           (highest (first (my-sort '> counts))))
5.      (if (count highest counts)
6.          (find-nearest-the-front
7.              (first (my-sort '< harmonic-notes))
8.              (get-relevant-analyses counts
9.                                     highest
10.                                    *analysis-lexicon*))
11.         (nth highest harmonic-functions))))
```

clear: "`(play (+ first-note 12)`," to play the variable "first-note" in octave transposition, or "`(get-smallest '(17 12 3 39))`," which returns "3."

Figures 2.10a and 2.10b show the functions `get-function` and `compare`. These intermediate-level functions are responsible for making the comparisons between gathered notes and harmonic functions. The function `compare` uses `count-harmonic-notes` (line 2 of figure 2.10b) to add up the number of matched notes between the chord notes and the notes in the various regions of the `*analysis-lexicon*` (shown in Figure 2.8). The LISP function `second` (line 2 of figure 2.10a) then retrieves the SPEAC symbol from the results of `compare`.

The function `weight-notes` in `analyze` (in line 3 of figure 2.11) weights its argument members by duration and dynamic. Notes with longer durations and louder dynamics are multiplied in strength by factors determined by a sliding scale. For example, notes that exceed 500 ticks in duration (eighth note) and 100 steps in dynamic (forte) are weighted five times stronger than those less than 250 ticks in duration (sixteenth note) and less than 75 steps in dynamic (mezzoforte). Also, notes that occur on the beat are given more strength. Such weightings are achieved by repeating stronger notes

**Figure 2.11** The function `analyze`.

```
1. (defun analyze (chords)
2.   (if (null chords) nil
3.     (cons (get-function (weight-notes (first chords)))
4.           (analyze (rest chords)))))
```

 **CD-ROM**

The function `analyze` (shown in figure 2.11) can be found in the file named sara-database in the sara source folder. This function takes a list of event-lists as in '(((0 79 250 1 100) (0 64 250 2 100) (0 48 500 3 100) (500 65 500 2 100) (500 50 500 3 100)))) and returns a list of SPEAC function names such as (a1). Running `analyze` with different lists of events can be a useful introduction to the analysis program. Tracing `analyze` and its various subfunctions, such as `get-function` and `compare` (see figure 2.10), can also be illuminating. Observing the functions `weight-notes`, `weight-note`, and `on-the-beat?` (all in the file sara-database) provides information on how SARA factors rhythm into the analysis process. ❖

so that they have more influence in determining function during harmonic analysis. A good example of this appears in the following sample runs of `weight-notes`:

```
(weight-note '(0 67 500 1 127))
(67 67)
(weight-note '(500 67 249 1 74))
(67)
(weight-note '(0 67 1000 1 127))
(67 67 67 67 67)
```

These repeated notes are then appended to the original collection of notes, which are then compared (by `compare` in `get-function`; see figure 2.10a) to the various chord definitions located in the *analysis-lexicon*. In this manner, `analyze` can interpret subtle gradations and nuances of harmonic function that otherwise could produce misleading results.

Chapter 6 of *Computers and Musical Style* (Cope 1991a) discusses the potentials of "varying the interpreter protocols." In both EMI and SARA, such variations are accomplished by revising the definitions in the `*analysis-lexicon*` (see figure 2.8). Thus, SPEAC functions can be attached to any assemblage of notes that the user wishes. This is particularly useful when analyzing certain twentieth-century music or pre–common-practice works. Thus, the notes C–E–F (36, 40, and 41 and projections) could be analyzed as `C1` (tonic with C as root in C major in traditional terms), as an `A1` (subdominant with F as root, according to Hindemith [1939] acoustic root strengths), or in any other way desired. Such revisions can be particularly useful when using programs like SARA for analysis only. When using the program for composition, such analysis becomes critical for proper ATN: if analysis is not accurate, then disparately functioned measures can be joined, causing disruption of both output quality and style adherence.

## ■ ANALYSIS PROGRAM

The top-level function for analyzing music in SARA is `analyze` (see figure 2.11). It returns a list of SPEAC names that are the result of applying `get-function` (in line 3) to its argument, which has been appropriately weighted by use of the function `weight-notes`. As described in the text accompanying figure 2.7, EMI and SARA rely on Schenker-inspired layer analysis for composing music with tonal backgrounds. In SARA this structure is formed by preexisting code and not by analysis (see the relevant description of the functions `schenker-plot`, `translate-urlinie`, and `translate-ur` in figures 5.22 and 5.23). In EMI, however, such structure is based on the analysis of music in the loaded databases. Such analysis follows two separate processes. First, ordered phrases in a database are treated as contiguous members of a section of a work. Thus, although music is stored by phrase in EMI, the analysis program can analyze structure. Second, structural analysis is an integral, active part of the composition process. Phrases completed as parts of balanced pairs are analyzed for their SPEAC components, and second phrases are composed using the projected logic of this analysis.

Structural analysis of both of these types follows the same principles as those described in conjunction with figure 2.7, the difference being that this compositional SPEAC analysis is accomplished "on the fly" rather than being stored in databases. Because both the derivation of work structure and the just-composed phrase structures must occur at the time of composition, these types of analyses significantly prolong compositional run times. This is the principal reason for omitting them in SARA. On the other hand, the importance of these types of dynamic analyses in the creation of larger forms is one of the most elegant sophistications found in many EMI compositions.

For example, figure 2.12 shows an EMI-composed composition in the style of Robert Schumann called *Childhood Scene*. This work is based on Schumann's *Kinderszenen* ("Scenes of Childhood"), op. 15 (1838) and other of Schumann's piano works. It is a good example of how the EMI analysis code operates. The melody follows straightforward layer processes moving $\hat{5}-\hat{4}-\hat{3}-\hat{2}-\hat{1}$ over the course of the work, with measures 1 to 16 a prolongation of the dominant D in G major. The cadence of the first section in measure 16 ends with the dominant in the melody, whereas the repetition of the same section (beginning in measure 17) ends with the tonic G in the melody in the final measure of the work. The $\hat{4}$, $\hat{3}$, and $\hat{2}$ scale degrees (or the notes C, B, and A) of the *Urlinie* occur in measures 23, 24, and 26, respectively, and are given extra weight in the repeated section by the final cadence. This *Urlinie* was composed by the program rather than derived from Schumann's music, though clearly this piece is based primarily on the brief work called *Von fremden Ländern und Menschen* ("From Foreign Lands and People"), part of which is shown in figure 2.13. Interestingly, Schumann's short piece uncharacteristically shows no appreciable melodic difference between repeated sections, though it does have agogically altered cadential notes in the accompaniment in its final measures.

The progressions of the EMI and Schumann works are different but related (i.e., the Schumann work was not a network for the EMI-Schumann). Each work's opening eight measures provide most of the functions used in the measures that follow. The Schumann work explores the tonic, subdominant, dominant, and secondary dominant of the dominant regions (C1, P1, A1, and S1), whereas the EMI-Schumann uses the tonic, subdominant, dominant, supertonic, and secondary dominant (leading tone) of the dominant areas (C1, P1, A1, P2, and S1; only one function difference). The second section of the Schumann uses the supertonic (present in the first measures of the EMI-Schumann) and the dominant of the submediant along with the chords of its first eight measures, whereas the EMI-Schumann uses the submediant as well as the other chords of its opening section.

**Figure 2.12** The EMI-Schumann *Childhood Scene.*

**Figure 2.13**  Schumann's *Von fremden Ländern und Menschen* ("From Foreign Lands and People"), from *Kinderszenen*, op. 15, no. 1.

Of interest here is the secondary diminished-seventh chord of the dominant (C♯–E–G–B♭) at the beginning of measure 2 in the EMI-Schumann. It resolves to the tonic in root position rather than to its normal dominant function, the expected chord from standard tonal functional protocol (or `S1` to `C1` in `SPEAC`). This variation probably is less the result of apparent creativity on the part of the program than it is of finding a variation of it in another work in the database: *Der Dichter spricht* ("The Poet Speaks"), no. 11 of *Kinderszenen* shown in figure 2.14. In measures 3 and 4 of this piece, the secondary harmony of the dominant moves to the tonic six-four (a dominant-type function), paving the way for the analytic code to produce a similar variation in the EMI-Schumann.

Although the Schumann *Von fremden Ländern und Menschen* was not used as a transition network for the EMI imitation, the analysis of the form, harmonies, and progressions of harmonies of figure 2.13 obviously served the program as a model. Even the fermata in measure 14 of the Schumann was encapsulated by the program (seen in measure 16 of the EMI-Schumann and symbolically rather than temporally represented in the data). Also, the triplet rhythm of the accompaniment, the stepwise voice leading, and the basic shape of

**Figure 2.14** Schumann's *Der Dichter spricht* ("The Poet Speaks"), from *Kinderszenen*, op. 15, no. 13.

the various lines all serve both works well. Analysis of the original Schumann works, particularly regarding the ways in which these various elements interlock and imitate, helps to fuse the EMI-Schumann into a work that is separate from but related to the originals.

# THREE

## The Pattern-Matching Component

Whereas the analysis components of EMI and SARA focus on analyzing musical data for storage in databases for recomposition, the pattern-matching (recognition) component ensures that perceived signatures will remain intact in the output. Pattern matching assumes that recombinant music, no matter how intelligently its parts are analyzed and refitted together, will lose an integral part of its style without ensuring that some patterns, larger than a part size, will survive the process.

Patterns take many forms. However, to be detected by a pattern matcher these patterns must have some shared reference. Leonard Meyer has attempted to encapsulate just such a commonality:

> The apprehension of a series of physically discrete stimuli as constituting a pattern or shape results from the ability of the human mind to relate the constituent parts of the stimulus or stimulus series to one another in an intelligible and meaningful way. For an impression of shape to arise an order must be perceived in which the individual stimuli become parts of a larger structure and perform distinguishable functions within that structure. A shape or pattern then . . . is meaningful and significant because its consequence can be envisaged with some degree of probability. (Meyer 1956, p. 157)

Pattern matching can help create compositions more true to a given style (Cope 1990), with musical style defined as "the identifiable characteristics of a composer's music which are recognizably similar from one work to another" (Cope 1991a, p. 30). The recognition of these signatures can aid in the perception of that composer's musical style. These signatures may be varied to some degree at each appearance but nonetheless remain perceptible as variations of the same musical idea.

My research has shown that signatures are typically two or more beats in length (see also Cope 1991a). They are generally locationally dependent and size specific. Figure 3.1 shows two versions of a classical cadential signature from Mozart, with choice of key, number of notes, and type of accompaniment being variations. The intervals of both melodies are exactly the same, with variations occurring in rhythm. The harmony is virtually the same for both examples functionally, although there are discrepancies in the voicing and doubling.

Once the EMI and SARA pattern matchers discover signatures, they protect them from recomposition. Without this protection, signatures would get lost in a Pandora's box of confused musical ideas. Once signatures are protected, the remainder of the music can be reconstructed according to the appropriate metric subdivision.

**Figure 3.1**  Two versions of a signature of Mozart:
a) Piano sonata, K. 330, third movement, m. 110. b) Piano sonata, K. 547a, first movement, mm. 181–82.

## ■ TESTING THE SIGNATURE THEORY

I have attempted, on numerous occasions, to evaluate the effectiveness of signatures in communicating musical styles to listeners. Although in each case I have tried to verify at least some of the qualifications of the subjects used for these evaluations, I have not been able to specifically define either the test or the control groups in any scientific manner. However, the findings here are more than anecdotal and, barring a more formal set of tests, seem useful at least in providing testimony for enhanced style recognition when signatures are present. In 1991, I asked eighteen students midway through their second year of music theory to evaluate twenty-five examples of Mozart and machine-composed Mozart. These students averaged 10.4 years of study on a musical instrument at the time of this experiment. Six of the students were pianists and the others primarily guitarists and vocalists. There was one violinist and one clarinetist in the group. The students professed to have studied (on average) 9.5 works by Mozart on their instruments and to have heard (on average) 28 works by Mozart. In addition, their theory teacher had assigned the following analyses of Mozart during the first half of the year: the development sections of the first movements of K. 570 and K. 576, the first movement of K. 331 (all piano sonatas), and the so-called Dissonance string quartet, K. 465.

The test consisted of a questionnaire regarding the above-named qualifications followed by twenty-five multiple-choice questions. The students were instructed to respond whether the played example (on tape) was Mozart. The examples consisted of (1) phrases of Mozart chosen from the lesser-known sonatas to avoid easy recognition, (2) phrases of machine-composed music without signatures, and (3) phrases of machine-composed music with signatures. In all cases, the machine-composed examples that were perceived to be the best examples of stylistic replication were used. All phrases were then randomly mixed so that signature and nonsignature examples were not differentiated in any way. The test examples were played twice, with a ten-second delay between each playing. The students were not told the number of actual Mozart examples present.

Sixty-seven percent of the students recognized the Mozart phrases as Mozart. Sixty percent of the students identified the machine-composed examples with signatures as Mozart. Thirty-eight percent of the students identified the machine-composed examples without signatures as Mozart. Breaking the scores down by instrument yields interesting results as well. By far, the single most successful results came from the lone violinist in the group. This individual recognized eighty percent of the real Mozart and thought that sixty percent of the machine-composed music with signatures and twenty percent of the machine-composed music without signatures were Mozart. Aside from the violinist's scores, the pianists scored the highest: seventy-two percent for real Mozart, sixty-four percent for machine-composed music with signatures, and thirty-six percent for machine-composed music without signatures. The lone clarinetist scored twenty percent for real Mozart, forty percent for machine-composed music with signatures, and eighty percent for machine-composed music without signatures. The six guitarists scored seventy percent for real Mozart, fifty-seven percent for machine-composed music with signatures, and thirty-five percent for machine-composed music without signatures. These latter scores suggest some correlation between Mozart's available repertoire for the respective instruments represented in the class and style recognition. However, the information from the scores regarding the number of years studied and works known was unrevealing. Scores were uneven, and they generally increased and decreased in parallel (i.e., as Mozart recognition increased, so did the recognition of style in machine-composed signature and nonsignature works).

This study, of course, falls outside the framework of scientifically valid research. It does, however, indicate that signatures can contribute to style recognition on the part of some listeners. Although it may take years to establish absolute proof of this assertion, it would seem that perceived style may survive recombinant processes if certain elements such as signatures are retained by that process.

A test similar to the one just described was presented at a special three-day demonstration during the 1992 conference of the American Association for Artificial Intelligence (AAAI) in San Jose, California. Called "Artificial Intelligence and the Arts," this test pitted machine-composed examples with signatures in the style of Mozart against actual Mozart. Almost two thousand individuals tested their ability to recognize Mozart. Results usually hovered near the fifty percent mark, suggesting that the audience was unable to distinguish between machine-composed Mozart and the real thing. Although the participants could not be prejudged for competence (and thus the test has absolutely no scientific value), the results do indicate that the machine-composed music has some stylistic validity and that, for the layperson at least, real Mozart is hard to distinguish from artificial Mozart containing Mozart signatures.

## ■ PATTERN-MATCHING TECHNIQUES

Although it may seem obvious, it must be noted that music entered into a pattern matcher must itself have style if matching is to produce useful signatures. Pattern matchers can detect style only to the extent that it is present in the source material. However, pattern matching music for signatures can be one way of determining whether certain music has a definable style recognizable by signatures.

The pattern matchers for EMI and SARA operate on two fundamental components: pitch and duration. The style of the music under analysis must reside in one or both of these variables. Musical styles that are distinguished principally by their timbral, dynamic, or other qualities are not capable of being analyzed by these programs (more recent implementations of EMI include timbre and dynamics; see chapter 7). A minimum of two works, or coherent parts of works, need to be entered into a database for the pattern matcher described here to operate. These should be coded (and clarified) in certain ways so that the pattern matcher can do its job efficiently (as described in chapter 2). Obviously, using just pitch and duration in the process has significant limitations. Missing are all the inflections of timbre, articulation, place within the bar, relation to beat, and so on. However, these elements can be factored into the pattern-matching process by additional code in strategic locations.

As discussed in chapter 2, one should eliminate pitches shorter than a certain duration when preparing databases. Typically, notes of 100 or less in duration (less than a thirty-second note) should be discarded to make pattern matching easier. On a more complex level, key and mode should be homogenized to C major. Removing modulations is also extremely important for melodic pitch pattern matching. Data should be in one key from beginning to end to ensure the legitimate matching of chromaticism. Removing modulations involves transposing the part of a phrase in a new key to the original key before ultimately transposing the entire phrase to C major.

Pattern matching can be aligned in a variety of ways with quite different results. For example, a serial alignment can eliminate patterns at the point where they fail a given test, thus avoiding further non-illuminating tests. Parallel alignment can, however, allow patterns that pass a certain number of tests to succeed. Figures 3.2a and 3.2b show how serial and parallel alignments of tests work with two simple input patterns using two tests: correct interval and direction matching. In the serial pattern match of figure 3.2a, although the patterns pass the interval test, they fail the direction test and thus do

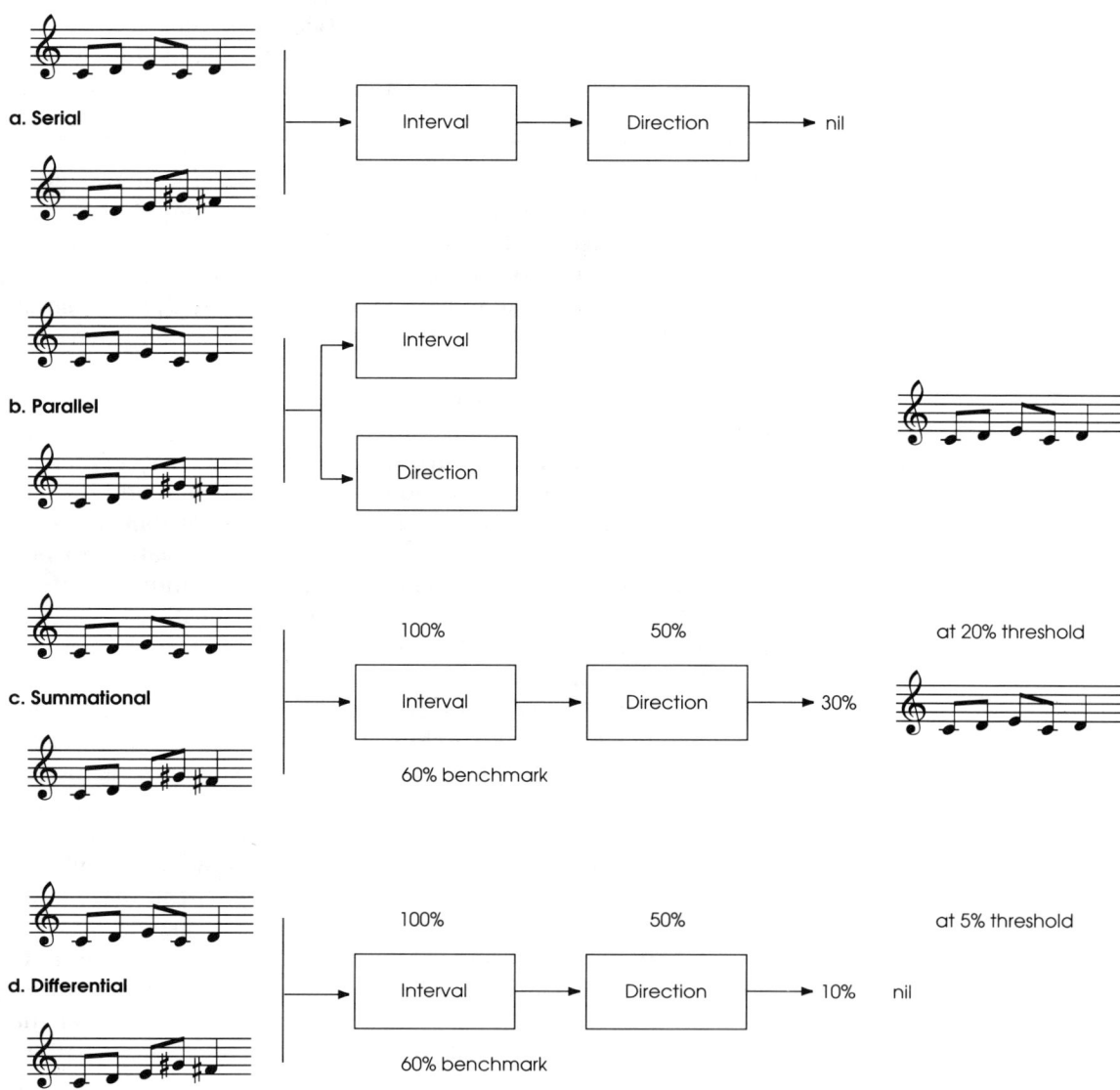

**Figure 3.2** Serial and parallel matching examples with summational and differential refinements.

not match. However, in the parallel pattern match of figure 3.2b, the patterns pass the interval test and therefore succeed.

Tests can also act cooperatively rather than pass/fail so that patterns gain weight with each successful trial. Thus, patterns can fail certain tests and still succeed if their resultant weights surpass a certain threshold. The summational form of pattern matching adds the various pattern-matching test results in relation to a provided benchmark. In figure 3.2c, the output must surpass the threshold for the match to succeed. Thus, in figure 3.2c, comparing interval and direction tests at 100 and 50 percent correct, respectively, with a benchmark of 60 percent, produces a summational result of 30 ([100 − 60] +[50 − 60]). In figure 3.2d, because the results represent a deviation, the output must fall below the threshold for the match to succeed. Thus, the differential form of pattern matching returns the absolute value of those test results below a provided benchmark. Therefore, in figure 3.2d, the comparison of interval and direction tests at 100 and 50 percent correct, respectively, with a benchmark of 60 percent produces a result of 10 (0 + [50 − 60]). Refinements and combinations of pattern-matching strategies can produce useful results.

EMI uses both serial and parallel forms of pattern matching with both summational and differential weightings. Such test strategies have the advantage of being able to detect very subtle pattern variations. These strategies also have the disadvantage of having to set literally hundreds of controllers, each setting of which having the sensitivity to pass or fail widely different sets of patterns. To save users the onerous task of setting and resetting such a large number of controllers, SARA uses a simple serial type of pattern matcher with pass/fail nodes. As will be seen later in this chapter, the matcher is still quite capable of detecting signatures, though sensitivity is exchanged for simplicity and ease of use.

There are also many ways to gauge accuracy in pattern matching. For example, *tonal* and *real* approaches to variation in the melodic portion of the pattern matcher's operation can produce quite different results. The term *tonal* simply means that the variant conforms to the half-step, whole-step patterns of major and minor keys, whereas the term *real* reflects an exact intervallic match. Pattern matchers set to *real* forms of comparison may miss patterns that conform to *tonal* variances unless controllers are set so wide as to allow many nonsignatures to pass as well. Pattern matchers set to *tonal* forms of comparison may not be able to distinguish between variations of chromatic and/or nontonal patterns.

Figure 3.3 shows a very simple musical line with three variants of the same four-note motive. The pattern is unmistakable to the ear—

it is a *simple* tonal pattern, sequencing stepwise down the C major scale. I emphasize the word *simple* because to the ear it is exactly that. For a computer program, however, these motives do not appear to be repeating patterns at all except in direction. If we chop the music into three motives, it looks like figure 3.4a in numeric notation. Transposing the second and third examples of figure 3.4a to the starting note of the first example of figure 3.4a gives figure 3.4b, and the problem is clear. The second and third notes of the second example of figure 3.4b do not match the second and third notes of the first example of figure 3.4b, nor does the third note of the third example of figure 3.4b match the third note of the first example of figure 3.4b.

By referencing the process to a major scale, however, and sliding the sequence around, the original four-note motive of figure 3.3 appears as three notes up a scale and includes a leap back to the original note as shown in figure 3.5. Moving the original pattern around in this list shows that each example falls exactly into place. We now have a kind of moving reference that follows the motive (i.e., step up, step up, two steps down, without stating what kinds of steps) and allows the patterns to match tonally. Thus, all the matches are recognizable even though the numerical intervals differ. Melodic matches in tonal music could be detected without this reference point but only with a level of fuzziness that would necessarily allow all sorts of nonmatching motives to match. *Real* approaches to pattern matching do not discriminate between patterns that conform to *tonal* scales and those that do not. However, as will be seen, *real* approaches to pattern matching can be particularly effective in detecting similar chromatic patterns.

We have seen a few of the ways that motives vary from one another and yet the ear is able to identify them as a match. There are virtually thousands of ways to vary motives. There are relatively few methods, however, that are both used by composers and apparent to the ear. For example, extended retrogrades (backward variations of motives) rarely occur and, when they do, are rarely recognized. The EMI pattern matcher allows only those forms of variation that can be easily heard to pass successfully. Almost all the more recognizable variations can be found in Beethoven's famous Fifth Symphony, so I will use examples directly from that work.

The principal motive of the Symphony no. 5 is shown in figure 3.6a. Beethoven weaves an incredible panoply of variations from this motive. These variation types must be recognizable by a pattern matcher. Some of Beethoven's variations are shown in figures 3.6b–j. Figure 3.6b is a simple tonal transposition of the motive. Note

*Figure 3.3*  A simple musical line with three variants of the same motive.

*Figure 3.4*  Numeric equivalents for figure 3.3 in exact numbers (a) and in transposition (b).

    **a.**  (72 74 76 72)  (71 72 74 71)  (69 71 72 69)

    **b.**  (72 74 76 72)  (72 73 75 72)  (72 74 75 72)

*Figure 3.5*  Using a major scale as reference for the motives of figure 3.3.

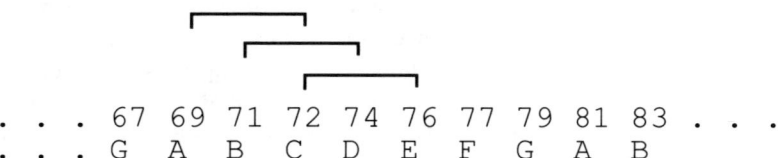

*Figure 3.6*  Motive variations of Beethoven's Symphony no. 5, first movement: a) Mm. 1–2 (violin 1); b) Mm. 8–9 (violin 1); c) Mm. 16–17 (violin 1); d) Mm. 35–36 (violin 1); e) Mm. 65–66 (cello and bass); f) Mm. 94–85 (bass); g) Mm. 146–47 (violin); h) Mm. 152–53 (viola and cello); i) Mm. 167–68 (flute); j) Mm. 188–89 (flute).

how the interval now forms a minor rather than a major third. Figure 3.6c is a combination of a tonal sequence and the filling in of the minor third with an intervening second. Figure 3.6d involves inversion-extension, with a minor third projecting upward from an initial note a major third above the original entrance. Figure 3.6e is an interval augmentation-inversion, a tonally conceived variation extended to a perfect fourth in the upward direction. Figure 3.6f is an interval diminution, and figure 3.6g is an inversion of the variation given in figure 3.6c. Figure 3.6h shows a transposition of figure 3.6c with interval diminution (minor second instead of a major second last interval). Figure 3.6i is a scalar interpolation of figure 3.6e transposed two octaves. Figure 3.6j demonstrates interval diminution and skeletonization. All these forms of variation, and several others, are accommodated by both the EMI and the SARA pattern matchers.

As previously mentioned, the EMI and SARA pattern matchers rely on *controllers* (and tonal matching in the case of EMI) to address the issues of what constitutes a match if one motive does not exactly match another version. This *almost* capacity of a matcher is extremely important to its usefulness. There are musical *almost*s that are recognizable to the ear but virtually unrecognizable in data form. Different composers have varying motivic development. Beethoven, as we have seen, manipulates material within a given rhythmic framework. A pattern-matching window for Beethoven's music can be very small and still be successful. As will be seen, Chopin, by contrast, varies by ornamenting lines with embellishments such that if the window to include intervening notes is not extremely wide a variation of a pattern will be lost. Such extension, although it occurs in Beethoven, is not his primary focus.

Figures 3.7a and 3.7b should be compared to the previously described Beethoven variants. Note how Chopin's theme in figure 3.7a is very much present in the second example and the ear hears it without much difficulty. However, a pattern-matching program will have problems recognizing the similarity unless it has the flexibility to allow the interpolated notes to pass without effect. The circled notes in figure 3.7b indicate the position of the notes of figure 3.7a. Note how Chopin reinforces the ear's interpretation of the first part of figure 3.7b as a variation by using contiguous pitches of the original pattern in measure 2. In measure 3 of both examples, the comparisons seem problematic at best, although with a sensitive performance the thematic elements clearly surface. Measures 4 and 5 again reassure the ear of the theme's presence. Measures 6 and 8 of figure 3.7a and measures 6 and 7 of figure 3.7b also prove contrasting in nature, though the ear still captures the inherent relations.

**Figure 3.7**  Chopin's Mazurka, op. 17, no. 4: a) Mm. 5–11. b) Mm. 13–19.

Measure 7 of figure 3.7b condenses bars 7 to 8 of figure 3.7a to a single measure with significantly altered note order and durations (e.g., the C of beat 1 in measure 8 of figure 3.7a is octave displaced as note 2 in measure 7 of figure 3.7b). As will be seen, such variations require a combination of controller settings for detection. Chopin typically varies his music in this way, as do certain other composers (e.g., Scriabin). Calibrating the size of certain controllers to allow such variations to pass while not admitting various nonvariations requires some combination of a good ear, knowledge about the composer, and experimentation. Algorithms can also intelligently automate the process of adjusting the controllers to some extent (see Cope 1992 and the discussion in chapter 7 of this book).

**Controllers**  On one level, pattern matching can be a rather simple process. This is particularly true when attempting to match patterns exactly. On another level, however, pattern matching can be an approximating process that requires programming nuance and insights where, with certain groups of controllers set to appropriate levels, signatures appear easily and clearly. With other groups of controllers and less appropriate settings, nothing that even remotely resembles stylistic signatures appears. For EMI and SARA to achieve this approximating process, they require certain variables, called *controllers*, to narrow the field of found patterns to those legitimately reflective of a composer's musical style. Controllers help pattern matchers find signatures when patterns are musically comparable yet not exactly the same. Controllers also help pattern matchers avoid identifying too many patterns as signatures, thus rendering databases immutable. In essence, pattern matching can be compared to the action of a sieve in which controllers define the width of the sieve's mesh.

When EMI or SARA attempts to match two patterns and encounters a variance, they apply a series of tests to determine whether (1) the variance adheres to one of the program's allowed variation techniques and (2) the amount of the variation falls within tolerable limits. Each of these tests relies on a specific variable, or controller, to determine the extent of allowable difference. These controllers each have a user-assignable value. As a simple example, imagine a pattern of two repeating notes matched against a pattern of two notes a minor second apart. Imagine as well that the matcher employs a comparison test with a controller called *difference* gauged in integers signifying half steps. With this *difference* controller assigned a value of 1 or more, the two patterns would succeed. With *difference* assigned a value of zero, they would not match. EMI has many such controllers that act in concert so that many different kinds of tests are performed. Thus, it is important to provide access to the pattern matcher through these controllers, as composers' styles, and thus signatures, differ as they appear in variation.

The pattern-matching controllers I will describe first are those present in various incarnations of EMI. These descriptions will help to clarify both the variety of possible controllers and the subtle interplay between them. I will then describe the controllers available in SARA and, through a sample pattern-matching session, demonstrate how these controllers can be set and reset to produce effective results.

### ■ Controllers in EMI

As mentioned previously, EMI takes two very different approaches to melodic pattern matching. The first (or tonal) approach matches pitches and compares patterns to a tonal scale as shown in figure 3.5. The second (or nontonal) approach matches the intervals derived from pitch patterns. Some patterns, particularly diatonic patterns, will resolve well using tonal controllers, whereas others require nontonal controllers. To ensure that both approaches have an opportunity to participate in the pattern-matching process, tonal and nontonal controllers are applied in parallel (see figure 3.2); success from either model is forwarded as successful. Controllers in each separate process (i.e., tonal or nontonal) are arranged serially (again see figure 3.2) using summational techniques so that patterns that do not match any single test can still match by successfully passing enough incremental portions of tests.

It should be noted that EMI does not employ combined pitch/rhythm pattern matching or controllers. Instead, it employs (at user discretion) a separate pattern matcher to discard patterns with seriously different rhythmic proportions and temporal interrelations before they enter the main interval/pitch pattern-matching sequence. Thus, a pattern consisting of four eighth notes will match any pattern consisting of equal or nearly equal durations. However, a pattern consisting of significantly varying durations will be rejected from this attempted match. EMI also employs a separate rhythm matcher that allows patterns with similar rhythms to succeed (see the *rhythm* controller description below). Melodic and harmonic pattern matching also fall into different categories because they require different controllers. However, melodic signatures are bound to their harmonic counterparts (and vice versa) when signatures are protected from recomposition by the program.

The principal controller in EMI, *allowance*, defines how far a melodic match can deviate in half steps. This controller affects the behavior of many other melodic controllers (i.e., both tonal and nontonal controllers), as it provides the maximum variance each controller may have from exactness in an attempted match. A high number (e.g., 10) in *allowance* can cause very different patterns to match. A low number (e.g., 1) allows few and sometimes no matches. An appropriate value (e.g., between 1 and 10, depending on composer) allows patterns with slight variations to match. In general, every effort should be made to keep the value of *allowance* low, as it tends to allow noise to enter the pattern-matching process.

Figure 3.8a shows a Mozart signature and a series of tonal variations. This signature typically appears in slow movements of Mozart's piano sonatas in varying guises. For a pattern matcher to substantiate this pattern as a signature, the variations must be allowed to match. Concomitantly, the latitudes enabling the variations to match must not be so extreme as to allow nonsignatures to succeed as well.

Figure 3.8b presents a variation of figure 3.8a. This variation is an inversion of the original with diminuted intervals between notes

***Figure 3.8*** Tonal variations of a Mozart signature:
a) Motive: K. 330, second movement, mm. 19–20; b) Inversion: K. 333, third movement, mm. 154–5; c) Augmentation: K. 279, second movement, mm. 56–57; d) Diminution: K. 309, second movement, mm. 4–5; e) Interpolation: K. 333, first movement, mm. 133–134; f) Fragmentation: K. 281, second movement, mm. 25–26; g) Order: K. 545, second movement, mm. 7–8.

4–5 and 5–6. These two patterns would not succeed in a nontonal pattern match, as the interval amounts for the first four notes, for example, do not match (2 2 1 as opposed to −1 −2 −2). For a nontonal match to occur, the *allowance* controller would have to be increased. This would in turn allow a large number of nonsignatures to also succeed. A tonal match on the other hand, occurs naturally as both the original and the inversion fall naturally in their respective keys (or as transposed to C major). The *p-inversion* (p for pitch) controller checks for inversions such as this during pattern comparisons and would need to be set to 7 (because 7 notes have created inverted intervals) to catch this variation.

Figure 3.8c shows a more severe variant of the original pattern. Here the fourth note moves a sixth, rather than a second, requiring the use of the *p-augmentation* controller (set to 1 to succeed in this instance). The first three notes are also a minor second apart, a nontonal relationship that, as is the case with figure 3.8d, requires the *p-diminution* controller. Both figures 3.8c and 3.8d also have durational variations in their second halves. However, the proportions remain roughly the same, and thus the rhythm matcher utilized at the onset of the process will pass these variations successfully. Figure 3.8c has an inverted second half that requires a combination of the *p-diminution* and *p-inversion* controllers for a successful match.

Figure 3.8e includes a single interpolated note (D, note 5) that requires a *p-interpolation* controller setting of 1. Figure 3.8f appears in retrograde form (*p-inversion* controller) without the ending sixteenth or thirty-second note turn and requires a setting of 1 in the *p-fragmentation* controller for a successful match. Figure 3.8g is an order variation of the signature and requires the use of the *p-order* controller. As in many of these cases, the patterns must also be transposed for the pitch match to succeed.

Figure 3.9a shows a simple Mozart four-note motive consisting of two minor seconds on either side of a diminished third along with a series of nontonal variations. This motive occurs in some form or other in all of Mozart's piano sonatas as a part of significant themes as well as less important transitions and accompaniments. In all probability this short figure is part of a larger signature rather than a signature itself. Because this chromatic pattern cannot easily be normalized to a diatonic scale, it matches more logically using intervals (*real* approach to pattern matching) instead of pitches.

The *i-inversion* (i for "interval") controller uses intervals and allows for real inversions of patterns to succeed as matches. Such inversions may pertain to one or more intervals of a pattern.

**Figure 3.9** Nontonal variations of a possible signature from Mozart's sonatas: a) Motive: K. 533, second movement, mm. 63–64; b) Inversion: K. 545, third movement, m. 30; c) Augmentation: K. 279, first movement, m. 6; d) Diminution: K. 283; first movement, mm. 80–81; e) Interpolation: K. 309, second movement, m. 27; f) Fragmentation: K. 310, first movement, mm. 94–95; g) Order: K. 310, second movement, m. 19.

Figure 3.9b shows an exact inversion of the entire motive shown in figure 3.9a. The *i-inversion* controller setting is cumulative so that a setting of 3 (three intervals for four pitches) would be required to catch this variant.

Figure 3.9c shows a variation of the original motive, the first interval being augmented by a half step. The *i-augmentation* controller determines the number of intervals that can be augmented for a match to take place (one in this case). The aforementioned *allowance* controller determines the acceptable amount of interval augmentation possible during matching (set to 1 to catch this variation). The *i-diminution* controller is the opposite of the *i-augmentation* controller in that it detects interval contraction rather than expansion. Figure 3.9d shows the original motive with its first interval contracted to a unison. The *i-diminution* controller would need to be set to 1 to allow this variant with the *allowance* controller set likewise.

The *i-interpolation* controller allows for intervening notes between the principal notes of the motive being matched. The *i-interpolation* controller is refreshed from melodic note to melodic note rather than being cumulative. In Figure 3.9e, the original motive appears as the intervals created by notes 1–2, 2–5, and 5–6. The intervening notes are considered to be interpolations, and the *i-interpolation* controller is set at 2 (the most number of intervening notes) to allow this match to succeed.

The *i-fragmentation* controller catches patterns where one or more notes have been removed from a variant. In Figure 3.9f, the first note has been extracted, leaving only the diminished third and its resolution. The *i-fragmentation* controller would require a setting of 1 to account for this missing note and allow a successful match to take place. The *i-order* controller determines how critical the order of the notes must be for two patterns to match intervallically. Figure 3.9g shows an example where the first interval is reversed. The *i-order* controller would need to be set to 1 to catch this variant.

The first controller mentioned in this section, the *allowance* controller, does not depend on the tonal or nontonal nature of a match. There are other such general melodic controllers. For example, the *contour* controller sets the amount to which the general contour of two motives must conform to one another. Figure 3.10 shows a musical example where the variants follow the same basic contour of the original but do not always follow the exact intervals, only their directions. This example would require a *contour* controller setting of 2 for the original motive to match this variant (to catch the low B and F♯ variances).

**Figure 3.10** An example of contour from Chopin's Prelude, op. 28, no. 6: a) Mm. 1–2. b) Mm. 3–4. c) Mm. 23–24.

The *rhythm* controller determines the amount to which rhythmic matches alone can allow patterns to succeed. In figure 3.11, the *rhythm* controller allows the duration match to supersede the lack of exact pitch or interval match. The *rhythm* controller, if set with a high enough number, overwhelms many of the other controllers and should be used with great care. As will be seen, SARA pattern matching may be switched completely to rhythm for the detection of rhythmic signatures. Usually, however, rhythm pattern matching succeeds in finding numerous examples of local motives rather than more global signatures.

The *pattern-size* controller determines the size of the patterns chosen for comparison. With the exception of the interpolation and fragmentation controllers (which allow larger and smaller segments of music to be selected for comparison), the *pattern-size* controller remains fixed during each pattern-matching attempt. The *pattern-size* controller requires some experience, as a setting too small will catch only parts of signatures and one too large will void the potential of finding signatures at all.

The threshold controllers indicates lower (floor) or upper (ceiling) levels of matches. The *floor-threshold* controller ignores matches that do not achieve significant successful comparisons to be considered signatures. The *ceiling-threshold* controller ignores matches that, like scales or other simple patterns, occur too frequently to be real signatures. Most likely settings fall between 5 and 10 for floor levels and between 20 and 30 for ceiling levels.

**Figure 3.11** An example of rhythmic variations in Chopin's mazurkas: a) Op. 17, no. 2, mm. 1–2. b) Op. 17, no. 4, mm. 5–6.

The *variants* controller determines the depth to which signature variations can be plumbed to allow for variants of signatures to be protected during recombinant composition. Set at ∞, this controller protects all forms of the found signatures, whereas set at 0 it protects only the original figure. Although these extremes provide good examples, usual settings are between 5 and 20.

As suggested by some of the previous examples, controllers usually work in combination rather than separately. This is particularly important in pattern matchers where patterns fail if they do not pass all tests. Figure 3.12 demonstrates how pattern variations can successfully match using many controller settings. Finding the variational aspects of this figure requires that a pattern matcher find the location of the members of the measures of figure 3.12a in the subsequent two examples without regard for rhythm and intervening notes. As previously mentioned regarding figure 3.7, the ear recognizes such note combinations as obvious variants, although the eye (and indiscriminating computation) does not. The *p-interpolation* controller would require a setting of 4 for either figure 3.12b or figure 3.12c to match figure 3.12a, as both have cases with four interpolated notes between elements of the melody. The third example points toward a different ending note and thus would additionally require setting the *p-augmentation* controller to 1 and the *allowance* controller to 4. The *pattern-size* controller would only need to be set to 9 (the number of notes in the original pattern) and not larger because, as previously mentioned, the interpolation controllers allow for attempted matches beyond the size of the *pattern-size* controller. Finally, the rhythm pattern matcher that precedes the melodic pattern matcher must be circumvented to avoid the match's failing

**Figure 3.12** Extended example of interpolation in Chopin's Nocturne, op. 55, no. 1: a) Mm. 1–2. b) Mm. 27–28. c) Mm. 45–47.

before the melodic process begins, as the rhythm of these examples is quite different.

Melodic pattern matching is substantially easier than its harmonic counterpart. To match melodic patterns, the program pattern matches through pitch lists with patterns of varying sizes while comparing the pitches or intervals in the context of the various controllers. Finding the appropriate pattern size is obviously a critical matter. However, experimentation with this and the other controllers leads to a fairly straightforward pattern-matching routine. Harmonic pattern matching requires a different approach.

Harmonic pattern matching relies strictly on intervals rather than on pitch and intervals. Matches that are apparent to the ear may not otherwise be apparent to a pattern matcher. Different inversions of the same chords, with doubling at the octaves and manifestations in different registers, combine to make harmonies that sound very similar appear very different in numerical representation.

Defining what constitutes a chord can also be a complex matter. Given that nonharmonic tones can occur at any time and that harmonies can change at varying rates, just deciding what constitutes a harmonic entity can pose serious problems. EMI takes the approach that the attack point is the most important instance of a harmonic pattern, as any nonharmonic tones present should generally agree with another pattern for a match to take place. Note that harmonic analysis (SPEAC), which could not function within such a simple restriction, takes place separately from harmonic pattern matching. EMI uses beats as the basis for harmonic rhythm. Beat definition relies on the previously discussed clarification of databases (see chapter 2) to ensure that harmonic comparisons will be valid.

The mechanics of refining EMI harmonic patterns include (1) counting the intervals vertically in a chord (using minor seconds) from the bass up, always using the bass note as reference; (2) reducing all elements (by subtracting 12) to less than 12; and (3) removing redundancies. For example, all root-position major triads reduce to the two intervals 4 and 7, minor triads to 3 and 7, and so on.

Figure 3.13 shows three variants of a harmonic cadential signature in Mozart piano sonatas (for more information on this Viennese classical signature, see Cope 1991a, pp. 168–69). The *number-present* harmony controller allows for matches when one or more of the textures being matched differs in number by an amount equal to or less than that of the controller setting. The *number-present* controller is refreshed from chord to chord rather than accumulated. The setting of 2 for the *number-present* controller would capture the almost versions of the cadential signature of figures 3.13a and 3.13b (differing by 11 and 7 in chord 1 and by 7 in chord 2 respectively), whereas a setting of only 1 would be required for matching figures 3.13a and 3.13c (differing by 11 in chord 1). Harmonic pattern patching also includes the *pattern-size*, *threshold*, and *variants* controllers, which have basically the same meanings as they do with melodic pattern matching, though they often require significantly different settings.

Both melodic and harmonic controllers must be set separately for each specific composer or idiom. The aim of properly utilizing the full complement of controllers is to discover an efficiency curve, or the levels just prior to that of diminishing returns. The most efficient curve should have settings that will capture significant patterns without also producing spurious ones.

The EMI melodic and harmonic pattern matchers have two orders. The first order operates independently on each of the individual works in the database. The second order operates on the results of the first order, seeking patterns that are common to the works in the database. The product of the first-order pattern matcher can be conceived as a kind of image—a template of a work expressed as a list of patterns and their frequency of occurrence. The second-order pattern matcher compares these templates by seeking metapatterns that represent the signatures of the composer/idiom of the source music. These metapatterns are found, simply

**Figure 3.13** Harmonic cadence signatures from Mozart sonatas with reduced interval analysis: a) K. 332, third movement, m. 35. b) K. 332, second movement, m. 40. c) K. 311, first movement, m. 112.

but elegantly, by a superimposition of the lists. Such superimposition of work images is the key to the process of signature detection (see Cope 1991a, particularly chapter 5).

The product of the first-order pattern match process is a list of lists that contain two important classes of information. The first class is a list of pitch and melodic interval data and harmonic interval data that represent patterns that have been discovered within the boundaries prescribed by the matcher. The second class is a number representing how many times each pattern has been discovered in the first-order lists. These numbers are ranked from highest to lowest accumulations.

With a large work, one may find as many as four or five thousand instances or repetitions of a pattern at the beginning of the list to a minimum of two at the end. Patterns highest on the list might seem most likely to be signatures. However, these highly used patterns are most often parts of the major themes of individual works and are not signatures. True signatures more often fall in the middle range of these lists. Those patterns with the lowest frequencies tend to be insignificant.

The second-order pattern match first sums two or more first-order lists, producing a list of the frequencies of the local patterns. Many of the frequencies of patterns found in one work will remain largely unchanged, whereas the frequencies of global signatures will increase significantly. A superimposition function next reorganizes the combined list into one that is ordered by the amount of change rather than by total amount. Patterns whose frequency changes significantly in the superimposition process are more likely to be signatures than those with high totals but that do not change significantly. Note that the combined total frequency of signatures may still be substantially less than the total frequency of patterns local to one of the works in the database: the amount of change is significant, not the highest count.

When the second-order pattern match is complete, one must decide where to skim off the actual signatures ("cream") from the local material ("milk"). Cut too deep into the list, and themes from the individual works in the database are erroneously recognized as signatures; cut too shallow, and the signatures are diluted. The `*master-threshold*` floor and ceiling controllers perform these operations. These controllers function exactly as the previously described melodic threshold floor and ceiling controllers do.

Dealing with a list of various matched patterns leads to the question of which is in fact the signature. Protecting all the matched patterns can overprotect a database. However, choosing which of a matched set of patterns is the signature would require an incredible amount of code as well as a significant amount of programmer guesswork with the *variants* controller. EMI solves this problem by cross-matching databases. This means that, although the patterns in database "x" are matched against the patterns in database "y," the patterns in database "y" will also be matched against the patterns in database "x." Because different starting patterns can produce different matches, the pattern that accumulates the most matches (within the thresholds) will become the signature of choice—the one protected from recomposition.

■ **Controllers in SARA**

As mentioned previously, the calibration of EMI's pattern-matching controllers is a time-consuming, exhaustive process. Often, changing one controller will counteract the effects of another, and I have often found myself working at cross-purposes. Although the results of such intensive research can be illuminating, the efforts expended are often so monumental that one could hardly expect any but the fanatical to become so engaged. Thus, SARA (the program included on the CD-ROM accompanying this book) has a substantially reduced set of controllers and thus a less effective pattern matcher. However, the resulting matching process requires exponentially less time to operate.

The controllers used in SARA are *intervals-off*, *amount-off*, *pattern-size*, and *threshold*. Limiting the number of controllers for SARA helps to distinguish their use and effect. Unfortunately, such limiting also hampers pattern matching for the detection of more subtle signatures. SARA, unlike EMI, also uses intervals exclusively for melodic pattern matching, eliminating the time-consuming need for comparisons of motives to tonal scales.

The *intervals-off* controller dictates how many intervals may be incorrect for a match to occur. Obviously, if this controller is set too large, it might return an entire database as a set of matched patterns. If *intervals-off* is set too small or set at zero, only exact matches will be returned, often resulting in no matches. The effect of the *intervals-off* controller parallels that of the *allowance* controller in EMI.

The *amount-off* controller indicates how much an interval may be incorrect for a match to take place. Setting this variable too large allows distinctly different patterns to emerge from the pattern-matching process. Setting this controller too small or at zero allows only exact matches to emerge from the pattern-matching process.

Both `*intervals-off*` and `*amount-off*` work in serial; in other words, if the amount an interval is off exceeds the level of `*amount-off*`, the match fails regardless of the size of `*intervals-off*`. Concomitantly, even meeting a liberal level for `*amount-off*`, an interval will fail if `*intervals-off*` is zero.

The `*pattern-size*` controller indicates the number of notes gathered in motives for matching purposes. The SARA pattern-matching process is incremental rather than contiguous (i.e., patterns are chosen with every successive note rather than by beginning a new pattern after the first pattern terminates). The incremental approach requires $L \times N$ (where L is the length of time to match one motive and N the length of the motive) more time to process than the contiguous approach, but the incremental approach finds many more possible signatures in the process.

The `*threshold*` controller delimits the lower number (floor) of matches for a signature to emerge. Thus, only those matches that exceed the level of the `*threshold*` controller are returned as potential signatures. The lack of a ceiling `*threshold*` controller is due to the probable size (small) of databases usually employed in matching using SARA. As stated previously, in circumstances requiring larger databases, both floor and ceiling thresholds would be required for logical signature extraction from matched patterns.

The variable `Rhythm?` (not a controller per se but useful to discuss in this section) allows for the finding of rhythmic (duration) signatures. These signatures can be protected exactly as pitch signatures are protected. The controllers just described play the same role in pattern matching for rhythm as they do in pattern matching for pitch. However, the degree to which some controller levels affect the pattern-matching process must be severely exaggerated in rhythm matching. For example, a level of 1 in the `*amount-off*` controller for notes (i.e., a minor second deviation) is significant, whereas it is negligible in rhythm (500 to 501 represents a duration of only a thousandth of a quarter note). It should be noted that in the current version of SARA, rhythm and pitch matching are separate. Patterns of either type can be matched and protected in a database. SARA does not employ a composite of pitch and rhythm matching because doing so requires such an extraordinary commitment of computation time. As mentioned in the previous section on EMI controllers, matching rhythm as a prelude to pitch is possible and even typical where time and memory constraints are not a consideration.

## A Sample Pattern-Matching Session

The phrases shown in figures 3.14a–c are from a Mozart database and will serve as examples for pattern matching. The databases of these phrases are slightly clarified (see chapter 2), but such variations will not significantly alter the search for signatures. The phrases shown in figure 3.14 were chosen specifically because they have a distinct signature present. Such foreknowledge is not necessary for successful pattern matching. However, as has been mentioned previously, pattern matching is most effective when using music with a clearly recognizable style. Because such music probably has signatures, suspecting their presence is logical.

Note that no single set of controller settings exists that will work for many different styles. In fact, resetting previously successful controller settings is not generally useful even when pattern matching different music by the same composer. However, if the music in a loaded database has the same perceived style, one can usefully *begin* pattern matching with controller settings similar to those successfully used with music of that style and then set and reset the pattern-matching controllers until signatures become recognizable.

Figures 3.15 to 3.20 present an example of a typical SARA pattern-matching session. Following the settings shown in these figures when the databases are selected in the order shown in figure 3.14 will produce the results shown here. The settings shown in figure 3.15 are the default and produce the result shown in figure 3.16. The pattern in figure 3.16 (found originally in figure 3.14a) does not seem particularly recognizable as a Mozart signature. It is simply a common pattern used by many different composers of Mozart's time.

Figure 3.17 shows the setting of the controllers for a second attempt at pattern matching. In this match, the number of the controller `*amount-off*` has been reduced to 1 and the controller `*threshold*` has been reduced to 2 to allow for more matches. Raising and lowering controller levels requires a combination of aural skills developed through practice. Figure 3.18 shows the patterns found by pattern matching with the controllers set as in figure 3.17. Here, more patterns appear; however, again none are recognizable as a complete Mozartean signature. Note that the patterns of figures 3.18d and 3.18e are from the cadence of figure 3.14b and bear a faint suggestion of a classical Viennese signature. However, neither is complete and therefore might not be generally recognizable.

Figure 3.19 shows the setting of the controllers for another attempt at producing a signature. In figure 3.19, the `*pattern-size*` controller has been increased to 7 and `*intervals-off*` reduced to 0 in hopes that this will allow a more complete pattern to emerge. Figure 3.20 shows the recognizable signature that results

**Figure 3.14** Mozart's sonatas: a) K. 283, second movement, mm. 1–4. b) K. 330, third movement, mm. 104 ff. and c) K. 547 a, first movement, mm. 59 ff.

***Figure 3.15*** The default settings of the pattern matcher.

| Intervals off | 1 |
|---|---|
| Amount off | 2 |
| Pattern size | 6 |
| Threshold | 3 |
| Rhythm | no |

***Figure 3.16*** Results of an initial pattern match.

***Figure 3.17*** Variable settings for a second attempt at pattern matching.

| Intervals off | 1 |
|---|---|
| Amount off | 1 |
| Pattern size | 6 |
| Threshold | 2 |
| Rhythm | no |

**Figure 3.18** Patterns resulting from a second attempt at pattern matching.

***Figure 3.19*** A final setting for pattern matching for signatures.

| | |
|---|---|
| Intervals off | 0 |
| Amount off | 1 |
| Pattern size | 7 |
| Threshold | 2 |
| Rhythm | no |

***Figure 3.20*** Recognizable signature resulting from a final pattern-matching session.

from the match using the controller settings of figure 3.19. This signature is now a complete version of the variants shown in figure 3.18, and no further expansion of `*pattern-size*` is necessary. The signature found here appears in the last two measures of figure 3.14b. It can be described as 1 −4 −3 −2 −1 1 in intervals beginning on G♯. Some of the other examples in figure 3.14 show variations of this figure that are similar enough to be recognized by ear as variants of this signature and thus as probably responsible for its detection as a signature. For example, the last measure in 3.14a includes a melodic shape and resolution of similar design. The last measure of figure 3.14c is an almost exact duplicate (melodically at the octave) of the found signature and most certainly was a significant factor in

*Figure 3.21* SARA output using the signature of figure 3.20.

the pattern-matching process. Note that signatures are situationally sensitive, which means that it is important that those, for example, that might appear more often near a cadence will do so again after recombination. For this reason, both EMI and, to some extent, SARA protect both signatures and their locations.

Figure 3.21 reproduces figure 1.22 and shows an example of SARA recombinant music using the signature found in figure 3.20. Note how the signature remains intact, whereas the prior material originates from a variety of sources (for details about locations, see figure 1.22). Signatures are protected from the recombinant process by attributes in their objects (discussed further in chapter 4) and by special use by the ATN program (see chapter 5).

Another example of signature use is seen in figure 3.22, which shows an excerpt from a suite in the style of Rachmaninoff by EMI. This work is based on databases of Rachmaninoff's Second Suite, op. 17, and his song "Before My Window," op. 26, no. 10. Figure 3.22 (beginning with measure 158) shows one of the main themes that is derived from the Rachmaninoff secondary theme of the introduction of his op. 17 (shown in figure 3.23 beginning at rehearsal mark 3). The melody of both examples occurs in the right hand of piano 2 (lower system). One of Rachmaninoff's signatures here is the harmonic progression of ii–V–iii–vi–IV–ii–V and so on. In SPEAC symbols, this

110  EXPERIMENTS IN MUSICAL INTELLIGENCE

**Figure 3.22** An example (mm. 158–70) from the EMI-Rachmaninoff Suite for Two Pianos.

**Figure 3.23** Rachmaninoff, Suite no. 2, op. 17, first movement, mm. 58–73.

**Figure 3.23** continued.

equates to `P2-A1-C5-C-P1-P2-A1`. In root intervals, this progression moves downward by fifths and thirds. It is also cyclic in that, once begun, it can continue in groups of five chords indefinitely (though Rachmaninoff is not prone to excessive repetitions). These progressions can be found in many of his works and, when found by EMI as a signature, are kept relatively intact, as in figure 3.22.

The first measure of the EMI imitation of figure 3.22 is very nearly a literal copy of the first measure of the original music in figure 3.23 and may be a matched signature itself. However, the second measure of the EMI imitation is a transposition of the fifth measure of the Rachmaninoff example and typical of EMI recombinancy (note the small variations in the accompanying parts due to recombinancy on sublevels, discussed in chapter 5). The third measure of the EMI imitation in figure 3.22 is a near exact repetition of the Rachmaninoff third measure in figure 3.23. The fourth measure of the EMI Rachmaninoff imitates the tenth measure of the original music, again an example of EMI recombinancy.

All this music is a clear example of EMI's recombining the original Rachmaninoff with slight variations. However, with the fifth and sixth measures of the imitation in figure 3.22, the process takes another route. Here, the music of the imitation reverts to the fifth, sixth, and seventh measures of the original, as shown in figure 3.23. This type of continuation is no accident; there are simply too many measures of Rachmaninoff's music for two pianos coded into the EMI databases for such contiguous music to be the result of chance. Likewise, there are too many conditions inherent in EMI's code to allow three measures of the original to exist side by side unless, of course, this example is a signature: a harmonic and melodic trait of Rachmaninoff found in more than one movement of the original suite. In the eighth measure of the EMI imitation, the music returns to recombinant techniques, and the music is derived from elsewhere in Rachmaninoff's work.

This example demonstrates how subtly signatures can be embedded in otherwise completely recombinant examples. This is not the case, however, in the example of EMI imitation in figure 3.24. The music in measures 246 to 248 is a metric transposition of the passage shown in figure 3.25 from the original Rachmaninoff, beginning three measures before rehearsal mark 2. Note that the music in the previous measure 244 of the EMI example is in a different key and of a much different character than the music in the measure that follows. This preparatory music is also much different than the music that precedes the Rachmaninoff original. Apparently, the signature here is of sufficiently unique character to require grafting at what the program considers an appropriate moment rather than

*Figure 3.24* Another example (mm. 245–49) from the EMI-Rachmaninoff Suite for Two Pianos.

**Figure 3.25** Rachmaninoff, Suite no. 2, op. 17, first movement, mm. 35–46.

the more natural threading found in figure 3.22. However, on hearing, the music in the EMI-Rachmaninoff seems natural to the style, suggesting that it may not be unlike Rachmaninoff to flagrantly force signatures into place. Rachmaninoff's "Before My Window" (see figure 3.26) for soprano and piano on Galinka's text provides signature verification for figure 3.25 and, as previously mentioned, was another of the works in the EMI database at the time of composition.

Figure 3.27, a third example from the EMI-Rachmaninoff Suite, demonstrates how melodic signatures can be divorced from their accompanying environments to create stylistic variations of merit. Figure 3.28 shows part of the original Rachmaninoff Suite third movement (beginning 11 after rehearsal mark 20), which was included in the database for the EMI imitation. The melodic signature begins on beat 2 of measure 55 in figure 3.27 and continues through measure 59. This melody is a transposition (down a diatonic step) of the original Rachmaninoff, beginning on the first beat of measure 28 of the example. Note that the harmonic functions of the EMI-Rachmaninoff do not follow the original and appear to be modulating during the example. The figurations of the original Rachmaninoff are lost either because the music here is from a different place or, as is often the case, because the database is not exactly the same as the music (for a discussion of the various ways databases are clarified, see chapter 2). Regardless of the singularity of the signature, it flows lyrically and simply into the melodic line.

**Figure 3.26**   Rachmaninoff, *Before My Window,* op. 26, no. 10, for voice and piano, mm. 14–15.

**Figure 3.27** Another example (mm. 52–59) from the EMI-Rachmaninoff Suite for Two Pianos.

**Figure 3.28** Rachmaninoff, Suite no. 2, op. 17, third movement, mm. 28–31.

In each of the three examples from the EMI-Rachmaninoff Suite, signatures play a significant role in the recognizability of Rachmaninoff's style. Whether threaded, spliced, or focused on a single aspect of the music, pattern matching holds important stylistic music together and helps maintain a significant degree of stylistic credibility in music that otherwise would suffer significantly from the recombinant procedures used in composition. Setting controllers appropriately helps to guarantee that found signatures will be of a proper length. This is important to ensure that signatures freeze a significant portion of the original music to help style recognition and yet not freeze so much music that the original work will be blatantly recognizable as a quote or make the recombinant music sound like a pastiche of the database being used.

## ■ PATTERN-MATCHING PROGRAM

The top-level function of the pattern-matching program is `top-level-matcher` (shown in figure 3.29). This function takes a list of phrase names as argument and returns a list of signatures in event notation. Each signature listing is headed by the number of occurrences of each matching set of patterns. The function `translate-`

---

 **CD-ROM**

Pattern matching is a fundamental part of the composing process in SARA. One can observe functions such as `top-level-matcher` (shown in figure 3.29 with its subfunctions shown in subsequent examples) by tracing logical functions of the SARA program and selecting the appropriate menu items under signatures. For those who wish to inspect or revise its operation, the full code for this menu item is located in the file called sara-match. For those interested in testing their abilities to determine real Mozart from machine-composed Mozart, the Hypercard program *Is it Mozart* is located in the folder named "hypercard is it mozart." This program uses the Macintosh speaker rather than MIDI, so no special equipment is required for performance. ❖

---

**Figure 3.29**  The function `top-level-matcher`.

```
1.(defun top-level-matcher (database-names)
2.  (rank-the-matches
3.    (challenge-the-matches
4.      (add-the-matches
5.        (match-the-database-music (translate-to-events
6.                                   database-names))))))
```

`to-events` in line 5 of figure 3.29 reassembles measure objects (see chapter 4) for pattern matching. This reassembly is not complicated or difficult, but it can be time consuming with longer phrases.

The function `match-the-database-music`, in line 5 in figure 3.29 and shown in full in figure 3.30, accomplishes what its name suggests: it matches the music in the selected databases using the lower level function `match-the-databases` (in line 4 of figure 3.30) which utilizes the framework of the previously discussed SARA controllers. The function `add-the-matches`, in line 4 in figure 3.29, adds matches that are similar enough to be counted as the same. The function `challenge-the-matches`, in line 3 of figure 3.29 and shown in figure 3.31, compares the match numbers to the `*threshold*` controller and returns only those that exceed its value (see line 3 of figure 3.31). These surviving matches are then sorted and ranked by the function `rank-the-matches` (line 2 of figure 3.29) by combining those matches that are similar enough to be counted as the same. This latter function is necessary because the basic pattern matcher progresses through a composition without removing previously matched events. Thus, a pattern that has many occurrences can be searched for more than once and thus appears in the output of `challenge-the-matches` as redundancies. With the use of `rank-the-matches`, these redundancies are removed so that only original signatures remain for placement in the signature dictionary and for protecting in the database.

As previously stated, the SARA pattern matcher thoroughly scans its argument for possible signatures by using an event-by-event progressing window on the channel selected for matching. This is an enormously expensive process in terms of both memory and time. For example, using more than ten phrases in the argument to `top-level-matcher` causes most eight-megabyte computers to stall during processing. Alternatives, such as accumulating

*Figure 3.30*  The function `match-the-database-music`.

```
1.(defun match-the-database-music
2.   (database-music &optional (length (length database-music)))
3.     (if (zerop length) nil
4.        (append (match-the-databases (first database-music)
5.                                     (rest database-music))
6.              (match-the-database-music
7.                 (append (rest database-music)
8.                         (list (first database-music)))
9.                 (next length)))))
```

*Figure 3.31*  The function `challenge-the-matches`.

```
1.(defun challenge-the-matches (finds)
2.   (cond ((null finds) nil)
3.         ((>= (very-first finds) *threshold*)
4.          (cons (first finds)
5.                (challenge-the-matches (rest finds))))
6.         (t (challenge-the-matches (rest finds)))))
```

patterns at termination points, forfeit many potential matches and reduce signature output to only those patterns that happen to match the termination points. This latter approach might randomly coincide with a composer's signature placement, but such is not likely.

Pattern matching need not be an active compositional component of an EMI-like program. Indeed, pattern matching could take place during analysis and the resultant signatures stored in the phrase databases. This would save enormous amounts of time. However, pattern matching is a personal process with different patterns interpreted as signatures depending on the user. Therefore, however long the process may take, pattern matching should be a session-to-session variable. Users who have fixed notions of signatures and who wish to bypass the often exhaustive pattern-matching process can save and load signatures via the signature-dictionary interface in SARA. Although such saving and loading does not alter the task of protecting signatures in the currently loaded databases, it does nullify the need to actually pattern match prior to composing.

As described earlier, the EMI and SARA pattern matchers are sensitive only to pitch and duration. However, within these arenas these pattern matchers are extremely versatile. Although the examples given are from Western musical traditions, these pitch- and duration-based programs have proven surprisingly successful in deriving signatures from non-Western idioms (i.e., ragas and Balinese gamelan). Only when patterns are deeply hidden (e.g., when they reside in more than one voice or channel) are weaknesses in the system apparent. Again, many musical styles are recognizable to the ear for reasons other than pitch and duration (e.g., timbre, instrumentation, dynamics, etc.), but the pattern matchers described here are not currently appropriate for them.

The EMI and SARA pattern matchers, as analytical tools for music theoreticians and educators, may help solve questions of style that have formerly been considered only in subjective and intuitive terms. EMI, for example, has been used to identify the distinctive signatures of specific composers, trace their influences, and examine their development over time. These programs should also enable researchers to study formerly intractable problems, such as investigating musical "what if" hypotheses (what if $x$ had been influenced by $y$; what if $z$ had lived longer; etc.).

As mentioned earlier, the signatures detected by the pattern matcher, when applied to a creative and recombinant composition program, can replicate musical style convincingly. The results of these replications may challenge one's aesthetic and philosophical premises concerning the limits of mechanical intelligence. However, they also portend a powerful new tool for composers and music researchers.

# FOUR

## The Object System

The EMI object system provides the analysis program with logical-sized music objects for recombinancy and lexicons for storing those objects as well as incipient gestures and cadences. The object system also enables the pattern matcher to protect signatures from recomposition by toggling the appropriate object attribute, voiding the need to protect note events individually and thus saving a significant amount of computer memory. Storing music in objects is both conceptually and functionally logical.

When Charles Babbage designed his first computer for calculating numbers in 1856, the word *computer* was defined as a person, "one who computes; a reckoner" (Webster 1828, p. 43). Babbage's dream was to free humans from the drudgery of calculations so they could accomplish higher aims—in his case, to navigate ships away from reefs and to design and engineer safe bridges. But as non-human computers evolved, so did the multiplicity and complexity of the languages required to operate them, and new layers of instructions were necessary for even the simplest tasks. Users of these computers often required more knowledge of how to operate the computers than was required to calculate the complex mathematics the computers were supposedly designed to make easier.

Researchers at the Palo Alto Research Center (PARC) in the mid-1950s, even if they were unaware of Babbage's vision, countered with interfaces both intuitive and simple in conception. They hid opaque instructions and dense data in what is now termed *object-oriented programming systems* (OOPS). Their mice, menus, and windows paralleled reality in such obvious ways that users could operate computers virtually without knowledge of low-level computer languages. In OOPS, complex instructions become a matter of pointing to and then clicking appropriate objects on the computer screen. More than a hundred years after Babbage's first computer designs, our silicon-based computers have finally allowed us to experience his dream: to escape being the "engines" and to become true "engineers."

Common LISP is a computer language not unlike those counterintuitive languages PARC intended to rectify. Common LISP, discussed at length in chapter 3 of *Computers and Musical Style* (Cope 1991a), relies on strict use of protocols and functions that act on data. The Common LISP Object System (CLOS) is LISP's counterpart to other OOPS programs. CLOS is LISP's OOPS.

CLOS is a standard for LISP object-oriented programming (Keene 1989; Lawless and Miller 1991). Like Common LISP itself, CLOS was designed to replace the plethora of object-oriented LISP extensions developed in the 1970s and early 1980s. Although each of these extensions was interesting and useful, their differences made communication between programmers difficult at best. CLOS can now be used by those who wish to write substantial object-oriented programs and expect them to have more universal value and not be subject to the whims of temporarily in-vogue approaches.

CLOS was designed and initially implemented by the X3J13 committee (Bobrow et al. 1988), formed at the 1986 ACM LISP and Functional Programming conference. As of the date of this writing, CLOS has all but achieved ANSI standardization. This means that the high-level documentation and testing required of approval by this board confirms that CLOS will remain the official object-oriented extension of Common LISP for many years to come. This is important when one considers the amount of time and energy required to learn CLOS. It is paramount that the program be supported in the future.

## ■ OBJECT ORIENTATION

In traditional programming, functions act on data. Such programs can be quite successful. For example, accounting and other mathematically based programs operate quite well in this kind of environment. However, in music programs, and particularly in EMI, data and attendant details for that data are arranged and rearranged in almost limitless orders to fit less certain goals. This recombinancy requires flexibility. Traditional programming operates less effectively when data must be compartmentalized and processed independently in this way.

In object-oriented programming, data is stored in objects with information on how this data is to be used. Because this process parallels the manipulation of objects in real life, object orientation is often referred to as *real-world programming*. Object-orientation serves well for simulation programs in that objects work as independent entities and as entities within a system: actors and re-actors. For approaches like EMI and SARA which use recombinancy, object orientation is a perfect environment. Recombinancy requires independent entities that can be clearly defined during deconstruction and re-assembled in many correct ways depending on the data and constraints each possess:

> Object-oriented programming is a type of modular programming built around abstract models of real-world systems . . . For example, a car object might contain an engine, tires and a chassis. Each of these components can be uniquely described . . . and manipulated independently or as a part of the system. For example, we perform actions on the car as a whole when we drive it but we view the parts distinctly when we take the car in for service. (Lawless and Miller 1991, p. 1)

Metaphors for object-oriented programs abound. IRCAM (Institute for Research and Coordination of Acoustics/Music, an important computer music center in Paris) has used a common parallel: genetics. One of its musical object systems (called Formes) employs object class names such as `grand-parent`, `parent`, `child`, and so on (Rodet 1984). Other researchers take a more musical approach to their object names as in `conductor`, `orchestra`, and `player` (Krasner 1980). Still other researchers adopt names like `piece`, `section` (Pope 1991), and so on. Whatever the example, the common concepts are hierarchy and inheritance. Each object name in the hierarchy (called class) has certain attributes that are inherited by all subsumed object classes.

Figure 4.1 shows a very simple hierarchy of musical objects. To the right of each object class is an attribute name (e.g., "name," "number," etc.) of that class and a distinguishing characteristic of that attribute name (e.g., "symphony," "1," etc.). Here, each subsequent (lower) object class inherits information from classes higher in the hierarchy. Thus, the measure object "duple" possesses all the information that precedes it in the hierarchy. This voids the need to redundantly store such information in each object separately.

Storing data in objects is an efficient way to make this data available for a wide variety of computational operations. Because data stored in objects follow a hierarchical model, search procedures and similar processes are simplified. For example, finding the number of `A1 SPEAC` functions in section "a" of Symphony 1 (see

**Figure 4.1** A simple hierarchy of musical objects.

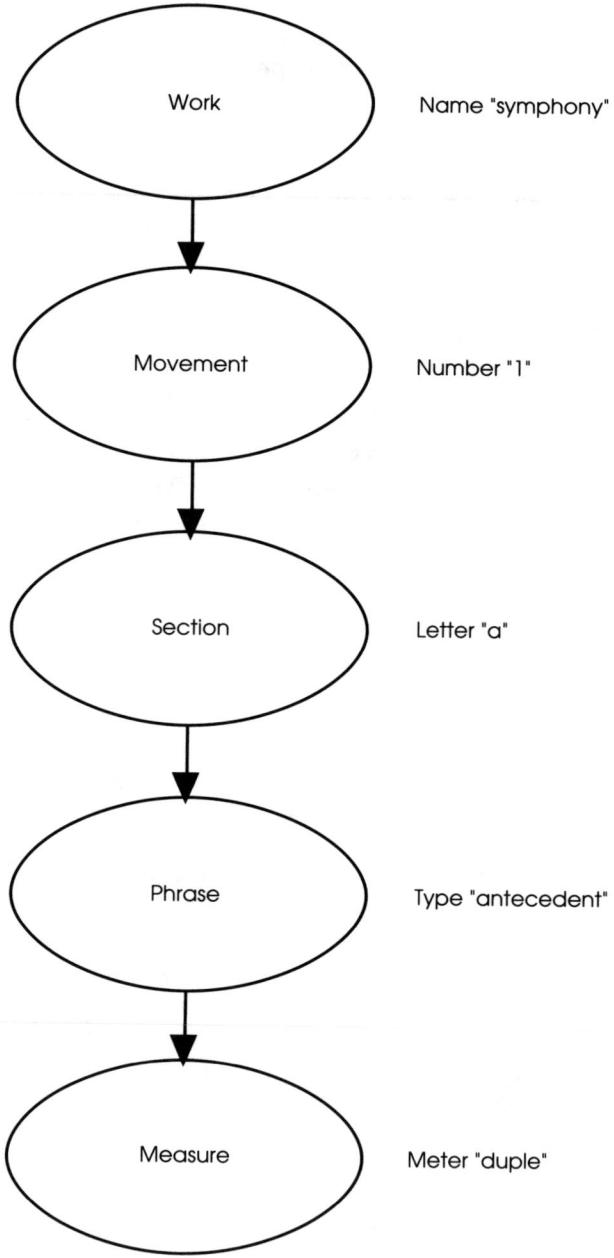

figure 4.1) can be a nightmare when data has been contiguously amassed in a single location. Even if the data has been organized clearly by measures (no guarantee in non–object-oriented databases), just searching all the various parts of the "a" section could be a nontrivial task. With object orientation, such a search routine is merely a matter of retrieving the desired objects from the section object where they are logically stored.

As a further example, the *Musikalisches Würfelspiel* on the CD-ROM that accompanies this book stores all the measures of eleven possible dice throws in a single location. The program then randomly chooses a measure from this collection of measures each time it "composes" a new composition. This is not an example of object orientation, nor need it be, as the choice of measures here requires nothing more than the equivalent of a throw of dice. Imagine, however, that the list of measures were a phrase from a work being used for recombinant music generation and that elements such as chord analysis, accompaniment type, and voice connectivity were needed for each measure. Even if such an analysis were completed prior to composition and stored with each measure, accessing the information, even in relatively short phrases of music, would be an incredibly time-consuming and potentially mistake-ridden task, to say nothing of the nearly unreadable nature of the long lists of data. Debugging such lists would require herculean feats of data searching, separation, and recognition. OOPS, on the other hand, ensures that measures are stored, along with their analysis, as separate objects and collected in appropriate lexicons where they can be sorted, accessed, rearranged, debugged, read, and so on in extremely user- and program-friendly ways.

In programs that employ recombinant approaches to composition like EMI and SARA, object orientation is almost a requirement. Just accessing single extended lists of events for making logical choices of given measures would be an incredibly complicated task. Augmented transition networks (see chapter 5), which require continuous sorting and resorting, exponentially multiply such complexity. Problems associated with cataloging and accessing incipient gestures and cadences would likewise increase.

The object-oriented software on the CD-ROM that accompanies this book (SARA) takes the form of `phrase` and `measure` (of varying meters) as names of its object classes. It could well have taken the forms shown in figure 4.1. In fact, a more extended form of EMI does just that. Such delineation more clearly denotes the hierarchy (large to small) and nature of the classes. However, for the purposes of explanation and for the condensed form SARA takes, `phrase` and `measure` are sufficient. Classes of objects that themselves have subclasses are called *superclasses*. Thus, in figure 4.1, all but the last example are superclasses. The `phrase` class in the accompanying software is a superclass, whereas, for example, `duple-measure` is a subclass with no inheritors.

Classes of objects have attributes. Attributes in CLOS are stored in slots, which are defined locations for data specific to a given attribute. In figure 4.1 all the terms to the right of the objects are attributes. The information in quotes to the right of the attribute names are the assigned values associated with these names. In SARA, the class of objects called `phrase` contains attributes for its name, mode, tempo, meter, and so on. The class `duple-measure` automatically inherits the values for these attributes plus the values for attributes of its own such as its music, analysis, destination, and so on. One of the advantages of inheritance is that it negates the need for duplication of attributes: once an attribute is defined for a superclass, it need not be redefined for any of its subclasses. Likewise, all the subclasses of this subclass will inherit the attributes of all their superclasses, voiding the need to repeat information that is in common between hierarchically associated subclasses.

Figure 4.2 gives an example of how one would create the classes of objects shown in figure 4.1. The LISP macro `defclass` defines a class or superclass of objects. Its argument (in parentheses to the right of the name of the class) is the name of any superclass(es) to which it belongs. Thus, in this example, `movement` is a subclass of `work` and `section` a subclass of `movement`. The list of descriptors following the first line of each defined class of objects comprises its attributes, which will be described in more detail shortly.

Specific examples of classes are called *instances*. Instances of classes possess all the attributes provided by their associated class and all superclasses to which they belong. Figure 4.3 shows how instances of objects are created using `setq` and `make-instance`. Inheritance and, by inference, hierarchy, can be shown by using *accessors* of the superclass on these instances. A sample run in figure 4.3 shows how these accessors work. Accessors act like functions in LISP. However, they are not defined by `defun`, but achieve function-like status by their association with their respective attribute in the `defclass` description or are inherited from a superclass of that class. Thus, `name` acts like a function in figure 4.3 by virtue of its being defined as an accessor in the superclass `work` in figure 4.2. The same is true of the accessors `letter` from the superclass `movement` and `phrase-type` from the superclass `section`.

The instance of `measure` here has inherited all the attributes of its superclass and those of its own class. However, `phrase` has none

**Figure 4.2** Defining the classes of objects shown in figure 4.1.

```
(defclass work ()
    ((name :initarg :name :initform 'symphony :accessor name)))
#<STANDARD-CLASS WORK>

(defclass movement (work)
    ((movement-number :initarg :movement-number :initform 1
      :accessor movement-number)))
#<STANDARD-CLASS MOVEMENT>

(defclass section (movement)
    ((letter :initarg :letter :initform 'a :accessor letter)))
#<STANDARD-CLASS SECTION>

(defclass phrase (section)
   ((phrase-type :initarg :phrase-type :initform 'antecedent
     :accessor phrase-type)))
#<STANDARD-CLASS PHRASE>

(defclass measure (phrase)
    ((meter :initarg :meter :initform 'duple :accessor meter)))
#<STANDARD-CLASS MEASURE>
```

of the attributes of measure (its subclass), as inheritance proceeds in only one direction in class hierarchy. As another example, observe how, in query (d) of figure 4.3, the instance of measure (the lowest rung of the hierarchy in figure 4.1) has inherited the attribute of name from the class work (the highest rung of the hierarchy in figure 4.1) without any explicit assignment of this information.

As was shown in chapters 3 and 4 of *Computers and Musical Style* (Cope 1991a), LISP promotes the idea of small, simple functions contributing to more complex combinations of functions. This promotes clarity of programming. It also makes use of the fundamental concept of small, specialized functions operating in concert to achieve powerful results. In LISP-like form, CLOS allows classes to be defined simply even though their manifestations may be complex. The functions that contribute to the more complex natures of specific instances of classes are called *generic* functions.

Generic functions differ from standard LISP functions in an important respect. Whereas a standard LISP function executes a single body of code on its arguments, generic functions have code that varies depending on the classes of their arguments. Generic

***Figure 4.3***  Instantiating the classes of objects shown in figure 4.2.

**a.**
```
(setq my-work (make-instance 'work))
#<WORK #x39D619>
```

**b.**
```
(name my-work)
symphony
```

**c.**
```
(setq my-measure (make-instance 'measure))
#<MEASURE #x397BB1>
```

**d.**
```
(name my-measure)
symphony
```

**e.**
```
(movement-number my-measure)
1
```

**f.**
```
(letter my-measure)
a
```

**g.**
```
(phrase-type my-measure)
antecedent
```

functions are sometimes called *polymorphic functions* for this reason (Gabriel, White, and Bobrow 1991). For example, a generic function called `play` could be used to play a single note (in the case of a call to an instance of a class of notes), a measure of notes (in the case of a call to an instance of a class of measures), or a complete phrase (in the case of a call to an instance of a class of phrases). In each of these cases, the data called by `play` would necessarily be in a different form (i.e., an event in the case of an instance of `note`, a list of events in the case of an instance of `measure`, etc.). The generic function would be called `play` in all three instances. However, the code that would be implemented will depend exclusively on the class of its argument. In other words, three different generic function definitions for `play` would need to exist.

This brief overview of CLOS should serve to introduce the reader to the basic elements of LISP object orientation. However, each element of CLOS requires more detailed explanation and examples as they pertain to music and the EMI and SARA databases, as the following hopefully provides.

## ■ CLASSES AND SUPERCLASSES

As previously mentioned, CLOS allows one to build classes from other classes (superclasses). These classes, often called subclasses, may also inherit from more than one superclass, thereby inheriting attributes of all their related superclasses. This is called *multiple inheritance*. Such multiple inheritances have precedence requirements in order from left to right (precedence to the left) in the argument of the inheriting class. Figure 4.4 diagrams one such complicated component system of superclasses and subclasses. For this example, the superclass `phrase` and `duple-measure` are defined in steps (a) and (b) as classes with no superclasses. In step (c), the class `mozart-measures` is defined as having the two just-defined classes as superclasses. Thus, as the queries of steps (e), (f), and (g) prove, an instance of `mozart-measures` (here called `my-mozart-measures`) inherits accessor functions and data from all its superclasses. This diagram further demonstrates that there may be many generations of superclasses, with the lowest subclass inheriting attributes from all superseding superclasses.

Interestingly, CLOS is implemented in CLOS. That is, standard CLOS object classes are themselves classes of other classes, with all such classes descendent of a single unique class. In CLOS this unique class is `t` (or `true`), which has no superclasses and which is a superclass to all classes except itself. This idea of writing CLOS in CLOS is called *metaobject protocol*.

## ■ SLOTS

Figures 4.5a–c show the lower level class- and object-defining functions used in one version of EMI. The function `define-phrase-class` in figure 4.5a uses `make-beat-objects` (shown in figure 4.5b) to move incrementally through the beats of music in its

**Figure 4.4** An example of multiple inheritance using the objects shown in previous figures.

**a.**
```
(defclass phrase nil
   ((creator :initarg :creator :initform nil :accessor creator)
    (matching-line-number :initarg :matching-line-number
     :initform 1 :accessor matching-line-number)))
#<STANDARD-CLASS PHRASE>
```

**b.**
```
(defclass duple-measure nil
   ((music :initarg :music :initform nil :accessor music)))
#<STANDARD-CLASS DUPLE-MEASURE>
```

**c.**
```
(defclass mozart-measures (phrase duple-measure)
    ((date :initarg :date :initform 1789 :accessor date)))
#<STANDARD-CLASS MOZART-MEASURES>
```

**d.**
```
(setq my-mozart-measures (make-instance 'mozart-measures))
#<MOZART-MEASURES #x3DA559>
```

**e.**
```
(date my-mozart-measures)
1789
```

**f.**
```
(music my-mozart-measures)
NIL
```

**g.**
```
(matching-line-number my-mozart-measures)
1
```

argument. The function `make-beat-objects` uses `make-instance` (line 7) to produce the new objects. The object EMI-object (see figure 4.5c) defines objects as a series of recordkeeping slots with embedded code. Because these recordkeeping slots include many necessary repetitions, they are not all shown in figure 4.5c but are listed by category below:

## THE OBJECT SYSTEM    133

*Figure 4.5*   EMI object definitions.

**a.**
```
(defvar object nil)

1.(defun define-phrase-class (name-of-phrase)
2.    (set (concat name-of-phrase '-beat-objects)
3.        (make-beat-objects name-of-phrase
4.            (eval-everything name-of-phrase))))
```

**b.**
```
1.(defun make-beat-objects
2.    (name-of-phrase phrase &optional (number one))
3. (if (null phrase) nil
4. (progn (set object (concat name-of-phrase '- number))
5.        (set (concat object '-beat)(first beats))
6.        (set (concat object '-second-beat)(second beats))
7.        (cons (set object (make-instance 'EMI-object))
8.              (make-beat-objects name-of-phrase
9.                (rest phrase)(1+ number))))))
```

**c.**
```
1.(defclass EMI-object nil
2.    ((precept-slot-ties :initarg :precept-slot-ties
3.                        :initform `(get-ties (eval
4.                            (concat (quote ,object) '-beat)))
5.                        :accessor precept-slot-ties)
6.     . . .
```

### CD-ROM

Figures 4.2 to 4.4 can be usefully run in the SARA Listener window, as can figure 4.12 with appropriate databases loaded. The files sara-objects and sara-menu provide examples of defining and calling objects in CLOS for music and windows, respectively. Writing new code for user-defined object classes and superclasses that inherit and have slots and methods will enhance the reader's understanding of how objects function within a hierarchy and provide a perfect environment for recombinancy in applications such as EMI and SARA. ✥

1. Precept (short for preinception) slots include information about ties (shown), first notes of each voice (`precept-slot-first-notes`), range of each voice (`precept-slot-tessitura`), analysis of SPEAC function (`precept-slot-function`), and accompaniment (`precept-slot-figuration`) such as alberti basses.

2. Incept (short for inception) slots, or the music of the object itself, include pitches (`incept-slot-pitches`), durations (`incept-slot-durations`), dynamics (`incept-slot-dynamics`), and articulations (`incept-slot-articulations`) of all voices.

3. Postcept (short for postinception) slots include information about the beat that follows the beat in the original music, including `postcept-slot-ties`, `postcept-slot-next-notes`, `postcept-slot-tessitura`, `postcept-slot-function`, and `postcept-slot-figuration`.

Each of these recordkeeping slots is represented by embedded code (shown following the `:initform` keyword in figure 4.5c). This embedded code remains unevaluated until an object instance is required to produce data. Such code can then produce significant amounts of context-sensitive data. Embedded code avoids possibly redundant data and huge data-laden objects in memory. The use of the LISP backquote macro here ensures that all but the object's own name (as in *object*) remain unevaluated at the time of the object's creation.

Figure 4.6 shows a few calls to the results of `define-phrase-class`. Note how using the accessors produces only lines of code. The evaluation of that code produces the data, which are not present in the object itself, thus the use of `eval` here. Using object systems such as the ones in EMI and SARA for storing groupings of notes larger than two- or three-note motives (such as measures) but less than phrases avoids huge lists of data where access is difficult and time consuming.

Figure 4.7 gives the definitions of the superclass `phrase` and one of its subclasses, `duple-measure`, as used in SARA. The `nil` argument following the `defclass` of `phrase` indicates that this class of objects has no superclasses. The sublists that follow this are slots that have names (first entry) followed by a series of initialization arguments and initial values. Thus, the `creator` slot has the initialization arguments and initial values: `:initarg` (the keyword `:creator`), `:initform` (initial value `nil`), and `:accessor` (initial value `creator`). Therefore, the `creator` slot's initial argument, `:initarg`, is the keyword `:creator`; its initial form, `:initform`, is `nil`; and its accessor function name is `creator`. The importance of these slots will become apparent as specific examples of these classes are created.

**Figure 4.6** Queries after a run of `define-phrase-class`.

```
(precept-slot-first-notes 'mozart-pf-one-281/3/1)
(get-first-notes (eval (concat (quote ,object) '-beat)))

(eval (precept-slot-first-notes 'mozart-pf-one-281/3/1))
(C4 E3 C2)

(eval (postcept-slot-next-notes 'mozart-pf-one-281/3/1))
(R R C2)

(eval (precept-slot-function 'mozart-pf-one-281/3/1))
P1
```

**Figure 4.7** SARA definitions for the classes `phrase` and `duple-measure`.

```
1.(defclass phrase nil
2.   ((creator :initarg :creator :initform nil :accessor creator)
3.    (matching-line-number :initarg
4.        :matching-line-number :initform 1
5.     :accessor matching-line-number)
6.    (mode :initarg :mode :initform 'major :accessor mode)
7.    (tempo :initarg :tempo :initform 60 :accessor tempo)
8.    (meter :initarg :meter :initform nil :accessor meter)
9.    (measures :initarg :measures :initform nil
10.      :accessor measures)))

1.(defclass duple-measure (phrase)
2.   ((music :initarg :music :initform nil :accessor music)
3.    (match? :initarg :match? :initform nil :accessor match?)
4.    (analysis :initarg :analysis  :initform nil
5.       :accessor analysis)
6.    (destination :initarg :destination  :initform nil
7.       :accessor destination)))
```

The slots in SARA's `phrase` objects defined in figure 4.7 include the previously mentioned `creator` as well as `matching-line-number`, `mode`, `tempo`, `meter`, and `measures`. The `creator` slot returns the name of the phrase and measure objects. The `matching-line-number` slot is used by the SARA pattern-matching program and indicates which channel should be used in searching for signatures. The `mode` slot stores information regarding the mode of the original music that can be useful for mode settings during playback. The `tempo` slot serves similarly to aid in tempo settings when playing databases and recombinant examples from a given database. The `meter` slot informs the user of the meter of the phrase and thus the type of measure (i.e., duple, triple, etc.) objects it contains. The `measures` slot stores names of all the measures associated with the phrase object and is very useful for reconstructing phrases for playback and so on. All of SARA's accessors use the same names as their respective slots.

The slots in SARA's `measure` (mono, duple, and triple) objects defined in figure 4.7 include `music`, `match?`, `analysis`, and `destination`. The `music` slot stores the music of the measure object as a series of events. If the `match?` slot is `t`, the object has been matched as a signature. This indicates that the original measure that follows it will follow it again during recombinancy so that signatures will remain intact. The default value of `match?` is `nil`. The `analysis` slot contains the SPEAC analysis of the measure object in a list of identifiers with one identifier per beat of music. The `destination` slot contains a list of the first notes of the original following measure and the SPEAC analysis of the original following measure. The `destination` slot is one of the most important slots of the EMI and SARA database storage systems in that it provides important information for the ATN recombinancy program. The destination slot can be expanded indefinitely (to the right) for deeper ATN and more sophisticated composition.

As previously mentioned, both the beginning and the ending of phrases are particularly important in the EMI and SARA recombinant processes. Thus, both `incipient` and `cadence` (shown in figure 4.8) are subclasses of the superclass `phrase`. Both these subclasses have slots for `music` (events), `match?` (whether or not the incipient measure or cadence is currently being protected from recomposition), and the SPEAC analysis of the current measure by beat. Each stored phrase of a database has representations of both `incipient` and `cadence`. Because all music does not have important or even extant pickup gestures or events, the `incipient` lexicon often does not contain any actual music.

**Figure 4.8** The incipient and cadence subclasses.

```
1.(defclass incipient (phrase)
2.  ((music :initarg :music :initform nil :accessor music)
3.   (match? :initarg :match? :initform nil :accessor match?)
4.   (analysis :initarg :analysis :accessor analysis)))

1.(defclass cadence (phrase)
2.  ((music :initarg :music :initform nil :accessor music)
3.   (match? :initarg :match? :initform nil :accessor match?)
4.   (analysis :initarg :analysis :accessor analysis)))
```

Lexicons are also important object classes in EMI and SARA. Lexicons are not superclasses, nor do they belong to a superclass. The incipience-lexicon in SARA contains a slot for first-measures (incipient object names). The cadence-lexicon in SARA contains slots for a half-cadence-list and a full-cadence-list. The half-cadence-list slot provides a list of the names of half-cadence combinations of measures in the database. The full-cadence-list slot similarly provides a list of the names of full-cadence (or authentic cadence) combinations of measures in the database. Figure 4.9 shows SARA definitions for both incipience-lexicon and cadence-lexicon.

The slots in SARA's standard lexicon class include mono-function-list, duple-function-list, triple-function-list, first-note-list, and last-chord. The first three of these contain appropriate lists of measure names, depending on the meter of the stored measure objects. The first-note-list slot stores a list of the first notes of each of the measure objects in the lexicon for easy access. The last-chord slot likewise provides a list of last-chord SPEAC analysis symbols for recombinancy.

Storing music in mono-measures can serve two purposes. First, it can naturally store music in mono-meters such as $\frac{1}{4}$, $\frac{1}{8}$, and so on, as the name *mono* suggests. Second, however, and more important, storing music in mono-measures allows for music in any meter to be stored by beat instead of by measure. Although this can be quite costly in terms of storage space (i.e., double and triple the number of object instances are required of duple- and triple-measure storage), it allows for a beat-to-beat rather than a measure-to-measure recombinancy. This can be very useful when using small databases, as composing can otherwise cause recognizability of the

**Figure 4.9** The SARA `lexicon` with the `cadence` and `incipience` lexicon definitions.

```
1.(defclass lexicon nil
2.   ((mono-function-list :initarg :mono-function-list
3.        :initform nil :accessor mono-function-list)
4.    (duple-function-list :initarg :duple-function-list
5.        :initform nil :accessor duple-function-list)
6.    (triple-function-list :initarg :triple-function-list
7.        :initform nil :accessor triple-function-list)
8.    (first-note-list :initarg :first-note-list :initform nil
9.        :accessor first-note-list)
10.   (last-chord :initarg :last-chord :initform nil
11.       :accessor last-chord)))

1.(defclass cadence-lexicon nil
2.   ((half-cadence-list :initarg :half-cadence-list
3.        :initform nil :accessor half-cadence-list)
4.    (full-cadence-list :initarg :full-cadence-list
5.        :initform nil :accessor full-cadence-list)))

1.(defclass incipience-lexicon nil
2.   ((first-measures :initarg :first-measures :initform nil
3.        :accessor first-measures)))
```

larger database measures. It is also useful when composing short phrases, where the number of larger measures required to compose a phrase could be very small and thus curtail creativity.

Beat-to-beat recombinancy has been used in many incarnations of EMI to great success, especially when employing complex ATN. In fact, it is in this mode of operation that EMI and SARA have produced some of their most interesting, creative music (see especially figures 5.11 and 5.12 and related text). Not only is the original database more obscured by the small samples used for composition, but the opportunity for highly novel progressions is significantly multiplied because the number of actual choices per phrase is so extensive. Users of SARA can produce or revise databases in any metric form they wish (see the user's manual on the CD-ROM accompanying this book). However, the one drawback with using beat-to-beat recombinancy is that the time required for composition increases significantly.

## ■ METHODS

One basic implementation of generic functions is called *methods*. Methods contribute to making instances of classes by helping to define certain aspects of that instance. As previously mentioned, generic functions, and hence methods, are similar to LISP functions. They take arguments and compute results. However, unlike normal LISP functions, methods are not called directly. Instead, methods are invoked during the existence of an instance of an object class. Also, because methods are generic functions, methods of the same name can perform quite differently depending on the class of objects being instantiated.

A good example of method creation and use is the generic function `initialize-instance` found in the file sara-menu on the accompanying CD-ROM. This method is redefined several times in this file with differing results, depending on the class to which the method pertains. In most cases, `initialize-instance` is responsible for describing instances of other classes, such as instances of button and table classes in windows. Each description is different and modifies the visual character of a different class of windows. Figure 4.10 provides an example of this behavior. Note that the function `defmethod` is the defining function for methods. This example of `initialize-instance` is bound to the class `about-window`, which is assigned to the temporary variable `window`. In this case, an instance of the `about-window` class will possess an instance of another object class called `static-text-dialog-item`, which, in this case, places the name SARA in the window at the designated location (see `view-position` in line 8). Other objects such as buttons, checkboxes, tables, and so on can also be placed in windows in this manner.

Methods often relate to instance behavior. For example, `before-methods` and `after-methods` are methods that are called at instantiation and dissolution of object instances. Primary methods tend to perform the primary functions of an object and exist between `before-methods` and `after-methods`. Around-methods and other forms of object-modifying methods also exist but are beyond the scope of this text. Suffice it to say, methods present a crucial link to understanding CLOS.

***Figure 4.10*** An example of the method `initialize-instance`.

```
1. (defclass about-window (window)
2.   nil
3.   (:default-initargs :window-type :document
4.     :window-title ""
5.     :view-position #@(10 40)
6.     :view-size #@(300 180)))

1. (defmethod initialize-instance
2.   ((window about-window) &rest initargs)
3.   . . .
4.   (add-subviews window
5.                 (make-instance
6.                   'static-text-dialog-item
7.                   :view-font '("athens" 26)
8.                   :view-position #@(76 8)
9.                   :dialog-item-text
10.                    "SARA")
11.   . . .
```

## ■ OBJECT PROGRAM

Each database file in SARA contains instances of four different object types: `phrase`, `incipient-lexicon`, `cadence-lexicon`, and `measures`. The first section of code in each database file defines a class of the phrase object. This object contains all the normal elements of a phrase object with the attributes that are common to all the elements of the incipient gesture, cadence, and measures of the phrase. When a database file is loaded, the `phrase` class for that database is defined, including matching-line number, tempo, mode, meter, and so on. Because measures (mono, duple, and triple) are subclasses of the class `phrase`, each measure of the loading database phrase inherits the current status of the just-defined phrase's attributes. This inheritance is class dependent. Thus, when another database is loaded with different attribute assignments, the measures of that newly loaded database will inherit those particular attributes, and the first-loaded database will retain its initial attributes.

The second section of code in each database file sets the database name and `-incipient` to the music of the pickup of the phrase, if one exists. Because incipient gestures will be added to incipient lexicons (i.e., groups of incipient gestures), the code must first ensure that a lexicon object exists before attempting to add the current gesture. Thus, each database has code to verify the existence of a lexicon and to create a lexicon if one does not already exist. The statement that follows the incipient gesture-creating code defines a network of `SPEAC` symbols useful for generating transition network compositions. This data can also be useful for initiating ATNs for more elaborate compositions.

The next section of code in each database file sets the database name and `-cadence` to the music of the cadence of the phrase. Because cadences, like incipient measures, will be added to lexicons (i.e., groups of cadence gestures), the code must first ensure that a lexicon object exists before attempting to add the current cadence. Finally, each database file contains a series of measure objects that contain attribute descriptions following previously described slots. Furthermore, each measure instance-creating code is followed by functions that add the measure name and its first notes to the associated slot positions in the appropriate lexicons (and create the lexicons if they do not already exist).

Figure 4.11 shows how the superclass `phrase` and subclasses `incipient`, `cadence`, and `triple-measure` occur in an actual database. Figure 4.11a shows how the class `phrase` is defined for a Chopin mazurka database. All the slots shown here are inherited by the instances of `triple-measure`, one of which is shown in figure 4.11d. Instances of `incipient` and `cadence` are shown in figures 4.11b and 4.11c along with code to include them in their appropriate lexicons (lines 3–5 of figure 4.11b and lines 7–9 of figure 4.11c). Note that, in lines 9 to 15 in figure 4.11a, the measure names in the particular phrase are listed for phrase reconstruction for performance and for setting multimeasure signatures into place. Figure 4.11 also shows how lexicons store appropriate measures of music.

The function `setf` (for "set field") here takes as arguments a list of the slot-value location and name of the field and the information to be set into that field. Thus, the code (`setf (slot-value 'chopin-maz-one-C1-lexicon 'triple-function-list)...`) in lines 10–11 of figure 4.11d places "..." in the `triple-function-list` slot of the `chopin-maz-one-C1-lexicon`. Thus `setf`, unlike `setq`, can assign and change an indefinite number of property values of, in this case, the `chopin-maz-one-C1-lexicon`. Furthermore, replacing "..." with a call to the function `cons` along with the data of "..." and `slot-value 'chopin-maz-one-C1-lexicon 'triple-function-list` adds "..." to the list in this location

*Figure 4.11* A basic database for a Chopin phrase.

**a.**
```
1. (defclass phrase nil
2.   ((creator :initarg :creator :initform 'chopin-maz-one
3.        :accessor creator)
4.    (matching-line-number :initarg :matching-line-number
5.        :initform 1 :accessor matching-line-number)
6.    (mode :initarg :mode :initform 'major :accessor mode)
7.    (tempo :initarg :tempo :initform 66 :accessor tempo)
8.    (meter :initarg :meter :initform 3 :accessor meter)
9.    (measures :initarg :measures :initform
10.    '(chopin-maz-one-17/1/1-mea-6
11.      chopin-maz-one-17/1/1-mea-5
12.      chopin-maz-one-17/1/1-mea-4
13.      chopin-maz-one-17/1/1-mea-3
14.      chopin-maz-one-17/1/1-mea-2
15.      chopin-maz-one-17/1/1-mea-1) :accessor measures)))
```

**b.**
```
1. (setq chopin-maz-one-17/1/1-incipient
2.       (make-instance 'incipient :music nil :analysis nil))
3. (if (not (boundp 'chopin-maz-one-incipience-lexicon))
4.     (setq chopin-maz-one-incipience-lexicon
5.           (make-instance 'incipience-lexicon)))
6. (setf (slot-value chopin-maz-one-incipience-lexicon
7.                   'first-measures)
8.       (cons 'chopin-maz-one-17/1/1-incipient
9.             (slot-value chopin-maz-one-incipience-lexicon
10.                        'first-measures)))
11. (setq chopin-maz-one-17/1/1-network
12.      '(c1 c1 c1 c1 p1 c1 a1 a1 a1 c1 c1 c1 c1 c1
13.        c1 c1 p1 c1 a1 a1 a1 c1 c1 c1))
```

**c.**
```
1. (setq chopin-maz-one-17/1/1-cadence
2.       (make-instance 'cadence :music
3.         '((0 43 1000 3 100) (0 65 1000 1 100)
4.           . . . .
5.           (5000 64 1000 1 100))
6.         :analysis '(a1 a1 a1 c1 c1 c1)))
7. (if (not (boundp 'chopin-maz-one-cadence-lexicon))
8.     (setq chopin-maz-one-cadence-lexicon
```

*Figure 4.11* continued.

```
9.          (make-instance 'cadence-lexicon)))
10.(setf (slot-value chopin-maz-one-cadence-lexicon
11.                  'full-cadence-list)
12.       (cons 'chopin-maz-one-17/1/1-cadence
13.             (slot-value chopin-maz-one-cadence-lexicon
14.                         'full-cadence-list)))
```

**d.**
```
1.(setq chopin-maz-one-17/1/1-mea-1
2.      (make-instance 'triple-measure
3. :music '((0 48 1000 3 100) (0 76 1500 1 100) (0 79 1500 1 100)
4.         . . . .
5.         (2000 79 500 1 100) (2500 75 500 1 100))
6. :analysis '(c1 c1 c1) :destination '((79 60 48) c1)))
7.(if (not (boundp 'chopin-maz-one-c1-lexicon))
8.     (setq chopin-maz-one-c1-lexicon
9.           (make-instance 'lexicon)))
10.(setf (slot-value chopin-maz-one-c1-lexicon
11.                  'triple-function-list)
12.       (cons 'chopin-maz-one-17/1/1-mea-1
13.             (slot-value chopin-maz-one-c1-lexicon
14.                         'triple-function-list)))
15.(setf (slot-value chopin-maz-one-c1-lexicon 'first-note-list)
16.       (cons (second
17.              (first
18.                (get-sounding-channel 1
19.                  (slot-value chopin-maz-one-17/1/1-mea-1
20.                              'music))))
21.             (slot-value chopin-maz-one-c1-lexicon
22.                         'first-note-list)))
  . . . .
```

rather than replacing it. Thus, in the case of figure 4.11d, the C1 lexicon of the chopin-maz section "one" may have an indefinite number of instances of measure names representing appropriate measures of like-functioned music. Data can be retrieved from any object in the database through the accessor names in the class definitions. This data takes the form of, for example, event lists (in the case of instances of the subclasses of the object superclass phrase) or lists of object instance names of measures (in the case of lexicons).

Figures 4.12a–e give an example of queries to a measure object that shows the dynamic nature of inheritance. Queries (a) to (d) demonstrate the inheritance of measure objects from the phrase objects whose class is defined at the onset of each database file as in figure 4.11. Query (e) show how the music local to each measure object can be retrieved for composition and performance (in conjunction with the original order of measures stored in phrase objects).

It is interesting to note that only a fraction of the code in a database is actual data. Most of the code sets the stage for recombinancy by creating and storing the various data in objects in logical locations. This can be likened to a situation in which one has but a few items of mail and thousands of mailboxes (a little data and lots of organization). Yet, unorganized and poorly prepared data is of little use, just as wrongly delivered mail has little value. EMI and SARA both strive to create object systems that arrange data in ways in which they can be most effectively utilized. This is the reason for the enormous care in data delivery and the rationale for the structure of the databases.

Figure 4.13 provides a good example of object use in composition. This EMI-Bach invention is based on a database and resultant lexicons of Bach's Inventions 5 and 15 shown in figures 4.14a and 4.14b. Note how the music in both hands of the EMI work imitates with variation the Bach Invention 15 transposed up one step. Measures 3 and 4 of the EMI-Bach borrow music from Bach's Invention 5, with the right hand of beats 2 and 3 of measure 3 of figure 4.13 drawn from the left hand of the second half of measure 2 of figure 4.14a. Determining the sources of measure objects in EMI recombinant music is often difficult because of the number of interrelated processes involved. In some cases, it is easier to observe measure grafting in the use of signatures, as seen in the Rachmaninoff examples of figures 3.22 to 3.28.

Figure 4.15 shows how the original Bach looks in database form; the objects and data are shown graphically to demonstrate its separateness and location in lexicons. Figure 4.16 then shows a possible source of the opening of the EMI-Bach imitation and how it might appear as a result of recomposition (again shown graphically to indicate sources). One can imagine the huge number of possibilities available when large numbers of databases are used and thus the use of the words *possible* and *might*.

***Figure 4.12*** Queries to objects showing inheritance of phrase information in measure objects.

**a.**
```
(meter chopin-maz-one-17/1/1-mea-1)
3
```

**b.**
```
(meter mozart-pf-one-281/3/1-mea-1)
2
```

**c.**
```
(measures mozart-pf-one-281/3/1-mea-1)
(mozart-pf-one-281/3/1-mea-6 mozart-pf-one-281/3/1-mea-5
  mozart-pf-one-281/3/1-mea-4 mozart-pf-one-281/3/1-mea-3
  mozart-pf-one-281/3/1-mea-2 mozart-pf-one-281/3/1-mea-1)
```

**d.**
```
(measures chopin-maz-one-17/1/1-mea-2)
(chopin-maz-one-17/1/1-mea-6 chopin-maz-one-17/1/1-mea-5
 chopin-maz-one-17/1/1-mea-4 chopin-maz-one-17/1/1-mea-3
 chopin-maz-one-17/1/1-mea-2 chopin-maz-one-17/1/1-mea-1)
```

**e.**
```
(music chopin-maz-one-17/1/1-mea-1)
((0 48 1000 3 100) (0 76 1500 1 100) (0 79 1500 1 100)
   (1000 55 1000 3 100) (1000 64 1000 2 100) (1000 60 1000 2 100)
   (1500 75 500 1 100) (1500 78 500 1 100) (2000 55 1000 3 100)
   (2000 64 1000 2 100) (2000 60 1000 2 100) (2000 76 500 1 100)
   (2000 79 500 1 100) (2500 75 500 1 100) (2500 78 500 1 100))
```

**Figure 4.13**  The beginning of an EMI-Bach Invention.

*Figure 4.14* The openings of Bach's inventions: a) No. 5 (BWV 776). b) No. 15 (BWV 786).

148   EXPERIMENTS IN MUSICAL INTELLIGENCE

**Figure 4.15**   Bach, Invention no. 5, m. 1, in objects (transposed to C).

:music
((0 48 1000 1 100) (500 60 250 2 100) (750 59 250 2 100)
(1000 36 1000 1 100) (1000 60 500 2 100) (1500 62 500 2 100))
Bach-invention-5-mea-1

:music
((0 64 1000 2 100) (250 60 250 1 100) (500 59 250 1 100)
(750 60 250 1 100) (1000 57 250 1 100) (1000 65 1000 1 100)
(1250 59 250 1 100) (1500 55 250 1 100) (1750 57 250 1 100))
Bach-invention-5-mea-2

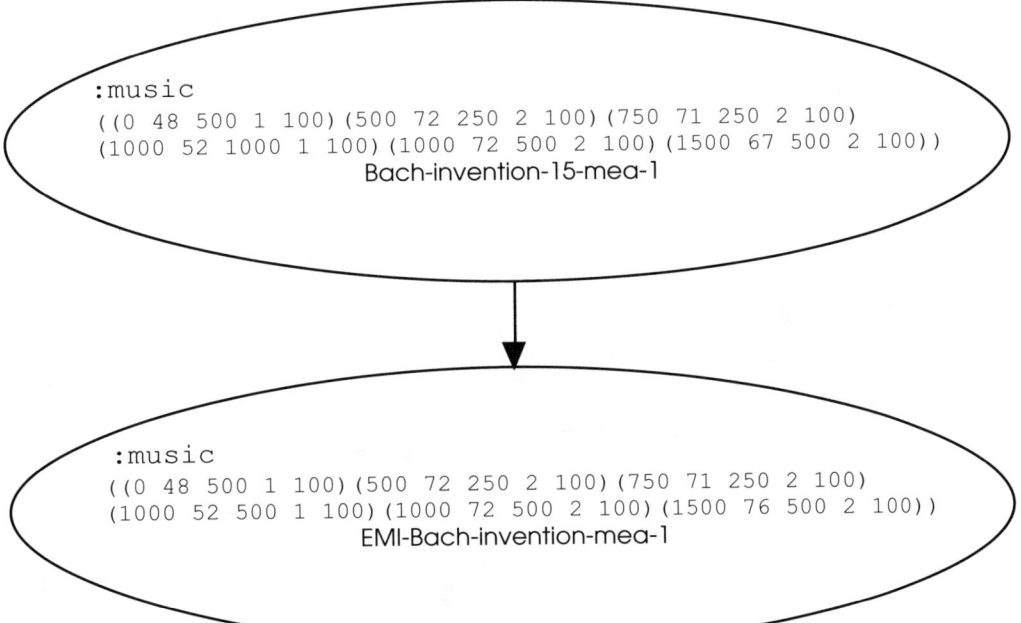

**Figure 4.16** One possible derivation of the EMI-Bach Invention.

# FIVE

## The ATN Component

The EMI and SARA augmented transition network (ATN) components attempt to ensure that the analyzed measures (stored in the object system files) and signatures (gleaned from pattern matching and protected in many of those objects) will be recombined in logical, musical ways. Augmented transition networks have been used successfully in automatic language analysis and generation (Bates 1978; Christaller 1979). They produce output that has predictable meanings but with numerous, different, and logical orders of words. They have proven valuable for human-machine interaction, where a natural flow of language is desired without redundancy.

We have seen in chapter 1 how finite-state transition networks (FSTNs) and recursive transition networks (RTNs) can effectively represent language. For example, the sentence "Jim sees the ball" could be analyzed by a simple set of four nodes and three arcs. Unfortunately, the result, an FSTN, would not be able to distinguish "Jim sees the red ball." An RTN, however, with simple recursive nodes to present subphrases of various lengths, could recognize both these sentences as well as hundreds of other variations. We also saw how ATNs were required to recognize transformational responses such as, in this instance, "The red ball was seen by Jim," and so on. Obviously, ATNs, with their various registers for storing conditional properties, are more sophisticated and flexible than either FSTNs or RTNs.

As a further example, observe the following sentences, the first as input and the other two as output from an ATN: "John was believed to have been shot" (see Woods 1970, pp. 603–4); "Someone believed that someone had shot John" and "Someone believed that

John had been shot." The transposition of these sentences resembles Chomsky's transformational grammar (Chomsky 1965). All three of these sentences are simple and have the same fundamental meaning. Yet the surface detail—the order of words—is different and interesting. People converse with such techniques all the time using countless varieties of word orders and choices. Machines do not naturally reorder words correctly in this way. Instead, they typically provide precise information in predictable orders. Augmented transition networks can analyze and create varied and logical output, making for more inventive interaction. When ATNs are applied to musical situations, especially situations involving recombinancy, they can produce diverse, logical musical compositions as well.

Figure 5.1 provides a more detailed example of how an ATN works. The basic sentence map in figure 5.1a is a complete sentence consisting of a noun phrase (subject—nps), verb phrase (vp1 or vp2), another noun phrase (object—npo), prepositional phrase (pp), and proper noun (pn). The two verb phrases represent optional versions of the transition. The word *jump* refers to a skipping of the step shown. The two interchangeable noun phrases are described in more detail in figures 5.1b and c. The representation *wh* in figure 5.1b stands for words such as *who*, *what*, *when*, or *where* used for queries. Other representations are as follows: *det* = determinator or article; *pn* = proper noun; *mp* = modifier phrase; *n0*, *n1* (and so on) = noun; and *p* = preposition. By applying certain viability tests (here between nodes 0 and 2 of the top diagram in figure 5.1a and shown in the code to be described) and inserting the various language parts that pass these tests, a variety of interesting statements and queries may be created from input of few actual words.

For example, recognition of the sentences "The man ate" and "The man ate the sandwich" proves that this network (figure 5.1) is capable of both FSTN and RTN parsing. The first sentence moves 0–1 by nps, 1–2 by vp1, and 2–3 by jump, and the second sentence moves 0–1 by nps, 1–2 by vp1, and 2–3 by npo. The network further proves its robustness as an ATN by recognizing "The sandwich was eaten by the man" as 0–2 by test, 2–3 by npo, 3–1 by test, 1–2 by vp–2, 2–0 by test, 0–1 by pp, 1–2 by jump, and 2–3 by jump. This sentence demonstrates transformational grammar in which the object precedes the subject. The various tests performed by the arcs in the diagram of figure 5.1 inform the nodal registers of the type (active/passive, tense, etc.) of choice that needs to be made in the subsequent state(s) of the network. For example, the passive voice created by "was eaten" must be evaluated by 3–1 by test and 1–2 by

THE ATN COMPONENT 153

*Figure 5.1* A context-free ATN.

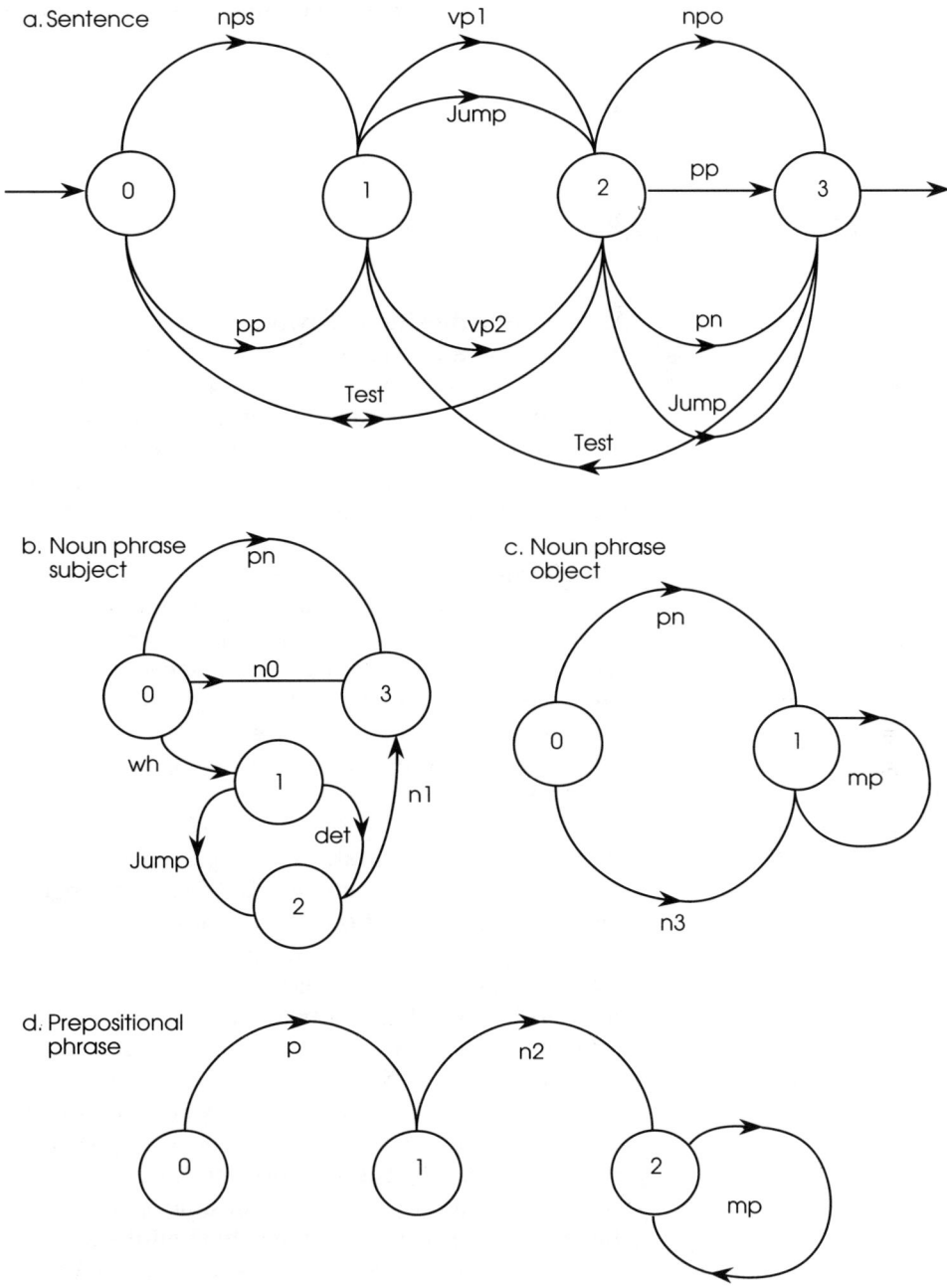

vp2 for 2–0 by test to observe the correctness of 0–1 by pp. Note that ATNs necessarily subsume FSTN and RTN capabilities and can successfully recognize sentences of these types as well as transformational examples. Also, ATNs are capable of generating correct sentences according to the same principles, given they have access to appropriately stored dictionaries of words.

## ■ ATN BASICS IN LISP

Augmented transition networks can be written effectively in LISP (see Gazdar and Mellish 1989; Watson 1991), partly because LISP involves symbolic computation, which lends itself well to assignments of words, abstractions, and arcs. The code presented here will produce questions and statements to show how ATNs can create logic in complex sentence generation. Two different *styles* of English language usage—William Shakespeare and Mark Twain—will be used as examples. These texts are provided in figure 5.2, which also shows my assignment of word types using the function `setf` to set them into appropriate dictionaries. Sentence parsing algorithms that *automatically* place words into dictionaries are relatively common in NLP and should not concern us here because they are both large and irrelevant to the point of demonstrating how ATNs can be applied musically. Figure 5.2c shows some of the variables required of the program defined by the LISP macro `defvar`. As mentioned earlier, it is proper protocol to set these variables before they are used.

The code shown in Figures 5.3–5.5 is self-contained and will reproduce output like that shown in figure 5.6 (see the file Shakespeare-Twain on the accompanying CD-ROM). Although this code does not generate transformational examples per se—both because such would require far more elaborate functions and because the chosen texts do not allow it—these functions contain tests, registers, and other ATN attributes that prove valuable by example.

Figure 5.3 shows the function `create-phrase`, the top-level function of the ATN program to be described here. The lexicon is reset in line 2 according to the lexicon argument used. This means that all the global variables representing word types will be redefined according to the appropriate lexicon grammar given in figure 5.2. The `question-or-not` variable is randomly set in line 3 so that it can affect and be consistent with the various sentence part choices. The variable `phrase` is then created from a combination of a `noun-phrase-subject`, the results of a test (lines 6–17) that

**CD-ROM**

The file Shakespeare/Twain contains all the functions and data presented in figures 5.2 to 5.5 and produces output like that in figure 5.6. The file Shakespeare/Twain/music contains an expanded version of this code, which includes the generation of music using the ATN engine (like that described here and in Cope 1992). The Hypercard stack titled "bach chorales" generates new instances of chorales based to some degree on the techniques described in figures 5.11 and 5.12 and the accompanying text. The Hypercard stack "chopin mazurkas" operates in much the same manner. The functions shown in figures 5.22 and 5.23 can be usefully run separately in SARA and demonstrate simple Schenker plotting. ❖

***Figure 5.2*** Shakespeare and Twain dictionaries:
a) *Othello,* act 1, scene 3, from *The Complete Oxford Shakespeare* (London: Oxford University Press, 1987), p. 1174.

**a.**
Rodrigo: "thou be fast to my hopes." Iago: "Thou art sure of me. I have told thee often, and I re-tell thee again and again. Thou canst cuckold him thou dost thyself a pleasure."

```
(setf (get 'shakespeare-lexicon 'grammar)
'(mapcar #'eval (list
  '(setq preposition '(to of))
  '(setq who-what-where '(dost canst wilt art))
  '(setq verb '(told re-tells))
  '(setq verb-phrase-1 '(canst-cuckhold art-sure
      be-fast has-told))
  '(setq verb-phrase-2 '(re-tell have-told))
  '(setq proper-noun '(rodrigo iago))
  '(setq pronoun '(i))
  '(setq determinator '(my a))
  '(setq noun-subject '(hope pleasure))
  '(setq noun-object '(thee him thyself))
  '(setq modifier '(again often))
  '(setq conjunction '(and)))))
```

***Figure 5.2*** Shakespeare and Twain dictionaries:
b) From *The Adventures of Tom Sawyer*
(New York: Harper and Row, 1978), p. 180.
c) Useful variables.

**b.**
"No it ain't, Huck no it ain't. It would ha'nt the place where he died. Lookyhere, Huck, I reckon we'll climb down there and have a hunt for that box. There — on the big rock over yonder."

```
(setf (get 'twain-lexicon 'grammar)
'(mapcar #'eval (list
  '(setq preposition '(for on over))
  '(setq who-what-where '(would lookyhere))
  '(setq verb '(reckon climb hunt ain-t have))
  '(setq verb-phrase-1 '(climb-down))
  '(setq verb-phrase-2 '(has climbed))
  '(setq proper-noun '(i we-ll))
  '(setq pronoun '(huck it))
  '(setq determinator '(the that a no))
  '(setq noun-subject '(box rock))
  '(setq noun-object '(the-place there))
  '(setq modifier '(over-yonder))
  '(setq conjunction '(and)))))
```

**c.**
```
(defvar preposition ())
(defvar who-what-where ())
(defvar verb ())
(defvar verb-phrase-1 ())
(defvar verb-phrase-2 ())
(defvar proper-noun ())
(defvar pronoun ())
(defvar determinator ())
(defvar noun-subject ())
(defvar noun-object ())
(defvar modifier ())
(defvar conjunction ())

(defvar preposition ())
(defvar who-what-where ())
(defvar verb ())
(defvar verb-phrase-1 ())
(defvar verb-phrase-2 ())
```

*Figure 5.2* Shakespeare and Twain dictionaries:
c) Useful variables (continued)

```
(defvar proper-noun '(i we-ll))
(defvar pronoun ())
(defvar determinator ())
(defvar noun-subject ())
(defvar noun-object ())
(defvar modifier ())
(defvar conjunction ())

(defvar the-chosen-subject 'proper-noun)
(defvar the-actual-subject ())
(defvar question-or-not ())
(defvar choice ())
```

associates proper nouns and questions with certain verb phrases and from certain choices on the basis of whether the sentence is a question (lines 19–30). These latter choices include a further test (lines 20–24) which provides another proper noun than the one already chosen for the subject and branches depending on whether the previously chosen word type creates a question. This combination of decisions based on question/statements and tests acts like registers to delimit output to a particular word type. They could just as easily be set to choose between genders, tenses of verbs, passivity of transformational sentences, and so on if the texts chosen for regeneration had required such consideration.

The function `noun-phrase-subject`, shown in figure 5.4a and called in line 5 of figure 5.3, begins (lines 2 and 3) by choosing from proper nouns, pronouns and questions (who, what, when, and where). Each of the three conditional questions (lines 5–9, 10–13, and 14–25) sets various program variables and the chosen subject to the actual choice of subject. Each of these is a fleshing out of the nps shown originally in figure 5.1b. Figure 5.4b shows the function `noun-phrase-object`, one of the functions called in lines 26–30 of figure 5.3. Lines 5 through 7 of `noun-phrase-object` randomly produce either an object with a modifier phrase (line 5) or simply an object (lines 6–7). In either case, `noun-phrase-object` avoids choosing the subject chosen already through the use of the LISP primitive `remove` (lines 4 and 7).

The function `prepositional-phrase`, shown in figure 5.5a and called in lines 26–30 of figure 5.3, returns a brief prepositional phrase. As in figure 5.4b, the actual subject is removed from the list

**Figure 5.3** The function `create-phrase`.

```
1. (defun create-phrase (lexicon &optional (output nil))
2.    (reset lexicon)
3.    (setq question-or-not (choice))
4.    (let ((phrase
5.           (nconc (noun-phrase-subject)
6.                  (let ((test
7.                         (list
8.                           (choose
9.                            (eval
10.                            (choose
11.                              (if (equal the-chosen-subject
12.                                         'proper-noun)
13.                                  '(verb verb-phrase-1)
14.                                  (if question-or-not
15.                                      '(verb-phrase-2)
16.                                      '(verb-phrase-1
17.                                        verb-phrase-2))))))))))
18.                    (if (first test) test))
19.                  (if question-or-not
20.                      (let ((test
21.                             (list
22.                               (choose
23.                                (remove the-actual-subject
24.                                        proper-noun)))))
25.                        (if (first test) test))
26.                      (funcall
27.                       (choose
28.                        '(prepositional-phrase
29.                          noun-phrase-object
30.                          jump))))))
31.      (if output (apply 'append phrase) phrase)))
```

of possible `noun-objects` so that duplication will not occur (lines 4–5). The function `modifier-phrase`, shown in figure 5.5b and called in line 5 of figure 5.4b, returns either a modifier or a modifier followed by a conjunction and another modifier. Because `modifier-phrase` is called only once, only one conjunction will result (use of `choice` in line 3). The function `jump` in figure 5.5c and called in lines 26 to 30 of figure 5.3 is an abstraction for `nil`. The function `reset` in figure 5.5d, found in figure 5.3, line 2, evaluates the grammar of its

*Figure 5.4* The functions `noun-phrase-subject` and `noun-phrase-object`.

**a.**
```
1. (defun noun-phrase-subject nil
2.   (setq choice
3.         (choose '(proper-noun pronoun who-what-where)))
4.   (cond
5.     ((equal choice 'proper-noun)
6.      (progn
7.        (setq the-chosen-subject 'proper-noun)
8.        (list
9.          (setq the-actual-subject (choose proper-noun)))))
10.    ((equal choice 'pronoun)
11.     (progn
12.       (setq the-chosen-subject 'pronoun)
13.       (list (setq the-actual-subject (choose pronoun)))))
14.    ((equal choice 'who-what-where)
15.     (progn
16.       (setq question-or-not t)
17.       (setq the-chosen-subject 'who-what-where)
18.       (if (choice)
19.           (list (choose who-what-where)
20.                 (choose determinator)
21.                 (setq the-actual-subject
22.                       (choose noun-subject)))
23.           (list (choose who-what-where)
24.                 (setq the-actual-subject
25.                       (choose proper-noun))))))
26.    (t
27.     (list (choose determinator) (choose noun-object)))))
```

**b.**
```
1. (defun noun-phrase-object nil
2.   (if (choice)
3.       (cons
4.         (choose (remove the-actual-subject noun-object))
5.         (modifier-phrase))
6.       (list
7.         (choose (remove the-actual-subject noun-object)))))
```

**Figure 5.5** The functions a) `prepositional-phrase`; b) `modifier-phrase`; c) `jump`; d) `reset`; and e) various utilities.

```
a.
1.(defun prepositional-phrase nil
2.  (append
3.   (list (choose preposition)
4.         (choose (remove the-actual-subject
5.                         noun-object)))
6.   (funcall (choose '(modifier-phrase jump)))))

b.
1.(defun modifier-phrase nil
2.  (append (list (choose modifier))
3.          (if (choice)
4.              (list (choose conjunction)
5.                    (choose modifier)))))

c.
1.(defun jump nil nil)

d.
1.(defun reset (lexicon)
2.  (eval (get lexicon 'grammar))
3.  (setq the-chosen-subject
4.        'proper-noun
5.        question-or-not
6.        nil
7.        the-actual-subject
8.        nil))

e.
1.(defun choice nil
2.  (nth (random 2 (make-random-state t)) '(t nil)))

1.(defun choose (list)
2.  (nth (random (length list) (make-random-state t)) list))
```

argument and sets the appropriate global variables to `nil`. The functions `choice` and `choose` in figure 5.5e are utility functions that provide random selection of `true` or `nil` (in the case of `choice`) and a random choice from a list (in the case of `choose`).

Figure 5.6 shows some sample output of this ATN program. Note that this generator often creates awkward results. Many more tests and conditions (which space limitations prohibit including here) must be coded to refine sentence production. However, and this is very important, music does not require as many ATN refinements as does language. As mentioned earlier, tense, singular/plural agreements, and so on are not essential to musical examples. Therefore, even a simple and rather crude generator such as this can be quite useful in creating logical examples of music. Note that the ATN code presented here can and has (see Cope 1992) created musical as well as language examples. However, such musical generation is understandably limited in scope (e.g., melody only); thus, because I wish to move on to more sophisticated composition, the examples and code that follow will not be directly built on the examples of this section.

*Figure 5.6* Output of the language program.

```
wilt my hope re-tell rodrigo
i canst-cuckhold him again and again
canst iago have-told rodrigo
rodrigo told to thee again and again
i have-told him
iago art-sure of thee
iago has-told of thee

huck climb-down the-place over-yonder and over-yonder
huck climb-down there
it climbed there
i hunt for the-place over-yonder and over-yonder
i ain-t for the-place over-yonder and over-yonder
we-ll climb-down for there
lookyhere we-ll has i
```

## ■ ATN BASICS IN MUSIC

To understand why ATNs are important for recombinant composing programs like EMI and SARA, it is useful to show how FSTNs and RTNs (see chapter 1 for definitions) can be used to generate music. Both FSTNs and RTNs provide some but not all of the requirements for effective recombinancy.

A *Musikalisches Würfelspiel* (see chapter 1) is a good example of an FSTN in that it is fixed in regard to a network of functions established by the composer but free in regard to which of an assigned group of measures such functions represent. Algorithmic programs that follow the *Musikalisches Würfelspiel* concept also follow FSTN principles. For example, analysis of a phrase of music according to the musical function equivalents of noun and verbs (e.g., tonics and dominants or SPEAC) can lead to the generation of new examples of music based on these progressions (nets). Thus, an analyzed I–IV–V–I (C1–P1–A1–C1) progression as a musical FSTN can provide a basis for musical exchanges producing equivalent progressions with different music for each function.

There are obviously severe limitations to the number and kind of choices FSTNs provide for both language and music. For example, a language FSTN has an established plan of word choices that cannot be varied without jeopardizing the correctness of output. The same is true of a *Musikalisches Würfelspiel* or musical FSTN. There are precisely n (usually 11, the possible outcome of the toss of two dice) ways to begin a *Musikalisches Würfelspiel*. A musical FSTN will be similarly limited by the number of analyzed phrases it uses as a net. Thus, one can tire of both a *Musikalisches Würfelspiel* and a musical FSTN quickly because what initially seems inventive soon becomes recognizable if not predictable.

There are many ways for music to be recombined using FSTN techniques. Of these, *linear* and *nonlinear* processes offer challenging potentials and another view of linguistic parallels in the creation of recombinant music. Figures 5.7 to 5.9 present the primary essentials of these combinatorial concepts. Figure 5.7 presents three Mozart phrases to be used as examples of these recombinant processes. These phrases are shown in their clarified form (see

*Figure 5.7* Mozart sonatas clarified: a) K. 279, first movement, mm. 1–4. b) K. 309, third movement, mm. 1–8. c) K. 284, third movement, mm. 1–4.

# THE ATN COMPONENT 163

chapter 2). References to these sources will take the form of example subletter, measure number, and beat number. Thus, *a.1.1* refers to figure 5.7a, first measure, first beat, and so on.

In *linear* processes, functions may exchange only with similar functions in the same phrase. Such linear processes assume that music in a single phrase is more likely to work with other music in that same phrase. This in-line exchanging requires that a phrase have a large number of the same types of functions present, or the results will sound very much like the phrase being used. This is due to the possibility that a given function will not appear elsewhere in the phrase and thus no function exchanges can take place. Figure 5.8 shows an example of linear recombinant music. Here, beat 1 is *a.2.3*, beat 2 is *a.1.2*, and so on. All the exchanges are the result of functional replacement in figure 5.7a only. Note that the program does not cancel a beat once a switch takes place. Thus, *a.2.3* occurs twice in the second half of measure 1.

In *nonlinear* processes, functions may exchange with any other similar function in any phrase in a complete database. In its simplest form, this process exchanges equivalent functions without regard for their similarities. The process here is thus more volatile than in linear exchanges, as the music exchanged can be of very different character. This nonlinear volatility may be controlled by choosing similarly styled music for databases. Figure 5.9 shows an example of nonlinear recombinant music. Note that there is no reason to exclude the originating phrase from the exchange process. Thus, nonlinear exchanges include linear exchanges. The template used for this example is that of figure 5.7b. Beat 1 is *a.1.1*, beat 2 is *b.1.2*, and so on.

However, both linear and nonlinear FSTNs still rely exclusively on a given set progression (net) as their harmonic cantus firmus. Thus, although providing interesting musical variations on these given progressions, musical FSTNs are quite limited in their ability to produce inventive new examples of music in a given style. Creativity with nonlinear FSTNs can be further curtailed as the music in a database must conform to fairly rigorous similarity constraints for the resultant recombinant music not to sound arbitrary.

Recursive transition network progressions elaborate FSTN networks of functions and can generate much more interesting musical output. For example, the progression I–vi–IV–V–I (C1–C2–P1–A1–C1) could be created by the logical assimilation of the I–vi–IV–I (C1–C2–P1–C1) and I–IV–V–I (C1–P1–A1–C1) progressions as I–vi–IV (C1–C2–P1) and IV–V–I (P1–A1–C1) can intersect through the IV (P1) chord and are permitted elaborations of these two progressions, respectively. Thus, completely novel chord progressions can be cre-

***Figure 5.8*** An example of "linear" recombinant music.

***Figure 5.9*** An example of "nonlinear" recombinant music.

ated by using common chords and otherwise following the succession rules of given phrases.

Unfortunately, the creativity allowed by RTNs exacerbates volatility as music of significantly varying ranges, types, and so on is forced together. One good method of solving this problem involves "rule inheritance," which incorporates connectivity between musical segments as well as their function choice. Rule inheritance requires the notion of "seeking," which means that the termination point of a given segment of music "seeks" certain destination points in the segment that immediately follows it. If another segment of music can be found that contains those same destination points but subsequently moves in different directions, a new coupling of segments can be created that follows all local rules of connectivity but that creates new music without the limitations of fixed FSTN networks. Programs that generate such combinations may know nothing about the local (beat-to-beat) rules of the music from which they compose but ultimately follow those rules precisely.

To understand how valuable the notion of seeking can be, let us examine the nature of one standard type of local rules. Bach's rules of part writing are similar to those of most composers of the Baroque era and, to some extent, to many of the composers who followed, especially those composing choral music. Thus, these rules provide an excellent example for demonstrating seek principles. Typically, Bach's voice-leading rules include the avoidance of (1) parallel fifths and octaves and (2) hidden fifths and octaves in outer sets of voices. Pitches that occur in successive chords (common tones) are generally maintained whenever possible. At least one voice moves in contrary or oblique motion. Spacing is kept to a maximum of an octave or less between each contiguous set of upper three voices, whereas the bass is allowed to move freely. Doubling rules follow these general dictums: (1) double the root if possible, except in diminished chords, where doubling the third is preferable; (2) double one of the primary notes of the key (tonic, subdominant, or dominant) if not the root; or (3) double the fifth of the chord if no other appropriate solution presents itself. Nonharmonic tones (passing tones, neighboring tones, suspensions, appogiaturas, cambiatas, echappées, etc.) each have particular contextual constraints. Suffice it to say, the practice of writing such chorales (a standard for music theory courses at the college level) is complicated and often requires years of study to achieve proficiency.

Coding these rules can be an extremely involved task. Programs producing only adequate output can run thousands of lines in length. Also, many of the rules compete with one another, significantly increasing the amount of required code. However, the previously mentioned notion of RTN seeking can produce quite striking and rule-correct results, with program length being similar to that shown in the simple language program of figures 5.2 through 5.5.

Figure 5.10 gives the first two measures of Bach *Chorale 40*. Because this music is entirely of Bach's origin, it naturally follows Bach's rules. Although this statement is rhetorical, it provides a useful reminder of where the rules actually reside (i.e., not in textbooks). Figure 5.11 begins with the first beat of Bach's *Chorale 40*. To focus on rule inheritance and seeking, let us assume that this first beat has been stored as an object in a database. Let us also assume that the destinations that this beat's voices seek are similarly stored. For example, the soprano has a stored (in the object's destination slot) C with a seek destination of B, the alto has a stored G with a seek destination of G, and so on, with the full set of destinations being G–D–G–B from the bass upward.

Now let us assume that a large database exists in which many Bach chorales are stored as beats or groups of beats in objects with their respective RTN seek destinations and that all these chorales have

***Figure 5.10***   J. S. Bach, Chorale no. 40, mm. 1–2.

***Figure 5.11***   An example of rules inheritance in the creation of a new Bach chorale. Beat 1 is from Bach Chorale no. 40, beats 2–4 from Chorale no. 187, beat 5 from Chorale no. 239, and beats 6–7 from Chorale no. 298.

been transposed to C major so that the numbers of similarly voiced chords have multiplied significantly (i.e., G–B–D in G major would transpose to C–E–G in C major, adding one more chord of that type for composition). With such a database of musical objects, it is not hard to imagine that there could be another chord in the database that begins with the notes G–D–G–B in the same octaves as the second chord of figure 5.10. This new chord could then replace the actual second chord of figure 5.10. It might then move to a different subsequent chord or at least offer different off-the-beat motions and different RTN seek notes than those of the current second beat of figure 5.10. This new combination would thus inherit all of Bach's local part-writing rules.

Figure 5.11 shows just such a case. The initial notes of the second chord of this example are the same as in the original music (see figure 5.10). However, the bass moves by eighth notes downward, and the following chord is then quite different from the original (again see figure 5.10). The ensuing beats vary significantly from the initiating chord's original following chords. Again, however, this new music follows all of Bach's local voice-leading rules.

Figure 5.11 extends this new composition by continuing the same process. The last beat of measure 1 in figure 5.11, now from a different chorale than that shown in figure 5.10, seeks E–B–E–G (from the bass upward) in their appropriate octaves. Such a chord was found by the program in another of Bach's chorales in the database, and the program replaced the original with the newly found music and its succeeding chord. Figure 5.11 shows how the process plays out into a full new phrase of music replete with all the rules of counterpoint inherent in Bach's extensive collection of four-part chorales. Thus, object orientation and RTN processing can play an important role in rule inheritance by keeping the amount of code required to produce new compositions to a minimum.

Figure 5.12 presents another example of rules inheritance to demonstrate the variety of functions, rhythms, and dissonances possible. Checking the appropriate chorales given in the figure legend will show how the various RTN seek destinations have remained absolutely faithful to the original music in terms of voice leading, doubling, and other inherited rules. The variations in the lengths of extracted music are somewhat arbitrary here, and longer segments are used so that the demonstration of the process can be made clearer. In more elaborate examples, signatures—discovered by pattern matching according to the principles found in chapter 3—could also be included in this process.

One might argue that the overall succession of chords in such music is not Bach's and that he may never have used either of the new progressions created in these examples. In fact, the new com-

**Figure 5.12**  Another example of rules inheritance in the creation of a new Bach chorale. Beat 1 is from Bach Chorale no. 127, beats 2–4 from Chorale no. 223, beat 5 from Chorale no. 187, beat 6 from Chorale no. 211, beat 7 from Chorale no. 223, and beats 8–12 from Chorale no. 239.

positions, although following the voice-leading requirements of note-to-note motion, ignore the overall semblance of progression unity. For example, it is quite possible that these quasi-Markov RTNs would scatter cadences randomly through the music such that phrases would be quite unbalanced in length and thus illogical. In other words, although the local note-to-note rules might be recognized, the higher level logic is not. Thus, this process, although excellent for rule inheritance, is poor at creating logical musical structures on larger scales.

One way to avoid this shortcoming is to combine the RTN seek process with an FSTN transition net. Such a net could follow, for example, given Bach progressions for phrases, ensuring cadences in appropriate locations, and Bach's own large-scale logic. This would require, at least, a separate component to store the functions and start notes of all the beats of one phrase of a chorale to use as a model. However, finding chords with the same function, start notes, and RTN seek destination notes would require incredibly large databases, as many of the chords substituted for the originals will otherwise (because of the restraints caused by the progression model) be near or often identical to the original music and include occasional passing tones or other off-the-beat differences.

There is a more useful way for RTNs to approach the problem of larger scale composition. Figure 5.13 presents a simple diagram of two-voice music demonstrating how rule inheritance can be used freely from an initial chord with the proviso that each successive choice of new chord be made from a list that includes, if possible, the next function of the original network in its most appropriate location. This means that if more than one iteration of the function occurs in a phrase, it will choose the most propitious one; otherwise, the net will be rejoined exactly where it first branched. The original net then creates a kind of background or superstructure for the explorations brought about as the result of rule inheritance. When the necessary vicissitudes of phrase length demand that a cadence occur, the RTN can be led back into the original network. This process imitates that of the language RTN, shown in figure 1.21, where subphrases expand on the initial net. The approach affords

*Figure 5.13* Using a TN during rule inheritance.

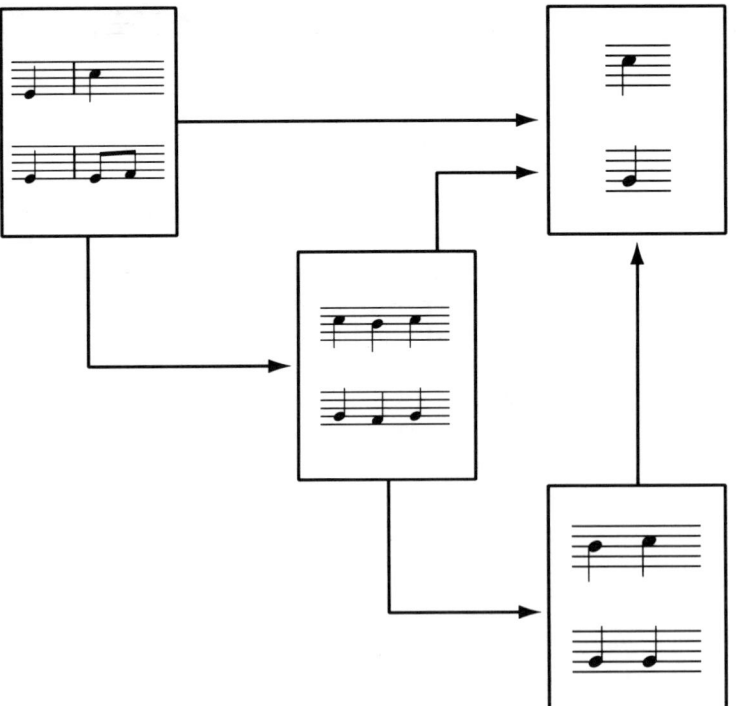

both a highly creative process and one that subscribes generally to the upper-level requirements of form. Unfortunately, the best that such RTNs can obtain from this "general subscribing" is rough approximations of phrase length and cadence location.

As we have seen, FSTNs in music produce predictable progressions of SPEAC functions on the basis of phrases in a database, and RTNs in music create more imaginative progressions but suffer from unpredictable phrase lengths. ATNs in music, however, just as their counterparts in language, produce creative composition with appropriately located cadences and proper phrase lengths. This transformational composition results from code that keeps track of previous choices while making new choices on the basis of the ability of those choices to properly fulfill larger structural requirements.

Figures 5.14a–e provide a simple musical example of how the ATN process can be useful in repositioning music instead of words when compared to FSTN and RTN processes. Figure 5.14a gives a short excerpt of music from Mozart. Figures 5.14b–d show repositionings of half-measure fragments of figure 5.14a. In the first random positioning of this example in figure 5.14b, the musical material seems forced together haphazardly, making little musical sense. The placement of the second half of bar 3 of figure 5.14a as the first half of the first bar of figure 5.14b alongside the first half of bar 1 of figure 5.14a produces awkward, stylistically uncharacteristic music. In the FSTN positioning of this example in figure 5.14c, the musical material seems somewhat more musical because the logic of the initial progression has been maintained. However, some connections (e.g., measure 3) seem stylistically uncharacteristic. In figure 5.14d the music is recombined following an RTN transition network. This example uses seek processes to enhance the musical logic that was lost somewhat in the FSTN recombination of figure 5.14c. However, the phrase length is uncharacteristic and the cadence seems forced. In figure 5.14e, however, the use of ATN creates a logical arrangement of segments such that the musical integrity of the original is maintained even though the selected parts of the music have changed places. Here, the nodes (half-measure points) remain informed of the potential short- and long-range consequences of the various choices; thus, phrase length, cadence, and other attributes fulfill both musical and structural needs.

Figures 5.15a and 5.15b give a more complex example of musical ATN. Figure 5.15a shows an eight-beat phrase of a Bach chorale with a traditional functional analysis and SPEAC symbols. Figure 5.15b links various chorale segments in a manner consistent with previous examples and provides both variety and rules inheritance while

**Figure 5.14**  a) Mozart, Piano Sonata (K. 545), mm. 1–4. b) A random recombination. c) A recombination using FSTN. d) A recombination using RTN. e) A recombination using ATN.

THE ATN COMPONENT 173

*Figure 5.15* A more complex example of musical ATN: a) First eight-beat phrase of Bach, Chorale no. 140. b) an ATN recombination.

adhering to the basic logic of phrase length and half-cadence function of the original music. Note that chords 4–5–6 of the original (figure 5.15a) are quite different from the new creation (figure 5.15b), although the cadential destination chord remains the same in voicing and function. The origin of each collection of beats is presented above the soprano voice of figure 5.15b as the number of the originating chorale and the measure numbers separated by a colon. Thus, one can imagine many strategies for creating new Bach-like chorales that follow both local and more global rules. Such combinations were used by EMI in the composition of the EMI-Bach chorale published in *Computers in Musical Style* (Cope 1991a, figure 5.40, pp. 194–96). However, unlike the rather simple examples presented here, the actual sources for the various beats of that chorale are difficult to trace, being based on over thirty similar works by Bach.

The difference between the progressions of figures 5.15a and 5.15b results from (1) allowable functional interchanges based on a combination of chord protocols inherent in rules-inheritance seek processes and (2) choices based on musical ATN register testing that has consequences beyond contiguous beats. This latter transformational concept is the same as that given with language shown in figure 5.1a. In figure 5.15b, the cadence represents node 3 in figure 5.1a, whereas the earlier chord choices in figure 5.15b represent the results of the "test" between nodes 3 and 1 in figure 5.1a. Interestingly, the last two beats of this music demonstrate an even more refined example of ATN. In figure 5.15b, the second chord of the second full measure (the last chord of measure 4 of the original Bach *Chorale 40*) connects with a noncontiguous but similarly functioning chord in the same chorale (measure 5, beat 3). This is made possible by the synonymous function and similar seek notes.

Augmented transition networks also allow for the generation of more convincing music in a style because position-sensitive signatures can be reconnected in ways that allow them to remain functionally (in musical terms) specific. Signatures, like cadences, require special alignment code to ensure that their connection to the destination phrase is logical, musical, and stylistically consistent. After all, if the initial and termination nodes of signatures are abrupt, their poor connection with surrounding music will nullify the very stylistic characteristics that their usage is designed to protect. Signature connections follow the same procedures necessary for potentially disruptive cadence connection: transformational arcs from the intersection nodes point back to the nodes of previous measures to guide them toward proper connectivity. Because the original order of the protocols is maintained, smooth connections for signatures help to create results that sound more like the music used for analysis while still being creative and unique. As mentioned previously, music (unlike language) need not have the tense, singular/plural, and other rules that make language ATNs so complex.

Micro-ATN (MATN) is to voices what ATN is to measures or submeasures. Whereas ATN selectively recombines music in a phrase, MATN selectively recombines voices within that music. As with ATN, EMI and SARA accomplish MATN through a complex process of lexicon matching, transposition, and register mapping. Whenever MATN recombines a measure, it first calls the SPEAC lexicon of the function of the chord. This ensures that the implied harmony of the original SPEAC lines will be maintained. To ensure the original connectivity of destination notes, only those voices (transposed or not) with similar initial and terminating pitches can be recombined. Thus, seek connectivity will be maintained with the new voice.

Figures 5.16a–c provide a simple demonstration of this process. The original music is shown in figure 5.16a. Note that the first notes of each beat are the seek destinations of the last notes of each preceding beat. Figure 5.16b shows another measure, found as a consultation with the S1 lexicon that both measures have in common. Figure 5.16c shows a newly constructed measure, a composite of figures 5.16a (top two voices) and 5.16b (bottom two voices). Note that the voices do not collide and that the material present in the new voices does not conflict with the remaining material of figure 5.16a. Also, the initial notes in the new measure still conform to those of the original measure of figure 5.16a (C–C–E–C from the bass upward).

Micro-ATN can produce slight variations of recombined music or entirely unique results not found in any of the databases in use. At its best, MATN invents exciting new combinations of voices that retain the stylistic traits of the original music. At its worst, MATN can produce problems that can destroy otherwise successful works. It is typically used with small databases that would otherwise create source-recognizable music and seems less necessary and interesting when applied to recombinant processes with large databases.

Observing ATN and MATN from the perspectives of large-scale composition can be useful. To this end, the beginning of an EMI-Mozart string quartet movement is shown in figure 5.17. Each measure of this work was drawn from Mozart's first (K. 80, 1770) and second (K. 155, 1772) string quartets, first and second movements. The first measure of the EMI-Mozart is a transposition (A major to G major) of the first measure of the second movement of K. 155, the first thirteen measures of which are shown in figure 5.18. The second measure of the EMI-Mozart is a slight variation (note the violin 2

**Figure 5.16**  a) Bach, Chorale no. 140 (beats 1–3, m. 1).
b) Chorale no. 241 (beats 2–4, m. 10).
c) Result of micro-ATN (MATN).

and cello parts) of the second measure of the first movement of K. 80, the first twenty measures of which are shown in figure 5.19. The variations are due to MATN, with each voice originating from some other location within the Mozart quartets in a similarly functioning measure. Note the ATN and seek connectivity in the upper voice in figure 5.17 with the first violin moving to a repeated G across the first barline. String quartets and instrumental music in general require less seek connectivity than do vocal works like Bach chorales. Thus, the other parts move more freely here.

The EMI-Mozart third measure is a transposed version from K. 155 (see figure 5.18, measure 3), whereas the fourth measure is the fourth measure of K. 80 (see figure 5.19) with a trill added via MATN. Such hocketing back and forth between sources is not unusual because, when transposed, such measures often connect logically between similarly metered movements.

Measures 5 and 6 of the EMI-Mozart continue the back-and-forth motion, returning to measure 5 of K. 155 (second movement) in transposition and measure 6 of K. 80 (first movement), respectively. Again, slight variations—here in the second violin part in the EMI-Mozart in measure 5 and the first and second violin parts in the EMI-Mozart in measure 6—result from octave displacements (see "Variations" in chapter 6) or possibly MATN. However, measure 7 of the EMI-Mozart breaks the exchanges by continuing K. 80, measure 7. Measure 8 of the EMI-Mozart then reverts back to a transposition of K. 155, measure 6, second movement.

This work uses a network chosen by the program from K. 80, measures 1 to 8. In traditional harmonic and functional terms, the progression is I–V–V–I–IV–I–IV–vii7/V–V). In SPEAC terms, this translates to C1–A1–A1–C1–P1–C1–P1–S1–A1. Although in some ways resembling each of the source works, the new theme has its own life and character because it follows strictly the basic mold of the Mozart model and adheres to the stepwise character of the lines of the original. In addition, little if any of the original style is lost in the reconstruction.

The next few measures of the EMI-Mozart are more creative and possibly interesting in their probable evolution. Measure 9 of the EMI-Mozart is a slight variation of measure 9 of K. 80. However, measure 10 of the EMI-Mozart is a radical variation (and transposition) of measures 45 (beginning on beat 3) and 46 (continuing to beat 3) of K. 155, shown in figure 5.20. The harmony of these two segments is alike even though the voicing between the violins differs significantly. Although the viola lines begin in a similar manner, the new work deviates (in measure 10 of figure 5.17) in apparent imitation of the previous measure's first violin part. Because no code was used

**Figure 5.17** The beginning of an EMI-Mozart string quartet.

**Figure 5.17** continued.

**Figure 5.18** The beginning of Mozart's String Quartet (K. 155).

**Figure 5.18** continued.

for such imitation, this seems to be the result of MATN. In other words, it was good fortune that some line of similar function and length from another part of one of these two quartets possessed the same melodic characteristics as the material in the previous measure in the first violin part. Note that throughout this passage the connectivity of the first violin and cello parts (particularly) exemplify stylistic stepwise motions due to extensive ATN activity.

However, measures 11 and 12 of the EMI-Mozart do represent program variations and are not of Mozartean origins. These two measures are a sequence at the interval of a perfect fourth from the previous two measures. Such sequencing is considered normal for tonal music but would be lost in all but vague terms from the original because of the deconstruction process. Therefore, they result here from specific sequencing code in the EMI program. However, the variation in the third beat of the viola part of measure 12 of the EMI-Mozart is the result of MATN, the origins being otherwise unclear.

The remainder of the EMI-Mozart second phrase (measures 13–16) is from measures 13 and 16 of K. 80 (see figure 5.19) and transpositions of measures 26 and 27 from K. 155 (not shown). The remainder of the EMI work is a similar compilation of materials, having interspersed techniques derived from code. What is not shown here, because of space limitations, is how the cadences and other key points are adjusted according to formal considerations so that, for example, the principal cadence points are each more final than internal cadence points and the various key centers, dictated to some degree by the borrowed Mozart network, conform to standard classical practices.

**Figure 5.19** The beginning of Mozart's String Quartet (K. 80).

***Figure 5.19*** continued.

# ■ ATN PROGRAM

Much of the ATN portion of the EMI and SARA programs resides in the analysis portion of the code. This is where SPEAC functions are analyzed and various destinations stored for the recombination process. Therefore, much of the measure-to-measure ATN code has been previously discussed (see chapter 4). There are, however, other levels of the ATN composition process that must be managed logically rather than by random selection.

**Figure 5.20** Mozart, String Quartet (K. 155), mm. 45–46.

The function make-best-choice, shown in figure 5.21, provides a simple but effective example of SARA connectivity necessary for proper ATN recombination. The first argument to this function, start-note-required, provides the seek-note destination of the previously selected measure. The measure-names argument is a list of appropriately functioned measure names from which to make a best choice. These are typically found in the lexicon of the appropriate SPEAC function. The final argument to make-best-choice, start-notes, is a list of beginning notes of the measures presented in the second argument. The function my-position in line 3 of figure 5.21 provides the position number of start-note-required in the start-notes of measure-names. This function will return a match if one exists but the use of find-closest in line 6 of figure 5.21 ensures that, if one does not exist, make-best-choice will still return a probable best match. In EMI, the equivalent function to make-best-choice tests all voices as well as texture, range, type of music, accompaniment, and even the relationship of the current choice to the impending cadence (see figure 4.5c and related text). In SARA, because of size and speed constraints, the function make-best-choice limits its parameters to one level: the destination of a channel 1 voice.

Managing higher level form functions for recombinant processes that do not otherwise account for such formal considerations falls

***Figure 5.21*** The function `make-best-choice`.

```
1. (defun make-best-choice
2.    (start-note-required measure-names start-notes)
3.     (let ((test (my-position start-note-required start-notes)))
4.       (if test (nth test measure-names)
5.           (nth (position
6.                   (find-closest start-note-required start-notes)
7.                   start-notes)
8.                measure-names)))))
```

under the umbrella of ATN. The function `schenker-plot` serves to create logical lists of SPEAC symbols that are ultimately translated into logical progressions for EMI and SARA. These SPEAC symbols serve as, for example, markers for cadential formation in large-scale forms. This ensures that final cadences of works have the tonic in, for example, the upper voice and that various internal cadences do not have tonic in their upper voice or otherwise lack completion. Figure 5.22 shows the function `schenker-plot`, which returns a list of melodic (*Urlinie*) notes for each phrase of a composition in the form of a list of descending numbers matching the number of phrases (sublists) in its argument. The function `layer-analysis`, called (in line 3) by `schenker-plot`, returns the actual list of *Urlinie* notes. Neither of these functions works with forms of less than six phrases, as such forms do not require this kind of care.

However, the function `schenker-plot` requires further translation into SPEAC symbols. This is accomplished by the function `translate-urlinie` (shown in figure 5.23a) used in the top level of the SARA program. This function takes the results of `schenker-plot` and returns a list of symbols indicating both SPEAC and level (f = foreground, m = middleground, or b = background) of the descending line numbers. These symbols are then translated into octave-independent scale degrees for the function `find-best-cadence`, which acts similarly to the previously discussed function `make-best-choice` but for cadences.

Figure 5.24 shows how the various layer analyses and projection functions coalesce into a unified whole to make the recombinant processes logical and coherent during composition. This layout can be seen as a representation of a Schenker framework and a transposed-to-C version of figure 5.17. The just-defined functions coordinate the upper voice (*Urlinie*) logic in a skeletal background,

***Figure 5.22*** The function `schenker-plot`.

```
1.(defun schenker-plot (form)
2.  (let ((number-of-phrases (length form)))
3.   (layer-analysis
4.    (create-raw-form (test-the-length number-of-phrases)
5.                     number-of-phrases)
6.    form)))
```

***Figure 5.23*** The functions a) `translate-urlinie` and
b) `translate-ur`.

**a.**
```
(defvar *plots* '(cb pb cm pm ab sb eb cf))

1.(defun translate-urlinie (plot)
2.  (if (null plot) nil
3.      (cons (translate-ur (first plot) *plots*)
4.            (translate-urlinie (rest plot)))))
```

**b.**
```
1.(defun translate-ur (plot-number plots &optional (test one))
2.  (if (equal plot-number test)(first plots)
3.      (translate-ur plot-number (rest plots) (add-one test))))
```

whereas the measure-to-measure SPEAC motions allow the harmonic direction to converge into logical cadences. The results help maintain coherence significantly beyond that of using prescribed forms. The subtleties of tonal (and to some degree non-tonal) music can be retained in music that otherwise succumbs to the exigencies of moment-to-moment composition. As a result, works really end and do not just stop, as so often is the case in computer composition not governed by some kind of background logic.

Modulation in EMI, and to some degree in SARA, results from a subtle combination of inheritance and manipulation. Momentary modulations (secondary functions of keys) can be captured in databases and reconstructed because both traditional functional analysis and SPEAC symbols allow for such nondiatonic representation. However, music that modulates for significant periods of time is transposed to C major, and modulating phrases are protected during

***Figure 5.24*** How *Urlinie* and SPEAC function together during composition (in this case for figure 5.17) in transposition.

database construction. The program then ensures their connectivity to appropriate new keys during recombinancy by not placing their cadences in lexicons. Such protected cadences are then treated like signatures during composition, and subsequent phrases are transposed to the appropriate new keys. Although low-level functions often require random procedures, it is imperative that high-level functions operate with this kind of musical integrity.

# SIX
# An Application-Level Program and Sample Output

The EMI and SARA application-level code coordinates the analysis system, the pattern-matching program, the object-oriented databases, and the musical ATN, creating a useful tool for composition. Although this combination may seem awkward, it turns out to be rather straightforward. Its success depends on connecting the various elements together in a logical order so that each can contribute its strengths without complicating the resultant mix of techniques.

## ■ PUTTING IT ALL TOGETHER

Each of the preceding chapters focuses on an important aspect of EMI and SARA and gives various examples of code regarding the concepts each chapter presents. The following discussion paraphrases each of these programs so that they can be seen at work in tandem and presents application-level code that calls the code previously described. This discussion then examines works created by SARA, the software that accompanies this book on CD-ROM.

Figure 6.1 shows a portion of the function `insert-music`, the primary code responsible for creating databases in SARA. Although the process of creating databases is not used directly by the composing program, it represents the principal analytical process of both EMI and SARA. The function `insert-music` takes numerous arguments, the first of which relates the name of the proposed database. The argument `pulse` represents the meter of the work being

**Figure 6.1** The function `insert-music`.

```
1. (defun insert-music
2.    (database pulse incipience matching-line-number mode tempo)
3.       . . . . .
4.    (set (concat database '-network)
5.         (nthcdr (if incipience pulse 0)
6.                 (analyze *music-in-beats*))) . . . . .
7.    (buffer-insert *temporary-buffer*
8.                   (insert-music-into-database
9.                      (get-section database)
10.                     database
11.                     (concat database '-network)
12.                     pulse
13.                     incipience
14.                     matching-line-number
15.                     mode
16.                     tempo))
17.   (enter-database *temporary-buffer*
18.                   (insert-into-file
19.                      (if incipience
20.                          (rest (eval database))
21.                          (eval database))
22.                     database
23.                     (eval (concat database '-network))
24.                     pulse
25.                     (get-section database)))
26.   (compile-file *path* :output-file . . . . .)
```

stored in a database, and `incipience` indicates the presence of a pickup measure (treated as a special case in SARA). The remaining arguments should be self-explanatory. The full code of `insert-music` (too large to reproduce here, hence the ". . . . ." indicating missing code) creates databases as shown in figure 4.11, the database for a Chopin mazurka phrase. Lines 4 to 6 of `insert-music` set the basic network to the analyzed music for transition network recombinancy. Lines 7 to 25 effectively print the class and instance–creating code (i.e., make-instance, etc., for objects) and data (i.e., lists of events) for each database. Line 26 compiles files for fast loading.

***Figure 6.2*** The pattern matcher interface code.

```
1.((and (match? (eval measure-name))
2.      (if (next-measure measure-name)
3.          (match? (eval (next-measure measure-name)))))
4. (next-measure measure-name))
```

***Figure 6.3*** The ATN interface code.

```
1.(let ((pre-dominant-list (get-predominant destinations)))
2.   (make-best-choice
3.       (get-destination-note measure-name)
4.       pre-dominant-list
5.       (get-new-first-notes-list last-chord pre-dominant-list)))
6.   (t (make-best-choice
7.       (get-destination-note measure-name)
8.       (remove-matched-objects
9.           (remove-last-chord last-chord destinations))
10.      (get-new-first-notes-list
11.          last-chord
12.          (remove-matched-objects
13.              (remove-last-chord last-chord destinations))))))
```

Figure 6.2 shows how the pattern matcher (discussed in chapter 3) interfaces with the EMI and SARA composing programs. Pattern matching occurs prior to actual composition and sets the match? variable of loaded objects to t when signatures are detected and appropriately set in place. Such signature protection ensures that these objects will not be separated from their original succeeding objects during recombination. In figure 6.2, if match? is t and the following measure, if one exists, also has its match? slot set to t (see lines 2–3), the measure is returned rather than seeking a logical replacement.

Figure 6.3 shows a small example of how the composing program handles ATN (discussed in chapter 5) during the recombination process. The function make-best-choice provides the interconnections necessary during the various measure choices from inception to cadence during the creation of a new phrase of music. The newly chosen function then provides destination functions and notes for continued composition. This code also shows (in line 1)

***Figure 6.4*** The top-level functions `create-work` and `create`.

**a.**
```
1. (defun create-work nil
2.    . . . .
3.    (setq *meter*
4.          (meter (eval (concat (setq *phase-name*
5.                                      (first *selected-databases*))
6.                               '-cadence))))
7.    (setq *layer-tuner* (if (> (length *structure*) *limit*)
8.                            (translate-urlinie
9.                             (schenker-plot *structure*))))
10.   (setq *initial-composition*
11.         (transpose-b-section *structure* (create *structure*)))
12.   (if (null *initial-composition*)
13.       (message-dialog "Failed!")
14.       (progn (setq *history* (reverse *history*))
15.              (setq *new-work*
16.                    (make-instance 'new-work
17.                           :mode (read-from-string *mode*)
18.                           :tempo *tempo*
19.                           :meter *meter*
20.                           :music
21.                            (embellish
22.                              (make-playable
23.                                *initial-composition*
24.                                *meter*)))))))))
```

**b.**
```
1. (defun create (form)
2.   (let ((creator (concat *creator* '-(very-first form))))
3.     (if (null form) nil
4.         (cond
5.           ((and (member (very-first form) *save-form*)
6.                 (< *recombinance* 10))
7.            (cons (eval (very-first form))
8.                  (create (rest form))))
9.            . . . .
10.          ((get-form-from-dbs (very-first form)
11.                              *selected-databases*)
12.           (progn (push (very-first form) *save-form*)
13.                  (cons (set (very-first form)
```

**Figure 6.4**  continued.

```
14.                       (compose creator
15.                             *phrase-length*
16.                             (get-meter-from-dbs
17.                               *phase-name*)
18.                             (first form)))
19.                   (create (rest form)))))
20.            (t (create (rest form))))))))
```

the formation of the `pre-dominant-list`, which is part of the ATN necessary for ensuring that cadences have proper logic and connectivity.

## ■ APPLICATION-LEVEL PROGRAM

The application-level function of the SARA composition program is `create-work`, part of which is shown in figure 6.4a. This function contains many of the various user warnings and sets a number of variables that require resetting, including `*meter*` (lines 3–6) and `*layer-tuner*` (lines 7–9), the latter of which is responsible, in larger compositions, for controlling formal constraints. Because much of the application level is devoted to matters of "shopkeeping" rather than fundamental issues of composition, `create-work` is hardly a revealing or an informative function. However, in line 11 it does run the function `create` (part of which is shown in figure 6.4b), which offers a far better vehicle for describing SARA composition processes. The function `create` takes a list of form representations as argument and returns a new composition as a list of measures identified by function. Three collections of code follow the conditional `if` in `create` (line 3). These collections (1) terminate the function if its form is complete (line 3), (2) resurrect a previously composed phrase if in fact the current form letter representation is a repetition (lines 5–8), or (3) compose an appropriate new phrase (lines 10–19).

The function `compose` (called in line 14 of figure 6.4b) initiates the primary composing functions of the SARA program. Shown in part in figure 6.5, `compose`, depending on the level of the user-controlled variable `*recombinance*`, employs an FSTN (in lines 3–4) or an RTN

**Figure 6.5** The function `compose`.

```
1.(defun compose (creator number-of-measures meter form)
2.   (if (< *recombinance* *fstn-limit*)
3.       (finite-state-transition (first *selected-databases*)
4.                                meter)
5.       (append (choose-incipient-gesture creator)
6.               (let ((test
7.                      (simple-compose
8.                       creator
9.                       (choose-initial-chord creator meter)
10.                      number-of-measures meter)))
11.                 (if *repeat* (make-repeat test) test))
12.     . . . . .
13.               (list (splice-cadence-channels
14.                      (choose-a-cadence creator form)
15.                      (list-appropriate-cadences
16.                       (second form)))))
17.     . . . . .
```

(in lines 5–16). In line 5, `compose` chooses an incipient gesture and then, using the function `simple-compose`, progresses to the recombinatorial process. The function `splice-cadence-channels` (line 13) controls the MATN of the appropriately chosen cadence.

The function `simple-compose` (shown in figure 6.6) is perhaps the most revealing function in the composition code. The variable `*history*` (in line 3) stores the measure names chosen by this function. This variable is useful for examining compositions at a measure-by-measure level. Lines 4 to 11 ensure that cadences that are part of signatures remain intact with those signatures through the variable `*cadence-match*` (in lines 10–11). The function `interchange-channels` (line 12) regulates the MATN of the currently chosen measure. Note that `simple-compose` calls itself with the current results of its composition choice (lines 13–46 are a recursive call to `simple-compose`). The variable `pre-dominant-list` (lines 28–29) controls `simple-compose` as it approaches a cadence (two chords from the end as shown in line 27). This process helps to ensure that cadential choices will not be grafted into place. Otherwise, resulting progressions will sound odd at best or mismatched and without resolution at worst. In line 38, `remove-last-chord`

**Figure 6.6** The function `simple-compose`.

# AN APPLICATION-LEVEL PROGRAM AND SAMPLE OUTPUT

```
1. (defun simple-compose (name measure-name number meter)
2.    (if (zerop number) nil
3.        (progn (push measure-name *history*)
4.          (if (and (match? (eval measure-name))
5.                   (= number 1)
6.                   (null (next-measure measure-name))
7.                   (match?
8.                     (eval (concat
9.                             (get-phrase measure-name '-cadence))))
10.               (setq *cadence-match*
11.                 (concat (get-phrase measure-name) '-cadence)))
12.        (cons (interchange-channels measure-name meter)
13.              (let ((destinations
14.                      (get-destinations
15.                        name
16.                        measure-name meter))
17.                    (last-chord
18.                      (get-last-chord name measure-name)))
19.                (simple-compose
20.                  name
21.                  (cond
22.                    ((and
23.                       (match? (eval measure-name))
24.                       (if (next-measure measure-name)
25.                         (match? (eval (next-measure measure-name)))))
26.                     (next-measure measure name))
27.                    ((twop number)
28.                     (let ((pre-dominant-list
29.                             (get-predominant destinations)))
30.                       (make-best-choice
31.                         (get-destination-note measure-name)
32.                         pre-dominant-list
33.                         (get-new-first-notes-list
34.                           last-chord pre-dominant-list))))
35.                    (t (make-best-choice
36.                         (get-destination-note measure-name)
37.                         (remove-matched-objects
38.                       (remove-last-chord last-chord destinations))
39.                         (get-new-first-notes-list
40.                           last-chord
41.                           (remove-matched-objects
42.                             (remove-last-chord
43.                               last-chord
44.                               destinations))))))
45.                  (next number)
46.                  meter)))))))
```

guarantees that progressions of like functions will not suffer from excessive measure repetitions. The function `make-best-choice` (called in lines 30 and 35 and shown previously in figure 5.21), a primary ATN function in `simple-compose`, aligns destination notes and otherwise attempts to create the best progression and connectivity. It is important to remember that `make-best-choice`'s selection correlates directly to the quality, correctness, and size of the database being used. Large, well-honed databases allow `make-best-choice` to find multiple possibilities and thus excellent contiguous measures for composition. Small databases force `make-best-choice` into reconnecting previously connected measures or making poor choices.

# ■ INTERFACE

Designing and implementing application-level interfaces for computer applications intended for more universal uses present enormously complicated problems. Aside from the purely practical difficulties of selecting and ordering items for menus, windows, buttons, and tables, one must tackle the requirements of interface simplicity and program access. Interfaces should be straightforward and provide uncomplicated protocols for operating and controlling the primary program commands. Interfaces should also provide access to the program variables, which allow users to achieve diverse goals and personalize their creativity. Unfortunately, the requirements of interface simplicity and program access often contradict each other. Simple interfaces often produce demonstration-level programs incapable of diverse or sophisticated output because of their lack of access to the program variables. However, interfaces with extensive access to program variables are often counterintuitive and can allow poor choices, leading to ineffective output.

To solve this difficult problem, the EMI interface follows the guiding principle that, whenever possible, the values of program variables should be inherited from the databases used for composition and not set by users. This inheritance ensures that as many stylistic links as possible will be made between the databases used for input and the resultant compositions. Determining output phrase lengths serves as a good example of this principle. Although allowing users control over the output phrase lengths could be considered a valuable tool for composition, EMI assumes that users are most interested in retaining the style of input works. Thus, EMI creates output with phrase lengths inherited from those of the databases used for composition. Such inheritance avoids the possibility that users could create phrases with stylistically atypical lengths. On the other hand, allowing users to select the level of recombinancy and, by inference, the type of compositional recombinancy (FSTN and RTN at low settings and ATN and MATN at high settings) is an appropriate user-controlled variable as this information cannot be inherited from the database and different approaches can produce unique and successful results.

Pattern matching provides another good example of an interface complication arising from the dichotomy between interface simplicity and program access. As chapter 3 points out, a good musical pattern matcher may have dozens of controllers for pattern matching with different musical styles. However, providing access to such numbers of controllers can produce confusing interfaces. In such circumstances, controllers can often compete with one another or have conflicting definitions. Interfaces with access to large numbers of controllers present an imposing complex of choices for even experienced users of the software. However, a simple four-controller pattern-matching interface, given that the controllers are well chosen, can provide user access to the basic principles of locating signatures while not unnecessarily complicating the interface.

Choosing appropriate musical forms represents an even more complicated interface problem. Inheriting form can be enormously difficult. In some incarnations of EMI, works are stored in very large single files and then analyzed for form before or during composition. However, such analysis is time consuming and often crude at best. Other EMI implementations allow users to select letters representing sections such as A and B for AB (biparte form) or ABA (triparte form) output. However, as with the previously mentioned control of phrase lengths, users can create stylistically uncharacteristic forms and create combinations of section designations for which there are no loaded databases. A third type of EMI interface employs user selection of databases with section suffixes. This approach has proven to be the most successful balance between interface simplicity and program access and is the one used in SARA. The program produces simple forms on the basis of user-chosen databases that are ordered according to the selection sequence. Thus, selecting "marshal-x-one-7/22/354" and "marshall-x-two-7/11/1," for example, automatically creates an AB, ABA, or similarly standard form. The "intro" (for "introduction") section name provides the single exception to this rule and always comes first to avoid stylistic clashes of introductory material falling in nonintroductory situations.

Program speed is another important consideration for interface design. Loading and composing often require significant amounts of processing time. To avoid such extensive computation periods, good interfaces often break up tasks into more manageable subtasks that allow users the opportunity to develop their own strategies for composing. Separating pattern matching from composition, for example, allows two very time intensive activities to be treated independently and permits faster composition. Also, such separation allows pattern matching for signatures without composing. Knowing about such time constraints while designing the interface level can also help determine choices of, for example, the types of pattern matchers (serial, parallel, etc.—see chapter 3) or types of storage (phrase database files instead of work database files, etc.), choices that can greatly affect computational time.

Obviously, software that composes fast but creates poor output is not better than software that composes slow but creates good output. However, weighing the need for reasonable composition time against the need for quality output often leads one to choose program procedures more logically. For example, storing the analysis of the various measure objects in databases rather than making such analysis a part of the compositional process was the result of attempts to reduce composition time. As an indirect benefit from this time-saving approach, redundant analyses of works were factored out of compositional runs.

Some interface component settings cannot be inherited. Most pronounced among these is the use of counterpoint in composition. For example, both fugue and invention forms require conscious choice by users and cannot usefully be inherited from databases. As pointed out in *Computers and Musical Style* (Cope 1991a, chapters 4 and 5), counterpoint generally requires special programs that require output to adhere to specific rules pertinent to the particular chosen form. All EMI and SARA interfaces have user access for the choice of contrapuntal forms.

Finally, some aspects of the EMI interface provide superficial yet interesting variations of output. Choice of mode (major or minor), key, dynamics, and so on, although fully inheritable from the events and objects in databases, remain controllable at the interface level. Having the option to perform works freely in any mode, key, or dynamic seems fundamental to the curiosity of users regardless of the effect on the resultant style of the output works. These superimpositions, as well as all the previously mentioned interface commands and variables, are amply documented in the SARA user's manual on the accompanying CD-ROM.

## ■ VARIATIONS

Johann Philipp Kirnberger's *Methode Sonaten aus'm Ermel zu schüddeln* (1783; see the discussion and figure 1.5 in chapter 1) demonstrates the effectiveness of rewriting and converting musical materials until the original is no longer recognizable. This involves a variety of standard compositional techniques, such as the scalar filling in of leaps, the addition of anticipatory notes, the arpeggiation of chords, and so on. EMI has an extended program for just such conversions. SARA has an abridged version of this program that principally concentrates on the addition of scales to otherwise skipping figures. In EMI, the use of such conversion techniques is based on an analysis of their presence in the original databases used for composition. However, because such additions are not easily inherited and because they are not acceptable in all styles of music, their incorporation in SARA is not a matter of inheritance but rather a matter of setting the `*recombinancy*` variable high (see the discussion of recombinancy level in the SARA user's manual on the accompanying CD-ROM).

Adding scales to melodic leaps is a factor of interval distance and the duration of the initial note. In the case of the leaps of thirds, intermediary notes are added when resultant durations exceed a sixteenth note (250 ticks) in length. Adding scales to larger leaps can occur only when producing even divisions of note values (i.e., duplets and quadruplets but not triplets, as they are not common to all styles) and when added durations exceed a sixteenth note in length. This latter condition makes larger leaps increasingly difficult to fill with scales. Neighboring tones may be interpolated between repeated notes as well. In EMI, such additions result from musical considerations. In SARA, such additions are random because musical logic requires extensive analysis, which increases composition time exponentially.

Form in SARA is generated automatically according to an algorithm that bases its decisions on two factors: the data loaded and then selected for composition and the concept of balanced phrases. The first factor generates form containing all the sections available for composition. Thus, if only a "two" section has been loaded or selected, only variants of this section will be generated. If sections "one" and "two" have been loaded or selected, then only variants of these will be generated (see the previous section for examples). With the exception of section "intro" (for "introduction"), the order of formal generation is user selected rather than predetermined. In the second factor above, the form algorithm attempts to create balanced phrase pairs to complete logical periods or sections. This follows standard classical traditions. EMI, in contrast to SARA, creates form templates on the basis of program interpretations of music in ordered phrases in the loaded databases.

Treating mode superficially reduces the overall effectiveness of the currently implemented SARA program (in EMI, mode is an integral part of composition). Clearly, the choice of mode (major or minor) is an important factor for composers, and compositional techniques vary depending on this choice. However, introducing mode into the composition process can complicate code immensely. This complexity begins with the definitions of chord function (see chapter 2), which need to include all chord variants in minor as well as major, and extends to all functions which depend on diatonic transposition (principally certain forms of tonal pattern matching) for their operation. However, the SARA object system does contain an attribute for mode and some may wish to add mode sophistication to this aspect of the program.

Tempo, on the other hand, is an attribute of phrase objects and storing music of similar tempi in a consistent database is advisable and possible. Therefore, tempo can currently be a significant factor in composition in both EMI and SARA, if so desired. Other parameters such as timbre, articulation, and so on remain outside most current implementations of, and programs modeled on, EMI.

Modulation requires elaborate recognition, analysis, and composition code. EMI contains functions that analyze the key of the termination of phrases and includes cadences in new keys on the basis of a combination of inner-phrase modulation and formal considerations. SARA (see discussion in chapter 5) has an embryonic subprogram where the use of new keys is relegated to the need for contrast in larger forms and, more subtly, on the basis of modulations suggested by phrases in loaded databases. At present, this rather trivial approach allows for faster composition with less effect on memory but creates fairly restricted modulation in output.

The superior quality of the output of EMI vis-à-vis SARA is the result of (1) the difference in the sophistication levels of the programs (e.g., SARA's need for a fast, simple interface), (2) the quality and size of the EMI databases (often encompassing entire *oeuvres* of some composers), and (3) my own aesthetic judgments with EMI in eliminating works that I perceive to fail while elevating those that I perceive to succeed to performances and ultimately to recording and publication. However, many of EMI's successes have required herculean amounts of hard-disk and RAM memory and equally herculean time periods for composition (often a week or more). I do not know how many good compositions failed to emerge because of power surges or outages. SARA creates music in a minuscule fraction of the time and memory required of these original EMI goliaths. SARA suffers, however, from many shortcuts that were deliberately taken to make the program more user-friendly and accessible. Such are the trade-offs when creating more portable software.

# ■ SAMPLE OUTPUT AND EXTENSIONS

Figure 6.7 shows, in both notation and partially in event form, a composition produced by the software on the CD-ROM accompanying this book. This SARA-Joplin rag shows many of the attributes of the Joplin rag of figure 5.25 in *Computers and Musical Style* (Cope 1991a, p. 175). The events (see figure 6.7b) are shown here to demonstrate the appearance of the output of the program. Although the musical output of this program (and, for that matter, EMI at times) is not consistently of the caliber presented in this and other examples, it is sufficiently interesting and musical in most cases to be of value.

Figure 6.8 gives a diagram of the basic sources of figure 6.7. Here the program has used measures from the "palm" and "syca" files of the "intro" (introduction) database. A quick survey of the readable versions of these files on the accompanying CD-ROM will affirm the logical use of the remaining measures in this recombinant music. This example provides a typical compositional situation in which measure fragments of various phrases have been chosen and combined into new, viable phrases. The use of MATN and other individual voice manipulation has been kept to a minimum here to show the derivations.

Figure 6.9 presents a more dramatic example of recombinancy created by a more advanced version of SARA: the opening measures of a sonata first movement in the style (arguably) of Beethoven. This music demonstrates the influence of Beethoven's *Pathétique* and *Appassionata* sonatas shown in figures 6.10a and b. The chordal structures at the beginning of the machine-composed Beethoven clearly resemble transposed versions of those in the *Pathétique*. Less obviously, the melodic octaves seem drawn from the opening triadic outlines of figure 6.10b; however, the double octaves are replaced by single octaves, so perhaps the music has been drawn from another sonata (parts of at least ten Beethoven sonatas were in the database

## 202 EXPERIMENTS IN MUSICAL INTELLIGENCE

**Figure 6.7** a) A SARA-Joplin rag. b) Beginning of the event code.

```
(setq joplin-save-work '((0  72 250 1 100)    (0    60 250 2 100)
                         (250  71 250 1 100)  (250  59 250 2 100)
                         (500  69 250 1 100)  (500  57 250 2 100)
                         (750  72 500 1 100)  (750  60 500 2 100)
                         (1250 71 250 1 100)  (1250 59 250 2 100)
                         (1500 69 500 1 100)  (1500 57 500 2 100)...
```

# AN APPLICATION-LEVEL PROGRAM AND SAMPLE OUTPUT 203

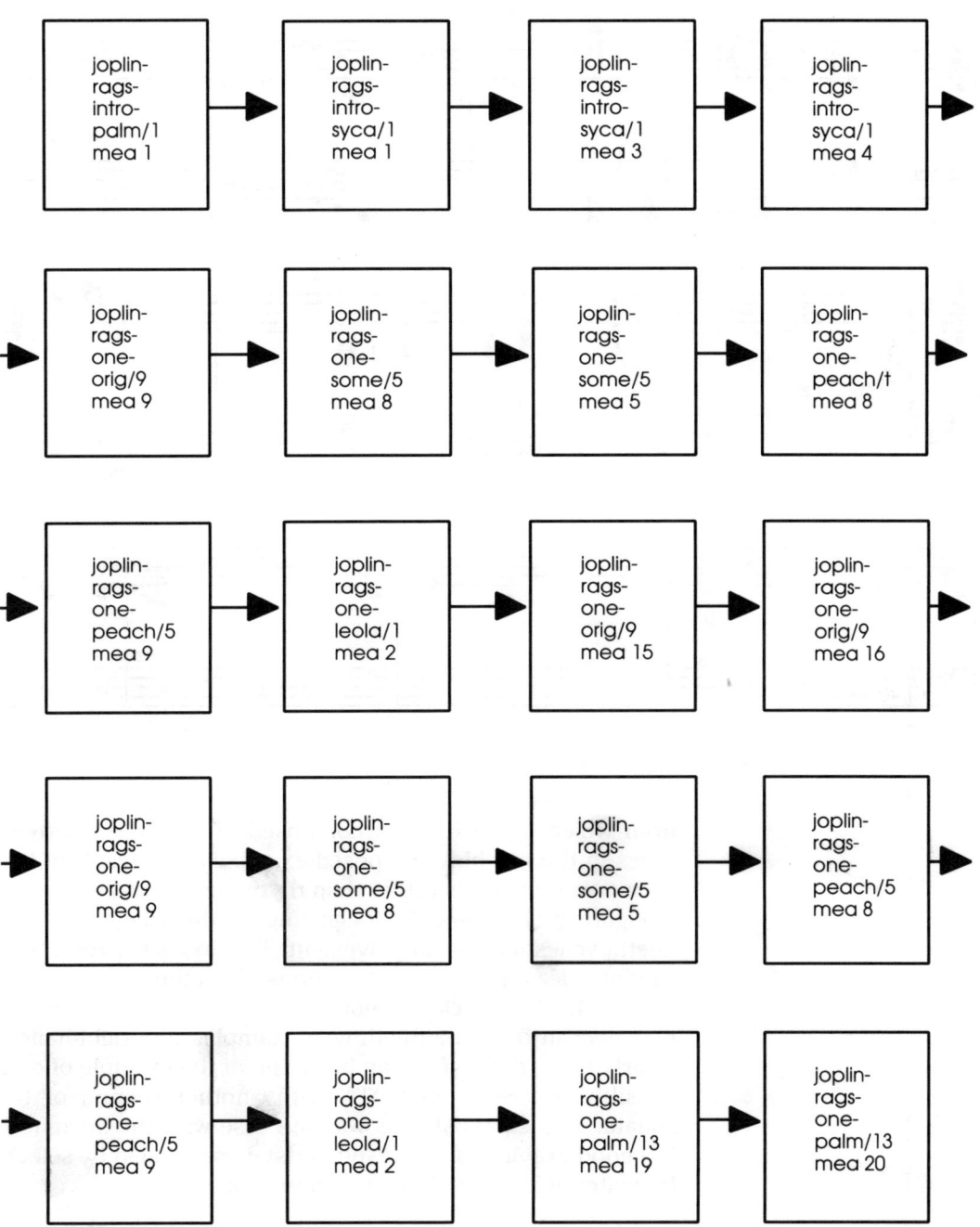

**Figure 6.8** Sources for beginning of the SARA-Joplin rag shown in figure 6.7

**Figure 6.9** An EMI-Beethoven piano sonata beginning.

from which figure 6.9 was composed). The double-dotted quarter notes in the machine-composed example are a result of ties across harmonic repetitions rather than rhythmic inheritance.

Figure 6.11 shows the beginning of the allegro section of the Beethovenesque sonata movement. This too is the result of an amalgam of at least two different sections of Beethoven sonatas shown in figure 6.12. The "rocking" motion of the left-hand accompaniment is prevalent in both the Beethoven examples, the right-hand material clearly being drawn from an inversion of the example of op. 2, no. 1, possibly the result of MATN with another section of that same sonata. This composite, as was the case with the opening material, is a good example of the result of databases honed by selecting similar material for recombinant composition.

**Figure 6.10** The beginnings of Beethoven's sonatas: a) Op. 13 (*Pathétique*). b) Op. 57 (*Appassionata*).

The transition from theme 1 to theme 2 of the SARA-Beethoven shown in figure 6.13 seems more drawn from Mozart's C-minor Fantasy (K. 475; see figure 6.14a) than Beethoven's sonatas. With the hands reversed and the rhythm augmented, these two examples seem quite related. Beethoven was particularly fond of this work by Mozart (also see the discussion on the related K. 457 in figure 1.12 and associated text). In terms of inheritance from Beethoven, the SARA-Beethoven seems derived as an inversion (MATN) of the left hand in the transition back to the recapitulation

*Figure 6.11* An EMI-Beethoven sonata beginning of an Allegro section.

***Figure 6.12*** Beethoven's sonatas: a) Op. 2, no. 1, first movement, mm. 19–30. b) Op. 13 (*Pathétique*), first movement, mm. 11–15.

## 208 EXPERIMENTS IN MUSICAL INTELLIGENCE

**Figure 6.13** An EMI-Beethoven sonata transition and second theme.

**Figure 6.14** a) Mozart, Fantasia in C minor (K. 475), mm. 173–74. b) Beethoven, Piano Sonata, op. 2, no. 1, first movement, mm. 95–104.

in Beethoven's op. 2, no. 1, first movement (see figure 6.14b). Again, the complexity of the various responsible code makes the absolute identification of the sources nearly impossible.

The secondary theme of the machine-composed example (shown in figure 6.13 beginning in measure 60) represents a composite of many different Beethoven themes. Therefore it is difficult, given the various competing processes involved, to determine an explicit inheritance. Figure 6.15 shows two similar examples: the first theme of a sonata and, interestingly, the main theme of a work Beethoven originally wrote as a second movement to his *Waldstein* Sonata, op. 53, but later discarded. This latter theme bears an uncanny resemblance to the second entrance of the theme in figure 6.13 (beginning

**Figure 6.15** Beethoven themes: a) Op. 2, no. 3, first movement, mm. 1–4. b) The beginning of Beethoven's *Andante favori*, WoO57 (1804), mm. 1–8.

in measure 70), especially because it was not in the database at the time of the composition of figure 6.13. Signatures may well be present here, but, with the possibilities of melodic, harmonic, and accompaniment MATN variations, it is quite difficult to discover them. At its best, EMI and SARA produce music with transparent seams between recombinant and signature elements. The closing theme of the SARA-Beethoven movement (shown in figure 6.16) appears to be an amalgam-signature of various of Beethoven's ending gestures, three of which are shown in figure 6.17 and all of which were in the database at the time of composition.

# AN APPLICATION-LEVEL PROGRAM AND SAMPLE OUTPUT 211

*Figure 6.16* EMI-Beethoven closing theme.

This SARA-Beethoven movement has moments of obvious sources (almost quotations). However, it has occasion to be spontaneous and ingenious in its interweaving of inherited materials. In many instances, such combinations of inheritance and spontaneity produce music of worth beyond that of simple interest. This kind of composition occurs as the result of program interplay and, most important, balance between the various constituent parts of the program, with none taking precedence. The music simply sounds in the style of the original and has no single recognizable source.

As previously mentioned, counterpoint is considered a special case by EMI and SARA. Contrapuntal forms cannot be inherited in quite the same way as homophonic forms. Inventions, for example, require code that alternatively exchanges voices and ranges such that an invention-like texture and imitation occurs. Figure 6.18 shows the beginning of an invention created by SARA using a Mozart sonata database, chosen to underscore the invention form rather than the more likely baroque idiom that typifies this form's appearance. One or more of the voices in the databases have been removed by the program, the resulting two voices demonstrating the simple but effective imitating aspects of the invention form.

Forms like the fugue may be achieved texturally by using ATNs for connections in all voices. For example, using a multi-fugue database and employing all channels to select exact destination notes results in a work with the same additive form as the fugues in the database. Rests will seek rests, notes will seek exact next notes, and so on. However, the resemblance stops at this point: the actual entering

212  EXPERIMENTS IN MUSICAL INTELLIGENCE

**Figure 6.17** Beethoven sonatas: a) Op. 13, last movement, mm. 205–210. b) Op. 7, third movement, mm. 139–49. c) Op. 2, no. 1, last movement, mm. 193–96.

**Figure 6.18** Beginning of a SARA-created invention using a Mozart database.

voices will not imitate one another. Creating a fugue proper is a special case requiring additional code.

EMI and SARA use a simple model to create fugues and other canonic forms. Composing music in these forms is traditionally difficult, partly because the rules require certain types of structured additive counterpoint, especially in their expositions. Both EMI and SARA create fugues by using subtractive counterpoint. The thickest texture is written first, then voices are subtracted gradually to create the additive texture when performed in reverse order. The concept is simple: if the thickest multivoiced texture created by a traditional ATN recombinancy is successful, then the program assumes, true or not, that the various thinner-voiced textures will also work. Thus, the code for creating fugues first composes a thick fugue-textured phrase, copies that phrase with one less voice, and then places this phrase before its former version. This process is repeated until a single voice is left. Thus, the fugue exposition, at least, is composed right to left so that the last material created is the first heard. Thus, with little added code, the program can create simple fugue expositions. Obviously, composing more intricate fugue expositions (including appropriate tonal and real answers, etc.) as well as fugue developments, strettos, and recapitulations lies beyond the scope of the SARA program as now constituted. However, EMI has composed substantial fugues using this type of process (see Cope 1991a, figure 5.38) as a fundamental principle.

SARA code can also be user-extended in a number of meaningful ways. First, adding databases can not only provide access to different composers and styles but also enhance those already provided with the application. Creating databases requires some skill and determination but can produce quite successful results. This process is an integral part of EMI and SARA, and users are encouraged to read the manual on the accompanying CD-ROM for instructions on how to select, prepare, enter, and save new databases. These new databases could, if so desired, further extend the program in areas such as mode and tempo recognition (see chapter 4) and further explore the program's potential for texture development (most of the included databases use only two or three of the sixteen MIDI channels available). Second, users with a general knowledge of LISP and CLOS can add variables to the pattern matcher by following the descriptions provided in chapter 3 or by defining their own. Third, work with honing and mixing databases can provide enlightening new perspectives on both musical style and computer composition. Finally, nurturing new styles by feeding new compositions back into the databases from which they were generated can be useful and fascinating. This *generational* composition has produced both useful and intriguing new compositional styles. SARA could be further expanded to include more complex forms described by either the program or the program's users.

Chapter 6 of *Computers and Musical Style* (Cope 1991a) discusses the mixing of musical styles (see especially figures 6.4 and 6.5 of that volume). Such mixing is possible with SARA by creating databases consisting of music from different styles. The results are sometimes useful but more often humorous. Because of the measure-level recombinancy in SARA, mixing styles tends to be terraced, and the shifts between the music of one style and another are usually clear. Using duple- and triple-measure databases emphasizes this fractured result. However, smoother compositions in which shifts of style are less focused can be created by using mono-measured databases, employing MATN, using variables such as *ties*, and allowing the program to randomly fill leaps and add other embellishments (available with high levels of recombinancy). This can produce interesting blends of styles and even new styles in which recognition of the original databases is difficult if not impossible.

The preface of this book suggests that SARA may be useful for composers, musicologists, and analysts, among others. There are a number of ways in which this may be possible. First, if the user is a programmer in LISP or has access to such a programmer, the SARA source code may be altered, augmented, or used as a model for larger, more sophisticated applications. EMI itself is a good model for just such expansion. Secondly, any one or more of the modules may be used separately to achieve a noncompositional goal. The various stages are stored in different files to make such use easier.

### CD-ROM

The manual for SARA provides important information on how the various application-level functions presented in this chapter connect to the various menus, windows, buttons, and tables of the user interface. Composing with SARA and then calling the variable *history* in the Listener window provides a source log of each composition run and a useful encapsulated view of the SARA compositional process. Loading, observing, and playing EMI files in SARA shows how the output of SARA conforms to that of EMI and, with the exception of EMI's longer forms and more elaborate databases, is a good opportunity to compare the quality of both outputs. ✥

# SEVEN

## Conclusions and the Future

Theorist Edward Cone has remarked, "It has been said that some of the most important scientific discoveries have resulted from taking seriously questions that are usually assumed to be trivial" (Cone 1968, p. 11). I hope this is true because I have steadfastly maintained that my research with EMI has focused on a very few simple ideas. These ideas are signatures (Cope 1991a), often called formulae (or clichés) by others, and the composing process (notably that it is recombination more than creation). These ideas can be seen as trivial, but I see them as significant and have devoted an enormous amount of time attempting to demonstrate their relevance to musical style and to the precepts of composition.

In this chapter, I will describe my attempts to expand the potentials of EMI. This will include a description of a reflexive version of EMI that composes without intervention from users. I will further detail my explorations with EMI beyond the realms of pitch and duration. I will also describe in some detail how EMI can be used effectively without MIDI. I will then attempt to develop some conclusions and deal with some of the controversial aspects of EMI and computer composition in general. Finally, I will speculate on the future of computer music composition, particularly that form of computer composition that strives to imitate either the music or the processes of human composers.

## ■ EXPANDING THE PARAMETERS

One more recent version of EMI incorporates a reflexive pattern matcher that identifies signatures without user input. This heuristic version of EMI requires only that it be loaded with music in a given style but otherwise is self-sufficient. The algorithm in figure 7.1 should serve as a useful outline of this program. The input works (A) are stored in standard database files as described in chapter 2. Instead of phrases, however, works are stored as single megalithic entities with cadences and phrases determined by the program when loading these files. These works are then statistically analyzed (B) for eventual comparison to the program's output to discover whether such output favorably matches the analysis of the program's input. This analysis includes such parameters as repeated notes, occurrence of leaps followed by steps, incidence and types of scales, tessitura of the various parts, and so on. The statistical analysis also initially sets the program's controllers (I and J) by loading the controller source file (K). The settings in this file are default values; "learned" values from previous program evaluations are stored in (L).

The pattern-matching process (C) locates signatures as described in chapter 3. The pattern matcher stores the signatures it discovers in a dictionary (D) that supplies these, along with the analysis of the works, for replication (E). The arrangement of signatures in replicated works is accomplished through the use of an ATN (see chapter 5) that maneuvers signatures and other recombinant material of varying lengths to logical rather than random positions. This positioning depends on factors inherent in the signatures themselves and how well they satisfy certain criteria.

Once created, new works (F) are analyzed statistically (G), and that analysis is compared (H) with the previously completed statistical analysis of the input works (B). If the comparison is successful, then the work is saved in a destination file (M). If the comparison is not successful, then the program's controllers are incrementally altered (I, J) and the program begins again. If a controller reaches a point where continued incrementing has little effect on the statistical analysis of output works, the next controller increases and the former one remains fixed at the level it created the most effect. Successful controller settings are saved for future use (L). The segmented arrows to the files (L) and (M) serve to highlight the fact that compositions and settings are not saved to destination files unless successful comparisons of their statistical analyses have

CONCLUSIONS AND THE FUTURE 219

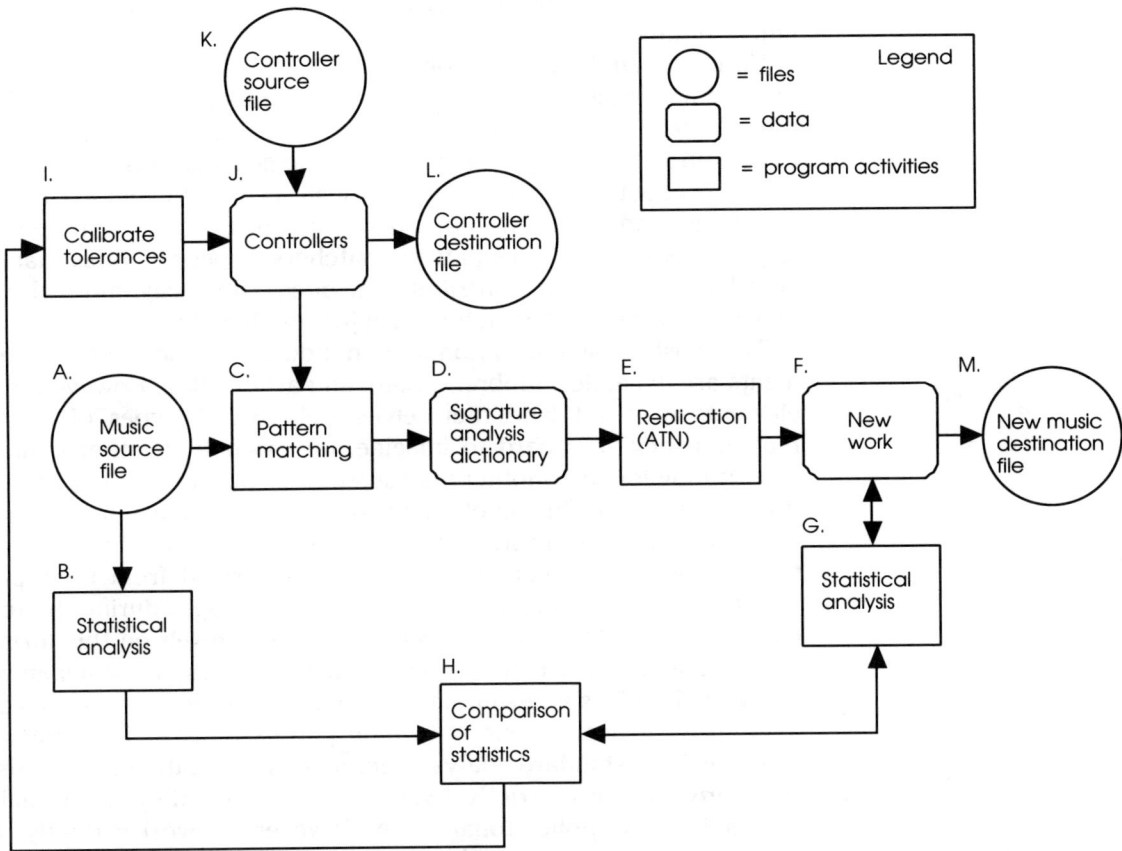

Figure 7.1  A reflexive algorithm for EMI.

occurred. Either the source file (K) or the destination file (L) of the controllers may be initially loaded, depending on whether default or previous altered settings are desired.

This version of EMI has the advantage of operating independently of user biases. As a consequence, the signature dictionary may produce more authentic signatures because the program is not being controlled by a user familiar with the music of the composer under study. It also can provide successful controller settings for pattern matching that can then be honed by users. Problems with this version of EMI include mistakes of cadence identification and key determination as well as problems with the use of idiosyncratic statistical models. At the same time, such a program provides an example of musical heuristics, with the resultant controller settings giving a firsthand demonstration of a self-controlled program learning, however crudely, the parameters of new databases and their inherent musical styles.

Until now, all the work accomplished with EMI has concentrated on pitch, duration, and (to some degree) texture and form. For similarly timbred tonal music (piano sonatas, string quartets, etc.), limiting composition to these parameters seems logical and has proven to be highly productive. However, tonal music of more extended timbral resources, and especially nontonal music of the twentieth century, requires more ubiquitous pattern matchers, especially ones that can correlate many musical attributes at once. Obviously, musical style depends on many other factors than just pitch and duration.

The most conspicuous nonpitch, nonduration, and nontexture elements are dynamics, timbre, rubato, and articulation. However, these elements may not lend themselves well to ATN types of musical recombinancy. It is hard to imagine, for example, another dynamic substituting for "p," another instrument for oboe, or another articulation for staccato. On the other hand, one can imagine, for example, the finding of dynamic signatures. Such signatures could then be protected from recomposition or even be separated from their pitch counterparts and reapplied to appropriate passages during the replication process. More recent EMI research has dwelt on this form of pattern matching. I call the results of such searches *hybrid* signatures.

Figure 7.2 gives an example from Varèse's *Hyperprism*. This work, for nine wind instruments and nine percussionists, does not conform easily to standard analysis techniques. The pitched sections of *Hyperprism* are not strictly twelve tone nor are they functional in even a liberally applied tonal sense. However, the work is tightly constructed with imitative rhythms and timbres on both large and small scales. A pattern matcher that simply searches for pitch and/or rhythmic patterns, although it may find signatures, cannot be as successful in its searches as a matcher more attuned to other elements. A hybrid pattern matcher, one that searches for particular rhythms in a variety of timbral circumstances, will yield more useful results.

Figures 7.3a–c shows a hybrid signature from Edgard Varèse's *Hyperprism* in a variety of guises. In figure 7.3a, the signature has a pitch content of C♯ and D, similar to but not exactly the same as the pitch contents of figures 7.3b and 7.3c. The minor second intervals between the notes provide a kind of logical glue for all three measures. However, single intervals do not suggest realistic signatures. The instrument choice (given as channel information in EMI) and the rhythmic relationships, however, are quite similar. In fact, the percussion parts are almost identical in figures 7.3a and 7.3b and very similar to figure 7.3c. This similarity provides the hybrid pattern

**Figure 7.2** The beginning of Varèse's *Hyperprism*.

© Copyright by G. Ricordi & C., Milan. Reprinted by permission of Hendon Music, Inc., Sole Agent.

**Figure 7.3** Varèse's *Hyperprism*: a) M. 5. b) M. 7. c) M. 66.

matcher, the one that catches this pattern, with enough data to identify these as clear signatures, especially when compared with similar motives from other of Varèse's works. Recognizing and protecting such signatures from recomposition in extended tonal and particularly nontonal music allows EMI to analyze and compose believable music in styles otherwise not easily imitated.

Composing using reflexive and hybrid pattern matchers and with timbre and dynamics has resulted in an EMI opera called *Mozart*. This opera was composed in 1992 and represents an interesting, but not ideal, collaboration between user and machine program. Understanding how the various pattern-matching and compositional elements coalesce in this work requires a description of this opera in some detail.

The libretto of *Mozart* is a rough translation from the original German of numerous letters authored by Wolfgang Amadeus Mozart that I chose and then set to EMI's music in Mozart's style. *Mozart* requires three performers: a vocalist and two shadow players. The stage for *Mozart* is a single platform with various pieces of electronic equipment scattered about. Screens surround the platform with projections of paintings of the characters to whom Mozart writes his letters during the performance. These projections slowly fade from screen to screen at thirty-second to one-minute intervals. The lead character, Mozart, attempts as best he can to direct his attention to these moving images.

The nonvocal music for *Mozart* may be performed by chamber orchestra or by MIDI controlled samplers. In either case, the orchestration should approximate that of one of Mozart's own operas. Both the singer and the accompaniment should closely follow Italian opera performance conventions. Setting the words to the music was particularly difficult in that the usual process for setting text involves the librettist writing the text first and then the composer setting the text to music. This latter process ensures that musical accent and meter will fit the desired poetic accent and meter. However, translating the libretto from German to English while setting the text to existing music was an advantage in that there are obviously many ways to correctly translate one language to another providing a helpful flexibility.

The opera begins in darkness. During the overture, the lights fade in, and two shadowy figures slowly exhume Mozart's body and carry him to the central platform, connecting it to various wires. Finally, these figures inject Mozart with a drug through a large hypodermic needle. As the overture concludes, Mozart, now alive, is the worse for wear. He sits unkempt atop the platform. His eyes are blackened, and dirt blobs hang from his eighteenth-century clothes. He is wired both electronically and as a puppet.

At the beginning of each act, Mozart appears vaguely alert. As he sings his letters and the act progresses, however, his enthusiasm wavers. As each act closes, Mozart weakens, only to be resuscitated by successive applications of the hypodermic needle by the shadow figures. During the finale, Mozart slowly succumbs a final time. As the finale ends, however, the audience hears new music in the style of Mozart never heard by anyone before (EMI has been composing anew in the style of Mozart during each performance). With a last burst of energy, Mozart smiles in such a way that we know he is pleased with this new work. He expires, and the two shadowy figures carry him back to his grave and bury him.

Figure 7.4 gives the opening measures of the adagio introduction of the EMI-Mozart overture and a sample from the allegro that follows. This music is based on databases from the *Don Giovanni* and *The Magic Flute* overtures as well as various phrases from other instrumental works. This EMI overture is the first example of music resulting from efforts to expand research beyond pitch and duration. Although these attempts are not particularly sophisticated, this example does demonstrate texture contouring as well as timbre and dynamic continuity resulting from a combination of heuristic and hybrid pattern matching and ATN. All the instrumental assignments and tempi were also machine produced as the result of recombinancy.

The timbral and dynamic aspects of this EMI-Mozart overture were controlled by the assignment of channels and dynamic values in the music stored in the databases. Each staff of the input orchestral works was stored as a separate channel (position 4 in the note events). In one sense, this process hardly represents a significant characterization of timbre. In another sense, however, as with pitch and duration, whatever salient features of style exist in the assigned parts of the original music will, at least to some extent, be inherited in the recombinant work. This is true, of course, only if proper care has been taken to ensure the survival of connectivity and signatures. In the case of this EMI-Mozart overture, connectivity roughly follows the examples presented in the creation of the various EMI-Bach chorales of chapter 5, and signatures exist as the result of the previously described reflexive pattern matcher.

Tempo inheritance in this EMI-Mozart overture was based solely on database design. In short, only slow Mozart music was used as a database for slow EMI composition and vice versa. Thus, the output music should be true to Mozart's predilections for composing certain styles of music for fast and slow music. Because database design relies on users rather than program control, little progress has been achieved in defining what differences exist between slow

CONCLUSIONS AND THE FUTURE 225

*Figure 7.4* EMI-Mozart *Mozart*, overture:
a) Beginning.

**Figure 7.4** b) Allegro.

CONCLUSIONS AND THE FUTURE    227

**Figure 7.4** continued.

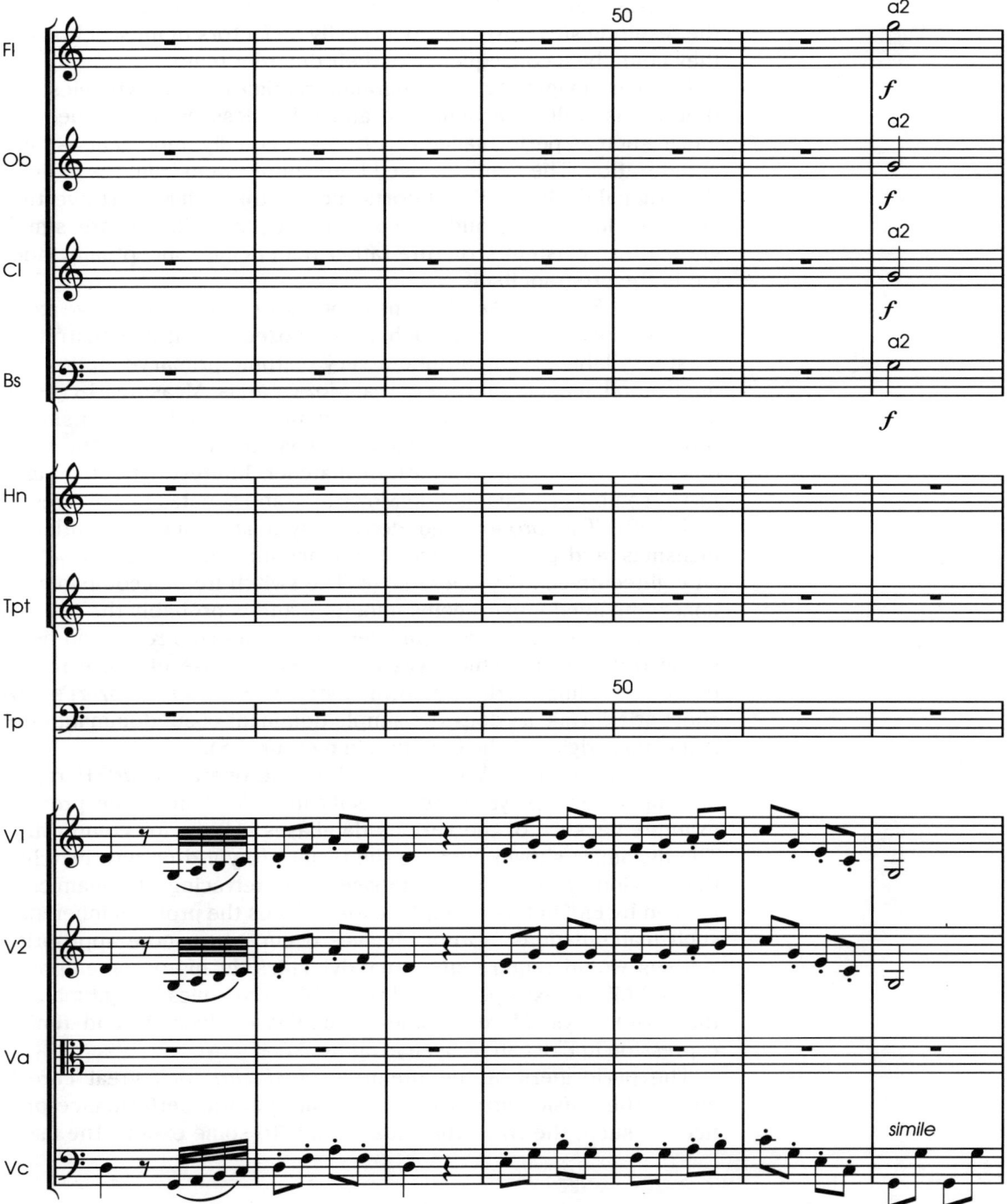

and fast Mozartean music except for the different types of signatures found in each type of music. Pattern matching the various databases can reveal different kinds of tempo signatures. However, the resulting signatures could as easily be factors of music choice as they could be a consequence of their different tempi.

One can imagine future programs treating tempo, dynamics, and timbre—as well as articulation and other less notated aspects of music such as performance practice—as equally important as pitch and duration. The methods used here simply stem from the limits of the original design of EMI. Efforts such as this EMI-Mozart overture, although interesting and to some degree meaningful, are simply grafts on an existent structure rather than being conceptually inherent in the program itself.

Figure 7.5 is from Act 2, Scene 8, of *Mozart*, a representative example of the use of text in a machine-composed aria. It demonstrates a mostly syllabic setting around a very diatonic primary-function harmonization, a common trait of real Mozart arias. Measures 18 (beginning on the fourth beat) and 19 (ending on the third beat) show a probable signature of Mozart's vocal style discovered by the previously described reflexive pattern matcher. Interestingly, this signature resembles those found in Mozart's piano sonatas (see figures 3.1 and 3.20). The pronounced dotted rhythms, lilting sixteenth-note melismas, and predominance of primary functions all contribute to an eighteenth-century opera style. The switch from accompanied to unaccompanied music seems unnatural and is probably the result of ill-applied ATN. The accompaniment here is a piano reduction of the orchestral original, which was necessary because of space restrictions. The simple triparte form matches well with Mozart's own short aria forms, as does the simple dominant-of-subdominant chromaticism (origins of the C natural in measure 18).

Figure 7.6 is from Act 3, Scene 2, of the opera *Mozart*. Here, the accompaniment plays a more significant role than in the previous example because of the various databases chosen for composition. The dynamics shown here are the result of hybrid pattern matching the previously mentioned databases. The terracing of dynamics as applied by EMI in this example tends to focus the problem inherent in such manipulations: abrupt changes occur when more appropriate settings would require smoother dynamics. In more contemporary styles, EMI can extrapolate and recombine dynamics in legitimate (to the style) ways. More complex examples of dynamic and timbral expression in EMI can be seen in figure 7.7.

The performers at the premiere of *Mozart* took great care to inform the music with proper classical operatic performance practice. As such, the trills, the rubato, and (to some extent) the use of

**Figure 7.5** EMI-Mozart *Mozart,* the beginning of act 2, scene 8.

# 230 EXPERIMENTS IN MUSICAL INTELLIGENCE

**Figure 7.5** continued.

**Figure 7.6** EMI-Mozart *Mozart,* act 3, scene 2.

**Figure 7.6** continued.

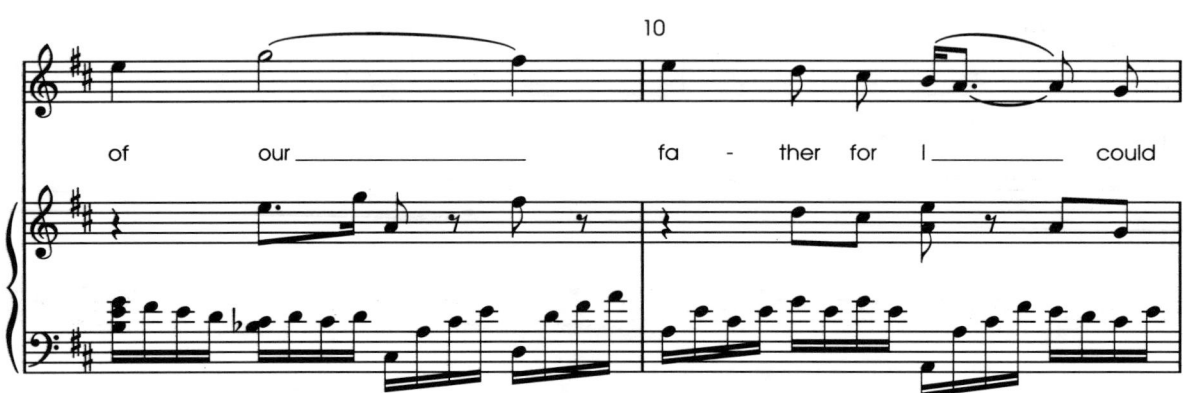

slurred notes are the result of performer scholarship, not inspired machine intelligence. Also, the balance of the accompaniment and vocal parts resulted from many attempts to create an aesthetic proper to the words of the aria as well as to the surrounding context of the opera as a whole.

EMI produced five to ten versions of each aria and recitative for this work. Because the program has no overview of the entire work or other context in which to create, I made the final choices between competing versions on the basis of the following criteria: (1) which followed the style of Mozart best, (2) which served the needs of the opera best, and (3) which were the most interesting aesthetically. Being a composer and being interested in creating a cohesive work rather than simply meeting some abstract stylistic goal, points 2 and 3 tended to influence my choices most.

*Mozart* is the result both of my conception, translation, and database selection and of EMI's reflexive and hybrid pattern matching, ATN, and object-oriented databases. The opera also integrates composition and performance practice. As such, while not the only model of human-machine collaboration, it does represent one logical form. One can imagine a significantly more interactive collaboration involving decision sharing on a more detailed level. However, the performers of the premiere of *Mozart* have provided audiences with a benchmark for future work in this area.

Many other researchers have also engaged in the difficult task of programming computers for musical rather than mechanical performance (Anderson and Kuivila 1991; Johnson 1991; Katayose et al. 1990; Widmer 1993). Accompaniment programs, especially those

**Figure 7.7** a) A portion of the score to the EMI-Cope *Horizons*.

**Figure 7.7** b) A trumpet expanded event. c) A translation table for some of the events in this work.

**b.**

```
(6500 69 6500 7 12 1 103 1 0)
```

**c.**
**TABLE:**

| position: | | | |
|---|---|---|---|
| 6 | 7 | 8 | 9 |
| **meaning:** | | | |
| enevelope | degree | mute | type |
| cresc/dim | 0-127 | 0/1 | st/cup |

using neural nets, have usefully accompanied live performances with appropriate musical nuance and imitative rhythms (Dannenberg 1985; Vercoe 1985). Such programs could serve in conjunction with composition programs to establish more complete machine-composition performance systems, unlike the collaborative approach required by *Mozart*.

## ■ BEYOND MIDI

MIDI offers an excellent interface between music sequencing software programs and connected hardware and software. However, its limitations are notorious. For example, one cannot communicate complex timbral effects for instruments such as muting, pizzicato, harmonics, and so on. Also, it is difficult to describe subtle envelope characterizations (e.g., "aftertouch"). These techniques require the user to select appropriate sounds on a synthesizer or sampler and (possibly) control these timbral aspects on those instruments. Because I often include very complex scoring details in my own music and because I wish EMI to use this information for its compositions in my style, I use a special expanded event form for encoding my music and then translate the results to standard notation rather than using MIDI.

Figure 7.7a shows five measures of *Horizons* for chamber orchestra. This composition was completed by EMI in 1994 and then translated directly to music notation without the aid of any MIDI devices. Note the controlled use of vibrato in the strings and the use of various mutes in the brass as well as the dynamic shaping of the notes. All these effects were stored in databases and utilized during the compositional process by employing the expanded event shown in figure 7.7b. This event includes not only the five-part information (start time, pitch, duration, channel, and dynamic) of a standard EMI event but also envelope, degree of dynamic change, mute, and type of mute information. These latter entries are keyed to tables (see figure 7.7c) of appropriate data that, in turn, are often keyed to other tables. Because this expanded information is nonstandard, it could be keyed to anything (i.e., tables of detailed microtonal information, etc.). Thus, orchestration can become an integral part of the EMI compositional approach, and, although often not currently useful as grist for pattern matching, this additional information can develop important connectivity for the appropriate levels of ATN.

*Horizons* is a work in three sections that follows the concept that no decipherable phrase delineation exists beyond the section level. There is also little perceptible metric feel, as if the music were virtually without barlines. This effect, almost antithetical to EMI, was accomplished by (1) using phrases of extended length as databases, (2) setting the phrase length to match the section length (i.e., a work length of three phrases), and (3) varying the measure length of stored measures using a default "mono" classification, thereby avoiding a metric "feel" and the rhyming quality of metered music. Because extensive ATN between all sixteen voices and ties often obliterates the connections between recombined musical segments, the actual segmentation cannot be discovered except by painstaking comparison between output and the original databases. The barlines here aid performance rather than indicate metric length in the database. The results of these processes makes *Horizons* sound very free in performance. There is no sense of reconstruction or recombination. Even at the two internal cadences, the music flows freely, without interruption.

Using the expanded event descriptions, avoiding MIDI, and using the metric blurring described above has produced a work reflective of what I would call my mature compositional style (unlike, say, *Vacuum Genesis* as described in *Computers and Musical Style* [Cope 1991a], figures 6.7 and 6.8). Taking advantage of the open architecture of both the EMI program and the manner in which EMI databases are constructed allows for better replications of twentieth-century musical styles. This is accomplished without detracting from EMI's ability to compose music in more classically oriented styles.

# ■ CONCLUSIONS

As with most things computational, algorithmic composition continues to receive its share of controversy, part of which evolves from poor output from programs created more for reasons of curiosity than musical expression. Certainly, computer composition has had plenty of examples of poor output. Yet, even when the output is interesting, musical, and/or insightful (as is occasionally the case with EMI), there are still few venues for performance/recording, and there often is significant controversy. When performances and recordings do come about, critics seem quick to discredit output with what often passes as philosophical rationale:

> The question is, is it even theoretically possible for a computer program, no matter how sophisticated, to produce good Mozart? I claim that it's not. The reason is because Mozart—the real Mozart—was a holistic analog phenomenon, not a reductionist digital phenomenon. The real Mozart had unconscious drives, turbulent flashes of emotion, and a sly sense of humor. (Aikin 1993, p. 25)

I am the first to concede that, on one level at least, machines will never replicate works on the aesthetic level of those that we have come to appreciate as masterworks. This is understandable, as those works were composed by humans for humans; and we *know* this to be true. We also know that this is not true in the case of machine composition, and that fact alone prohibits many from believing that machine composition can achieve an equal footing. On this level, regardless of how good a replication is, it cannot, a priori, be as good as the great works of tradition.

On a deeper level, however, such concessions provide few insights and may even confuse our real sensibilities. As I stated earlier in this book, computers do not compose, they *perform* programs. These programs are written by humans. Whatever intelligence EMI possesses, whatever abilities it has to compose and analyze, it has only because of my labors. Critics seem somehow oblivious to this by virtue of the intervening hardware. Let us be clear: computers add and subtract, and criticisms of algorithmic and computational composition are criticisms of the human programmers of those machines and not the machines themselves.

Yet, authorship of machine-created compositions is complicated and nontrivial to many:

> Who is the composer of a Bach-like invention produced by EMI? Obviously this is not exactly the work of Bach nor entirely of the computer nor especially of Cope. There is some essence of Bach that is perhaps equivalent to the essence of orange in orange-blossom honey—very pervasive but not always clearly discernible. The honey does not look or taste very much like an orange, but it looks and tastes even less like a bee, and we are happy enough to consider it an entity of its own kind. Although computer processing produces an EMI work, the result is hardly the consequence of a purely mechanical process, since it requires data segmented by Cope and algorithms devised and adapted to a particular task by him. (Selfridge-Field 1992, p. 543)

Authorship of a *Musikalisches Würfelspiel* (discussed in chapter 1) seems clear. Composers who deliberately write disconnected measures of music for the express purpose of having them selected according to some quasi-random process and then reconnected in numerous different ways are still the composers of all the resulting works no matter how staggering their number happens to be. This is also true of any EMI output that I perpetrate on my own music, as in the case of *Vacuum Genesis* (see Cope 1991) and *Horizons* (see figure 7.7). But this is not so clearly the case with the EMI-Bach, -Mozart, -Rachmaninoff, -Beethoven, -Schumann, and so on found in this volume. This music was forged from music not intended to be a *Musikalisches Würfelspiel* by a program I devised for this purpose. The original composers of the works used by the program are not the composers of these new works. I am not the composer of these works, at least not directly. To many, the ultimate responsibility lies with EMI, the entity that places this new music once removed from either the composers of the music or the creator of the program. In the final analysis, however, I am the one responsible for EMI, responsible for the database input into EMI, and responsible for the aesthetic selection of works from EMI's output. The operational word here, "responsible" (not "composer of"), represents a distinction that, although subtle, portrays the actuality.

To someone in the position of having spent over twenty percent of his life devoted to the enterprise of writing code for, and words about, algorithmic composition, I find such discussions curious. There is an almost nonchalant manner in which EMI is considered an entity unto itself—capable of being challenged as a machine entity. In the final analysis, however, as I mentioned in chapter 1, computers are not our rivals but our slaves. EMI acts as a "tool" in much the same manner that an instrument does during musical improvisation. Furthermore, many computer programs (such as EMI and SARA) use human-composed data as an integral part of their composing processes.

Beyond the fact that I created the EMI program, my own aesthetics are very much a factor in the choices of EMI output used in publication and recording. In many ways, it seems no less creative for expression to assert itself through this art of selection than through the art of creation. In fact, I think that *choosing well* is in many ways as hard as *composing well*, although clearly the number of decisions one must make compositionally far exceed decisions of selectivity. At the same time, winnowing out potentially great works from the thousands that can be almost instantly created by a computer program can be an incredibly difficult process.

Interestingly, when the output from a computer program is deemed good—so good that even informed critics acknowledge it—credit is often given to performers rather than the programmer. Although it is true that a good performance can greatly enhance the perceived quality of a work, especially when combined with the appropriate performance practice, good performances cannot save weak or unmusical works. Music is great because the proportions of that music match those proportions we deem artistically genuine. Whether those proportions exist because a human or a machine created or performed them is irrelevant.

There are some that argue that creating new music in a given composer's style, whether by computer or by human hand, tends to cheapen the value of the original music. This argument is strengthened if such imitations are very good and even more so if the imitations are numerous and popular. I would argue that such imitating often takes place anyway in film scores, popular music, commercials, and so on. In fact, no sooner does a unique work or style appear than it is copied and revised ad nauseam. As can be seen from chapter 1, and from even a cursory study of Mozart's era, Mozart's style was itself a copy of many styles and was then further copied by hundreds of would-be Mozarts. His music has survived these masquerades, and it will most certainly survive the music created by machine programs. Likewise, I think that the world cannot have too much good Mozart (real or digital) and hope that *many* other dead composers could be so resurrected.

I presented one such tangible example of such a resurrection in chapter 5 (pp. 176–182) of *Computers and Musical Style* (Cope 1991a): an EMI movement in the style of Prokofiev. This engaging work so impressed me that I have since orchestrated it for chamber orchestra and made a version for two pianos. Interestingly, it is but one movement of three (the second) completed in 1989 and possibly the least interesting of them in terms of compositional process. The first movement of that sonata, the instigator for creating the Prokofiev database in the first place, is based on the first forty-four measures of Prokofiev's unfinished tenth sonata, which are its initial music in clarified form. Figure 7.8 gives the first seventy-three measures of this work. Completing unfinished works by dead composers is a feat previously accorded only to humans (Mahler's and Beethoven's tenth symphonies are particularly notable examples). Computer programs may now offer extraordinary new potential for such completions.

After initially harmonizing the last few bars of the original Prokofiev (figure 7.8, mm. 1–44), the program repeats the first halves of measures 15 to 17 a major second up in measures 48 to 50 in augmented rhythm. This simple variation surpasses basic recombinancy by collecting a subsection of the original music for development. This is similar to what the program would do if the original music had been its own creation. Without commenting blow by blow on the succeeding material, it should be apparent that the measures extending the original Prokofiev are all based on it as a skeletal structure instead of depending on multiple databases from other of Prokofiev's works. Not that those other databases were not present during machine composition, for they were; rather Prokofiev had involuntarily supplied enough of the new work as to make total dependency unnecessary.

From a humanistic perspective (the perspective most critics of EMI claim they adhere to), one can hardly imagine both musicians and nonmusicians not being at least curious as to how EMI's imaginings of Prokofiev's completion of this movement would sound. Indeed, it could be useful and thought provoking to create a multitude of such possible extensions and compare them with other of Prokofiev's sonatas. At the least, these posthumous projections could provide imaginative appellations for the curious. For many, they might also provide a most sought-after continuation of a Prokofiev legacy, a new work in his style.

EMI and SARA have, in the decade or more since their inception, created hundreds (even thousands in one particular case that will be discussed later in this chapter) of new works in various styles. Beyond the arguments of human versus machine composition, the consequence of such creation seems immediately valuable: it facilitates research into areas such as musical style and pattern recognition and enhances the potential for composer-computer collaborations:

**Figure 7.8** The beginning of the first movement of EMI-Prokofiev Sonata 10.

**Figure 7.8** continued.

242  EXPERIMENTS IN MUSICAL INTELLIGENCE

**Figure 7.8**  continued.

> Many may find that they do not fully agree with the implications of such work: why have a computer attempt something that we can already do much better by ourselves? The answer is that in doing so we discover more about music as a system of the human intellect. (Casey 1993, pp. 1054–55)

Computers have allowed us to make enormous strides in the understanding of musical signatures that lead to yet deeper understanding of musical style. Signatures can differentiate styles and can, for example, identify characteristics of baroque versus classical styles, of German baroque versus Italian baroque, of individual German baroque composers, of Bach versus Handel, and even of early Bach from late Bach.

Such differentiation need not replace broader definitions of style, but it can augment them. It is unproductive to rely solely on generalizations of musical style, as do most analytic approaches, rather than developing strategies for describing specific examples of the signatures that in part define these styles. After all, defining common-practice music merely as a body of chord protocols and general voice-leading rules provides little insight into this music. Furthermore, computer composing programs using such definitions produce little more than correct realizations of those chord protocols and rules: neither good music nor musically good realizations. It is, after all, the exceptions to these chord protocols and rules that often provide insight into the styles of individual composers. Recombinant processes inherit such exceptions, whereas generalized rules prevent them from occurring:

> It cannot be assumed that the mechanical extraction of information such as the frequency of specific notes, phrases, harmonic progressions or rhythms will provide instant clues as to the natures of the creative processes which led to their generation. Whereas there can be little doubt that such repetitive processes of feature extraction can be executed accurately and at high speed by a computer, this justifies neither the method nor the value of the results. (Manning 1993, p. 132)

At the same time, devising and refining programs that attempt replications of diverse musical styles leads one to many useful insights about why, for example, such compositions differ in style, how relatively important the constituent elements that comprise them are, and how complex the temporal and musical mind is that appreciates them. Music theories and, for that matter, the theories of any art form need to rely on processes such as those exemplified in EMI. For, as in the sciences, if one cannot prove that a process works (with replication as one such proof), then that process remains in theory only and unproved theories, no matter how eloquent, have little value. Music theories can benefit from nonspeculative substantiation through computer re-creation, and for some this may be the only realistic way to reveal true substance.

## ■ THE FUTURE

> Turn it on and a concert of original music begins—music never heard before! A series of classical pieces are composed even as they are being played! Fugues, dance suites, chorales and concerti are composed and played on a host of instruments including piano, harpsichord and flute. No two compositions are ever the same, giving the listener an enjoyable infinite musical experience. (CPU Bach 1993, p. 1)

So goes the patter of one current ad for our future music: this an ad for a joystick television CD-ROM player from Panasonic. The advertisers would have us believe that composition is a sleight of hand, a flip of the switch—that the makings of great compositions lie within the grasp of complete novices. One must wonder about the possibilities.

Certainly, no truly inquiring mind can ignore the potential of the digital medium and the staggering potential for computer creativity. It is difficult to imagine, as algorithmic processes become more sophisticated, that our best creative minds will not be drawn to their possibilities, if not for inspiration or craft then at least for the curiosity of their output: "There has never been so powerful an instructor or decision-making tool for helping you determine which methods have promise and which do not" (Jaxitron 1985, p. 2).

Previous to the computer era, composers faced the same kind of blank canvases as painters do. In the future, however, composers may find themselves more like sculptors, already having malleable machine-composed foils to wrestle with as they begin. Whether composers will then be seduced into programming or not will depend on the level of their desire to understand the processes they use. The output of their programs will rely exclusively on the quality of both the programmer and the resultant musical compositions that the programmer's program produces and not, as previously discussed, on any magic, of lack of it, in the machine.

With just such thoughts in mind, I created a program that composed 5,000 works during the first few months of 1992. These included 2,000 multi-movement piano sonatas, 1,500 symphonies, 1,000 string quartets, and 500 assorted preludes and inventions for various solo instruments. The reason for creating this program was to enhance my opportunities to examine style formation as well as to provide works that I could "sculpt" as I desired. Under these circumstances, one can observe how style changes over time, how it becomes codified, and what kinds of anomalies create significant stylistic changes. This program uses databases constructed of chorale-like homophony from three of Stravinsky's works: the third piece of the Three Pieces for String Quartet of 1913, a homorhythmic chorale section from the 1947 version of the Symphony of Wind Instruments, and the final chorale passage from the Symphony in C of 1940. The style of these passages consists of repeated chords varied in duration, texture, and metric placement. I chose these passages because they have served to inspire my own work yet seem separate enough from it to allow objective perception of style and style development.

This program initially creates a small body of music and analyzes that music for basic chord types, protocols, voice leading, ATN, and so on. The program pattern matches the newly created works for signatures and places them in dictionaries for further generations of music. The program then creates another body of works that "gently" incorporates its analysis of past works. This "gentle incorporation" means that rules are not applied strictly but only when the opportunity exists. These signatures and the previously mentioned analysis are saved for study and comparison with other such data saved in chronological order. The program then creates new bodies of works, uses them in turn as databases, and incorporates ever increasing robustness in its application of signatures and analysis as constraints until they become the norm. Anomalies occur only when a constraint cannot be followed, in which case a previous, less stringent version of that constraint is applied until some earlier version applies successfully. This process follows basic inductance procedures that are similar to those used in many current machine-learning knowledge engineering programs.

Several techniques give the music variety. For example, three types of scales were allowed to exist between various notes in each voice. These included chromatic, octatonic, and whole tone—the three found most often in the analyzed Stravinsky and my own work. The number of voices present at any given time was random but generally consistent by phrase. A certain element of octavization (projecting a voice upward or downward by one octave) was also present to introduce various inversions for variety. Also, melody and voice leading followed principally stepwise motion.

The results have proven to be interesting and consistent. Figure 7.9 gives an example of the beginning of one of these works: *Sonata 293*. Here, the influence of the simple chorale-like database is pronounced, and the harmonies show very little sign of development beyond that present in the music from which it was drawn. However, figure 7.10, the beginning of a composition over a thousand works deeper into the output, shows an almost stagnant harmonic rhythm with melodic outbursts in octaves. Figure 7.11, a composition almost two thousand works later in the sequence (with numerous intervening preludes, quartets, and symphonies), has evidence of both the music of figures 7.9 and 7.10 yet a style that is different than either of these preceding works. I was personally so taken with these three randomly chosen examples that I included the works in a slightly varied form in my *Well-Tempered Disklavier* collection of forty-eight preludes and fugues (1992–94).

Creativity of this magnitude is not new, particularly to other arts than music. For example, Raymond Queneau of the collaborative group of writers known as Oulipo, created the book *One Hundred Million Million Poems* (Queneau 1983), which, as its title suggests, allows for the composition of a great number of poems not unlike the works of music created by *Musikalisches Würfelspiel* (see chapter 1).

In the first and last chapters of *Computers and Musical Style* (Cope 1991a), I waxed eloquently, or so I thought, about an EMI workstation. The code presented with this book does not compose on such a workstation, nor does one yet exist. The dream continues of a digital extension of myself that provides music from which I can extract at will. This music would be *in* my style and *of* the nature of my current work. The creation of *The Morning of the World* (Cope 1991, figure 6.12) represented a tactile beginning as *Horizons* represents a major step forward. I hope that the future holds many new compositions, yet unimagined, in which my work will be so jointly procreated that it will be difficult for anyone, least of all myself, to know which part was created by which entity. This is one view of the future: composers irreducibly joined with the tools of technology.

The previously mentioned posthumous completions of works by computer suggest that composers' creativity might extend beyond their lives and that such composers might even program their own databases before their death specifically for posthumous composing. Imagining that composers of our future could sculpt databases instead of individual works is not as far-fetched as one might think. None of this needs to be to the detriment of humanness. In fact, when that humanness fully expands into the extraordinary capabilities of those very tools that humans have created, then we will truly begin to achieve our full potential.

Hans Morovec believes that

> we are in the process of creating a new kind of life. Though utterly novel, this new life form resembles us more than it resembles anything else in

CONCLUSIONS AND THE FUTURE 247

**Figure 7.9** The beginning of EMI Sonata 293.

**Figure 7.10** The beginning of EMI Sonata 1755.

**Figure 7.11**  The beginning of EMI Sonata 3392.

the world. To earn their keep in society, robots are being taught our skills. In the future, as they work among us on an increasingly equal footing, they will acquire our values and goals as well—robot software that causes antisocial behavior, for instance, would soon cease being manufactured. How should we feel about beings that we bring into the world, that are similar to ourselves, that we teach our way of life, that will probably inherit the world when we are gone? I consider them our Children. (Morovec 1992, pp. 51–58)

Let us hope that these children inherit our musical and expressive sensibilities. For, as much as I embrace machine extensions of human endeavor, I cannot imagine a meaningful exchange between Mozart, be it the real analog Mozart or a digital reductionist phenomenon, and a robotic ear. Clearly, however, computers will play an ever increasing role in our future music. Computers will affect every aspect of how we compose, work, and live. There is no question that new algorithmic worlds await both us and our children, robot or not, and that these worlds will reveal startling new music.

I began this book with a discussion of early experiments with musical combinatoriality from the seventeenth and eighteenth centuries. These early experiments often took the form of diversions or games (*Musikalisches Würfelspiel*), and few have taken this work seriously since. It is certainly possible that my own research into twentieth-century recombinancy falls into a similar, soon to be ignored, experiment. However, it is important to note that Charles Babbage's calculating machine remained a novelty for many decades until a few engineers took it seriously and created our present-day computers. Maybe algorithmic composition and recombinancy will enjoy just such a rediscovery as we prepare for the music of the twenty-first century.

# Bibliography

Aikin, Jim. 1993. "Ghost in the Machine." *Keyboard* 19, no. 9 (September): 25–28.

Ames, Charles. 1987. "Automated Composition in Retrospect: 1956–1986." *Leonardo: Journal of the International Society for Science, Technology and the Arts* 20, no. 2: 219–50.

Anderson, David P., and Ron Kuivila. 1991. "Formula: A Programming Language for Expressive Computer Music." *Computer* 24, no. 7 (July): 12–21.

Bach, Carl Philipp Emmanuel. 1757. "Einfall einen doppelten Contrapunct in der Octave von sechs Tacten zu machen ohne die Regeln davon zu wissen." In *Historisch-Kritische Beyträge Aufnahme der Musik,* vol. 3, pt. 1, ed. Friedrich Wilhelm Marpurg. Berlin.

Barlow, Harold, and Sam Morgenstern. 1948. *A Dictionary of Musical Themes.* New York: Crown Publishers.

Bates, Madeleine. 1978. "The Theory and Practice of ATN Grammars." In *Natural Language Communication with Computers,* ed. Leonard Bolc, pp. 191–259. Berlin: Springer-Verlag.

Bezdek, James C. 1981. *Pattern Recognition with Fuzzy Objective Function Algorithms.* New York: Plenum Press.

Bobrow, D. G., et al. 1988. *The Common Lisp Object System Specification.* Technical Document 88-002R of X3j13 (June).

Buxton, William. 1978. *Design Issues in the Foundation of a Computer-Based Tool for Music Composition.* Toronto: Computer Systems Research Group.

Callegari, Antonio. 1802. *L'Art de Composer de la Musique sans en Connaitre les Elémens.* Paris.

Casey, Michael. 1993. Review of *Computers and Musical Style,* by David Cope. *Notes* 49: 1053–55.

Chomsky, Noam. 1965. *Aspects of the Theory of Syntax.* Cambridge: MIT Press.

Christaller, Thomas, and Dieter Metzing, eds. 1979. *Augmented Transition Network—Grammatiken.* Berlin: Einhorn Verlag.

Cone, Edward. 1968. *Musical Form and Musical Performance.* New York: W. W. Norton.

Cooke, Deryck. 1959. *The Language of Music.* New York: Oxford University Press.

Cope, David. 1977. *New Music Composition.* New York: Schirmer Books.

———. 1987. "An Expert System for Computer-Assisted Music Composition." *Computer Music Journal* 11, no. 4: 30–46.

———. 1988. "Music and LISP." *AI Expert* 3, no. 3 (March): 26–34.

———. 1990. "Pattern Matching as an Engine for the Simulation of Musical Style." In *Proceedings of the International Computer Music Conference,* pp. 288–91. San Francisco: Computer Music Association.

———. 1991a. *Computers and Musical Style.* Madison, Wisc.: A-R Editions.

———. 1991b. "Recombinant Music." *Computer* 24, no. 7 (July): 22–28.

———. 1992a. "Algorithmic Composition [re]Defined." In *Proceedings of the International Computer Music Conference,* pp. 23–25. San Francisco: Computer Music Association.

———. 1992b. "Computer Modeling of Musical Intelligence in EMI." *Computer Music Journal* 16, no. 2: 69–83.

*CPU Bach.* 1993. Hunt Valley, Md.: Music Prose Software, Inc.

Dannenberg, Roger B. 1985. "An On-Line Algorithm for Real-Time Accompaniment." In *Proceedings of the 1984 International Computer Music Conference,* pp. 193–98. San Francisco: International Computer Music Association.

Delange, Herman-François. N.d. *Le Toton Harmonique on Nouveau Jeu de Hazard.* Liège.

Duisberg, Robert. 1993. "1992 International Computer Music Conference, San Jose, California, 14–18 October 1992: General Remarks." *Computer Music Journal* 17, no. 2: 86–87.

Feil, Arnold. 1955. *Satztechnische Fragen in den Kompositionslehren von F. E. Niedt, J. Riepel und H. Chr. Koch.* Heidelberg: Gehrer & Grosch.

Forte, Allen. 1955. *Contemporary Tone Structures.* New York: Columbia University Teachers College.

Fry, C. 1984. "Flavors Band: A Language for Specifying Musical Style." *Computer Music Journal* 8, no. 4: 2–34.

Gabriel, Richard, Jon L. White, and Daniel G. Bobrow. 1991. "CLOS: Integrating Object-Oriented and Functional Programming." *Communications of the ACM* 34, no. 9 (September): 29–38.

Galeazzi, Francesco. 1791–96. *Elementi teorico-pratici di musica*. Rome.

Gazdar, Gerald, and Chris Mellish. 1989. *Natural Language Processing in LISP: An Introduction to Computational Linguistics*. Menlo Park, Calif.: Addison-Wesley.

Haydn, Joseph. 1793. *Gioco Filarmonico, o sia maniera facile per comporre un infinito numero di minuettie trio anche senza sapere il contrapunto*. Naples.

Helm, E. Eugene. 1966. "Six Random Measures of C. P. E. Bach." *Journal of Music Theory* 10: 138–51.

Hiller, Lejaren. 1970. "Music Composed with Computers: A Historical Survey." In *The Computer and Music*, ed. H. Lincoln. Ithaca, N.Y.: Cornell University Press.

———, and Leonard Isaacson. 1959. *Experimental Music*. New York: McGraw-Hill.

Hindemith, Paul. 1939. *The Craft of Musical Composition*. London: Schott.

Hoegi, Piere. 1770. *A Tabular System Whereby the Art of Composing Minuets Is made so Easy that any Person, without the least knowledge of Musick, may compose ten thousand, all different, and in the most Pleasing and Correct Manner*. London.

Huron, David. 1993. "The Humdrum Toolkit: Research Software for Music Scholars." Paper read at the joint meeting of the American Musicological Society and the Society for Music Theory, Montréal, November.

Iverson, Eric, and Roger Hartley. 1990. "Metabolizing Music." In *Proceedings of the 1990 International Computer Music Conference,* pp. 298–301. San Francisco: International Computer Music Association.

Janzen, Thomas. 1992. "Algorhythms: Real-Time Algorithmic Composition for a Microcomputer." In *Computer-Generated Music,* ed. Denis Baggi, pp. 199–209. Los Alamitos, Calif.: IEEE Computer Society Press.

Jaxitron. 1985. *Cybernetic Music*. Blue Ridge Summit, Pa.: TAB Books, Inc.

Johnson, Margaret L. 1991. "Toward an Expert System for Expressive Musical Performance." *Computer* 24, no. 7 (July): 30–34.

Katayose, H., T. Fukuoka, K. Takami, and S. Inokuchi. 1990. "Expression Extraction in Virtuoso Music Performances." In *Proceedings of the 10th International Conference on Pattern Recognition,* pp. 780–84. Atlantic City, N.J.

Keene, Sonya. 1989. *Object-Oriented Programming in COMMON LISP: A Programmer's Guide to CLOS*. New York: Addison-Wesley.

Kircher, Athanasius. 1650. *Musurgia Universalis*. Rome. Reprint, New York: Georg Olms.

Kirnberger, Johann Philipp. 1757. *Der allezeit fertige Polonoisen- und Menuettenkomponist.* Berlin.

———. 1783. *Methode Sonaten aus'm Ermel zu schüddeln.* Berlin.

Koch, Heinrich Christoph. 1782–93. *Versuch einer Anleitung zur Composition.* Rudolstadt and Leipzig.

Krasner, Glenn. 1980. "Machine Tongues VIII: The Design of a Smalltalk Music System." *Computer Music Journal* 4, no. 4: 4–14.

Lawless, Jo A., and Molly M. Miller. 1991. *Understanding CLOS: The COMMON LISP Object System.* Bedford, Mass.: Digital Press.

Lester, Joel. 1992. *Compositional Theory in the Eighteenth Century.* Cambridge: Harvard University Press.

Lidov, David, and A. James Gabura. 1973. "A Melody Writing Algorithm Using a Formal Language Model." *Computer Studies in the Humanities and Verbal Behavior* 4: 138–48.

Mahling, A. 1991. "How to Feed Musical Gestures into Compositions." In *Proceedings of the 1991 International Computer Music Conference.* San Francisco: International Computer Music Association.

Manning, Peter. 1993. Review of *Computers and Musical Style,* by David Cope. *Music and Letters* 74: 132–34.

Meyer, Leonard. 1956. *Emotion and Meaning in Music.* Chicago: University of Chicago Press.

———. 1989. *Style and Music.* Philadelphia: University of Pennsylvania Press.

Morovec, Hans. 1992. "Letter from Moravec to Penrose." In *Thinking Robots, an Aware Internet, and Cyberpunk Librarians,* ed. R. Bruce Miller and Milton T. Wolf. Chicago: Library and Information Technology Association.

Mozart, Wolfgang Amadeus. 1793. *Anleitung zum Componiren von Walzern so viele man will vermittlest zweier Würfel ohne etwas von der Musik oder Composition zu verstehen.* Berlin.

———. 1793. *Musikalisches Würfelspiel.* N.p. Reprint, Brighton, Mass.: Carousel Publishing Corporation, 1973.

Newman, William S. 1961. "Kirnberger's Method for Tossing Off Sonatas." *Musical Quarterly* 47: 517–25.

Plantinga, Leon. 1977. *Clementi, His Life and Music.* London: Oxford University Press.

Pope, Stephen Travis. 1991. "Introduction to MODE: The Musical Object Development Environment." In *The Well-Tempered Object: Musical Applications of Object-Oriented Software Technology,* ed. Stephen Travis Pope, pp. 83–106. Cambridge: MIT Press.

Printz, Wolfgang Caspar. 1696. *Phrynis Mytilenaeus oder der Satyrischer Componist.* Dresden.

Queneau, Raymond. 1983. *One Hundred Million Million Poems.* Translated by John Crombie. Paris: Kickshaws.

Rameau, Jean-Philippe. 1722. *Traité de 'harmonie.* Paris. Translated by Philip Gossett. New York: Dover, 1971.

Ratner, Leonard. 1970. "Ars Combinatoria Chance and Choice in Eighteenth-Century Music." In *Studies in Eighteenth Century Music Essays Presented to Karl Geiringer on the Occasion of his 70th Birthday,* ed. H. C. Robbins Landon. New York: Oxford University Press.

Ricci, Pasquale. N.d. *Au plus Heureaux jeux Harmoniques pour Composer des Minuets ou des Contredances au sort d'un dex.* N.p.

Riepel, Joseph. 1755. *Grundregeln zur Tonordunung insgemein.* Frankfurt.

———. 1757. *Gründliche Erklärung der Tonordnung insbesondere.* Frankfurt.

Roads, Curtis. 1984. "An Overview of Music Representations." In *Musical Grammars and Computer Analysis,* ed. M. Baroni and L. Callegari, pp. 7–37. Florence: Musicologia A Cura Della Società Italiana de Musicologia.

Rodet, Xavier, and Pierre Cointe. 1984. "FORMES: Composition and Scheduling of Processes." *Computer Music Journal* 8, no. 3: 32–50.

Rowe, Robert. 1993. *Interactive Music Systems: Machine Listening and Composing.* Cambridge: MIT Press.

Schenker, Heinrich. 1935. *Der freie Satz (Free Composition).* Vienna: Universal Edition. Translated and edited by Ernest Oster. New York: Longman, 1979.

Selfridge-Field, Eleanor. 1992. Review of *Computers and Musical Style,* by David Cope. *Journal of the American Musicological Society* 45: 535–45.

Simon, Herbert, and Kenneth Kotovsky. 1963. "Human Acquisition of Concepts for Sequential Patterns." *Psychological Review* 70: 534–46.

———, and Richard K. Sumner. 1968. "Pattern in Music." In *Formal Representation of Human Judgment,* ed. B. Kleinmuntz, pp. 219–50. New York: John Wiley and Sons.

Slawson, Wayne. 1985. *Sound Color.* Berkeley: University of California Press.

Stadler, Maximilian. 1780. *Table Pour Composer des Menuets et des Trios a l'infinie; avec deux Dez a Jouer.* Paris.

Steele, Guy. 1990. *Common LISP: The Language.* Bedford, Mass.: Digital Press.

Taubert, Karl Heinz. 1988. *Das Menuett.* Zürich: Verlag Musikhaus Pan AG. Originally published in Paris, 1786.

Vercoe, Barry. 1985. "The Synthetic Performer in the Context of Live Performance." In *Proceedings of the 1984 International Computer Music Conference,* pp. 199–200. San Francisco: International Computer Music Association.

Watson, Mark. 1991. *Common LISP Modules: Artificial Intelligence in the Era of Neural Networks and Chaos Theory.* Berlin: Springer-Verlag.

Webster, Noah. 1828. *An American Dictionary of the English Language.* New York: S. Converse.

Weizenbaum, Joseph. 1966. "ELIZA—a Computer Program for the Study of Natural Language Communication between Man and Machine." *Communications of the ACM* 9: 36–45.

Widmer, Gerhard. 1993. "Understanding and Learning Musical Expression." In *Proceedings of the 1993 International Computer Music Conference,* pp. 268–75. San Francisco: International Computer Music Association.

Winograd, Terry. 1968. "Linguistics and the Computer Analysis of Tonal Harmony." *Journal of Music Theory* 12: 2–49.

———. 1972. *Understanding Natural Language.* New York: Academic Press.

Winsor, Phil. 1987. *Computer-Assisted Music Composition.* Princeton, N.J.: Petrocelli Books.

Woods, William. 1970. "Transition Network Grammars for Natural Language Analysis." *Communications of the ACM* 13: 591–606.

Xenakis, Iannis. 1971. *Formalized Music.* Bloomington: Indiana University Press.

# Index

## A

about-window, 139
:accessor keyword. *See* keywords
add-the-matches. *See* SARA functions
after-methods, 139
Aikin, Jim, 236
Alberti bass, 37, 46, 55, 134
algorithmic composing programs, 23, 236–37
    Compass, 36
    Cypher, 35–36
    EMI, 25–27, 36
    Metamuse, 36
    SARA, 25–26, 36
*allowance*. *See* EMI variables
Ames, Charles, 23
American Association for Artificial Intelligence (AAAI), 82
*amount-off*. *See* SARA variables
*analysis-lexicon*. *See* SARA variables
analysis, 136
analysis slot. *See* measure object slots
analyze. *See* SARA functions
Anderson, David P., 25, 232
antecedent, 30. *See also* SPEAC
around-methods, 139
*ars combinatoria*, 1–2. *See also Musikalisches Würfelspiel*
ATN. *See* augmented transition networks
augmented transition networks (ATN), 40–48, 151–87
    accompaniments and, 31, 55, 76, 134, 184, 210, 228, 232
    defined, 40, 45
    harmony and, 46, 48, 73, 175, 210
    pattern matching and, 26, 136, 151, 168, 189, 191, 197, 218–20, 245
    signatures and, 26, 40, 46, 48, 109, 151, 168, 175, 187, 224, 245

voice-leading and, 48, 166–69, 177, 245
autocatalytic theory, 36
automated music, 23

## B

Babbage, Charles, 123–24, 249
Bach, C. P. E., 26
    *Einfall einen doppelten Contrapunct in der Octave von sechs Tacten zu machen ohne die Regeln davon zu wissen*, 3–7
    *Musikalisches Würfelspiel* and, ix
Bach, J. S., 12, 14, 243
    analysis of the musical style of, 166–70
    Cantata no. 67, 18
    Chorale no. 40, 166–67
    Chorale no. 140, 173, 176
    Chorale no. 241, 176
    chorale style and, 166–69, 171, 174, 177
    Invention No. 5 (BWV 776), 144, 147, 148
    Invention No. 15 (BWV 786), 144, 147
    inventions in the style of, 25, 48–52, 144
    St. Mathew Passion, 18
background, 66, 67, 69. *See also* Schenker, Heinrich
Barlow, Harold, 12
Bartók, Béla, 67
    Fourth String Quartet, 67
Bates, Madeleine, 151
Beethoven, Ludwig van, 239
    motives of, 201, 209
    Andante favori, 210
    Piano Sonata, op. 2, no. 1, 16, 20–21, 204, 207, 209, 212
    Piano Sonata, op. 2, no. 3, 20–21, 210
    Piano Sonata, op. 10, no. 2, 20–21
    Piano Sonata, op. 13 (Pathétique), 14, 15, 19, 20, 22, 201, 204, 205, 207, 212

    Piano Sonata op. 53 (Waldstein), 209
    Piano Sonata op. 57 (Appassionata), 201, 205
    Sonata, op. 7, 212
    Symphony no. 5, 86–88
before-methods, 139
Bezdek, James C., 33, 34
Bobrow, Daniel G., 124, 130
Brulé, 17, *Cil qui d'Amors*, 17
Buxton, William, 23
Byrd, William, 18
    O Lord my God, 18

## C

cadence-lexicon, 137, 140
cadence lexicon slots
    full-cadence-list, 137
    half-cadence-list, 137
*cadence-match*. *See* SARA variables
Callegari, Antonio, 8
Casey, Michael, 243
CD-ROM accompanying this book, 3, 26, 34, 58, 67, 72, 102, 118, 127, 133, 138, 154, 155, 189, 198, 199, 201, 214
*ceiling-threshold*. *See* EMI variables
challenge-the-matches. *See* SARA functions
choice. *See* create-phrase functions
Chomsky, Noam, 152
choose. *See* create-phrase functions
Chopin, Frédéric, 190
    Mazurka, op. 17, no. 2, 97
    Mazurka, op. 17, no. 4, 88–89, 97
    Nocturne, op. 55, no. 1, 98
    Prelude, op. 28, no. 6, 96
Christaller, Thomas, 151
clarifying, 29, 40, 55, 59–64, 83
classes, 125, 127, 128, 131, 139, 143, 190
Clementi, Muzio, 12–14
    Piano Sonata, op. 24, no. 2, 12–14

Common LISP Object System (CLOS), 26, 124, 128, 129, 131, 133, 139, 214
Compass, 36
compose. *See* SARA functions
computer programs. *See* Compass; CPU Bach; Cypher; ELIZA; EMI; Humdrum Toolkit; MAX; Metamuse; SARA; SHRDLU
Computers and Musical Style, 1, 24, 25, 26, 31, 38, 48, 73, 124, 174, 198, 201, 214, 235, 238, 246
Cone, Edward, 217
consequent, 30. *See also* SPEAC
controllers, 36, 38, 88, 89–118, 197, 218, 219, 220
Cooke, Deryck, 1, 12, 15, 23
counterpoint, 12, 35
  Bach, J. S. and, 48
  EMI and, 198, 211, 213
  SARA and, 69, 198, 211, 213
CPU Bach, 244
create. *See* SARA functions
create-phrase. *See* create-phrase functions
create-phrase functions
  choice, 158, 161
  choose, 161
  create-phrase, 154, 158
  jump, 158, 160
  modifier-phrase, 158, 160
  noun-phrase-object, 157, 159
  noun-phrase-subject, 154, 157, 159
  prepositional-phrase, 157, 160
  reset, 158, 160
create-work. *See* SARA functions
creator slot. *See* phrase object slots
Cypher, 35–36

## D

Dannenberg, 234
database, 57–59, 83, 118, 127, 166, 168, 175
  EMI and, 102, 113

SARA and, 54–59, 83, 104, 119, 120, 136, 137, 138, 140–41, 144, 189
defclass. *See* LISP primitives
define-phrase-class. *See* EMI functions
Delange, E. F., 8
destination slot. *See* measure object slots
des Prez, Josquin, 17
  *Qui velatus est*, 17
*difference*. *See* EMI variables
Duisberg, Robert, 24
duple-function-list slot. *See* lexicon object slots
duple-measure, 128, 131, 134, 135

## E

ELIZA, 41
embellishments, 62, 65, 88. *See also* ornaments
EMI. *See* Experiments in Musical Intelligence
EMI variables,
  *allowance*, 91, 93, 95, 97, 102
  *ceiling-threshold*, 96
  *difference*, 90
  *floor-threshold*, 96
  *i-augmentation*, 95
  *i-diminution*, 95
  *i-fragmentation*, 95
  *i-interpolation*, 95
  *i-inversion*, 93, 95
  *i-order*, 95
  *master-threshold*, 101
  *number-present*, 99
  *p-augmentation*, 93, 97
  *p-diminution*, 93
  *p-fragmentation*, 93
  *p-interpolation*, 93, 97
  *p-inversion*, 93
  *p-order*, 93
  *pattern-size*, 96–97, 99
  *threshold*, 99, 102, 103, 104, 119
  *variants*, 97, 99, 102
EMI functions, 131–35
  define-phrase-class, 131, 134, 135

make-beat-objects, 131, 132
event, 57, 118, 19, 123, 143, 224, 235
Experiments in Musical Intelligence, 1–102, 109–18, 123–27, 131–35, 144, 146, 149, 177–83, 217–49
  ATN and, 19, 26, 40, 45, 48, 73, 109, 127, 136, 138, 151, 162, 174, 175, 177, 181, 183–86, 189, 191, 197, 211, 213, 218, 224, 235
  Bach, J. S., 25, 48–52, 144–49, 237
  Beethoven, Ludwig van, 204–6, 208, 211, 237
  Chopin, Frederic, 141–43
  Cope, David, 25, 233, 237
  Joplin, Scott, 25, 201
  language and, 19, 25
  *Mozart*, 223–32
  Mozart, W. A., 25, 47, 178–79, 181, 205, 210, 213, 237
  objects and, 109, 123–49, 151
  pattern matching and, 25, 26, 28, 36, 37, 40, 45–46, 53, 57, 60, 64, 65, 79–121, 136, 151, 189, 191, 197, 198, 214, 218, 219
  Palestrina, Giovanni, 25
  Prokofiev, Sergei, 238–42
  Rachmaninoff, Sergei, 109–18, 237
  Schumann, Robert, 74–77, 237
  signatures and, 11, 25, 26, 36, 37, 40, 48, 54, 79, 90, 102, 103, 109, 112, 113, 115, 118, 120, 121, 123, 151, 175, 218, 219, 220, 224, 243
  Sonata 293, 247
  Sonata 1755, 247
  Sonata 3392, 248
  statistics and, 218
  Stravinsky, Igor, 25, 245
  Varèse, Edgard and, 220–23
extension, 30. *See also* SPEAC

## F

Feil, Arnold, 10
find-closest. *See* SARA functions

## INDEX

finite state transition networks, 40–45, 151, 152, 154, 162, 164, 165, 169, 171, 193, 197
`first-measures` slot. *See* `incipience lexicon` slots
first-note-list slot. *See* lexicon object slots
first-order pattern matcher, 99, 101
`*floor-threshold*`. *See* EMI variables
foreground, 69. *See also* Schenker, Heinrich
Forte, Allen, 67
Fry, C., 23
FSTN. *See* finite state transition networks
`full-cadence-list`. *See* cadence lexicon slots
function, 70
    computer, 70, 124, 128, 129, 130, 134, 184, 185
    musical, 28–33, 46, 66, 71, 73, 74, 115, 162, 169, 170, 174, 175, 177, 184, 193, 228

### G

Gabriel, Richard, 130
Gabura, A. James, 23
Galeazzi, Francesco, 10, 11
gamelan gong kebyar, 67, 121
Gazdar, Gerald, 44, 154
generational composition, 214
generic functions, 129–30
`get-function`. *See* SARA functions

### H

`half-cadence-list`. *See* cadence lexicon slots
Handel, George Frederick, 14, 243
    *Messiah*, 20
harmonic pattern matching, 98, 99
harmonic progressions, 28, 109, 164, 177
harmony, 20, 28, 31, 33, 35, 37, 46, 48, 67–73, 99, 100, 101, 175, 210. *See also* function, musical, harmonic pattern matching, and harmonic progressions

Haydn, Franz Joseph, 14
    *Musikalisches Würfelspiel* and, 7, 9–10, 38
    Symphony no. 103, 17
hierarchical techniques, 28, 30, 33, 36, 45, 46, 70. *See also* augmented transition networks (ATN); Experiments in Musical Intelligence (EMI); Schenker, Heinrich; SARA; SPEAC; Urlinie; Ursatz
Helm, E. Eugene, 5, 6
Hiller, Lejaren, 23
Hindemith, Paul, 73
`*history*`. *See* SARA variables
Hoegi, Pierre, 8
    *A Tabular System Whereby the Art of Composing Minuets Is Made so Easy that Any Person, without the Least Knowledge of Musick, may Compose Ten Thousand, All Different, and in the Most Pleasing and Correct Manner,* 8
Humdrum Toolkit, 35
Huron, David, 35
hybrid pattern matching, 220–32

### I

`*i-augmentation*`. *See* EMI variables
`*i-diminution*`. *See* EMI variables
`*i-fragmentation*`. *See* EMI variables
`*i-interpolation*`. *See* EMI variables
`*i-inversion*`. *See* EMI variables
`*i-order*`. *See* EMI variables
`incipience-lexicon`, 137, 140
`incipience lexicon` slots
    `first-measures`, 137
incipient, 136, 137, 141
`:initarg` keyword. *See* keywords
`:initform` keyword. *See* keywords
`initialize-instance`. *See* LISP primitives
`insert-music`. *See* SARA functions
instances, 128, 139, 190

`interchange-channels`. *See* SARA functions
interfaces, 191, 196–98
    EMI, 189, 196–98
    SARA, 196–98
`*intervals-off*`. *See* SARA variables
IRCAM, 125
Isaacson, Leonard, 23
Iverson, Eric, 36

### J

Janzen, Thomas, 23
Jaxitron, 144
Johnson, Margaret L., 232
Joplin, Scott, 25, 201–3
`jump`. *See* `create-phrase` functions

### K

Katayose, H., 232
Keene, Sonya, 124
keywords, 134
    `:accessor`, 134
    `:initarg`, 134
    `:initform`, 134
Kircher, Athanasius, 1
    *Musurgia Universalis*, 1, 2
Kirnberger, Johann Philipp, 3
    *Der allezeit fertige Polonoisen- und Menuettencomponist*, 2–3, 4, 11
    *Methode Sonaten aus'm Ermel zu schuddeln*, 12, 13, 26, 45, 199
    *Musikalisches Würfelspiel and*, 7, 10
Koch, Heinrich Christoph, 10
Kotovsky, Kenneth, 34
Krasner, Glenn, 125
Kuivila, Ron, 25, 232

### L

language models for music, 15, 19, 151–54, 162
    augmented transition networks (ATN), 19, 151, 153, 154
    finite state transition networks (FSTN), 151, 152, 154
    natural language processing and, 19, 25, 28, 40, 42–45, 154

recursive transition networks (RTN), 151, 152, 154
`last-chord` slot. *See* `lexicon object` slots 137, 141
Lawless, Jo A., 124, 125
`layer-analysis`. *See* SARA functions
`*layer-tuner*`. *See* SARA variables
Lester, Joel, 11
`lexicon object` slots, 137, 141
   `duple-function-list`, 137
   `first-note-list`, 137
   `last-chord`, 137
   `mono-function-list`, 137
   `triple-function-list`, 137, 141
lexicons, 137, 141, 144, 154, 187
Lidov, David, 23
linear transition networks, 162, 164–165
linear recombinant music, 162, 164, 165
linguistics, 40; NLP and, 40
LISP primitives,
   `defclass`, 128, 134
   `initialize-instance`, 139, 140
   `make-instance`, 128, 132
   `setf`, 141, 154

## M

Mahler, Gustav, 14, 20, 239
Mahling, Andreas, 36
`make-beat-objects`. *See* EMI functions
`make-best-choice`. *See* SARA functions
`make-instance`. *See* LISP primitives
Mannheim rocket, 14
Manning, Peter, 243
markov chain, 169
Marpurg, Friedrich, 6
`*master-threshold*`. *See* EMI variables
`match?` slot. *See* `measure object` slots
`match-the-database-music`. *See* SARA functions
`match-the-databases`. *See* SARA functions
`matching-line-number` slot. *See* `phrase object` slots
MATN. *See* micro augmented transition network
MAX, 35
`measure object` slots
   `analysis`, 136
   `destination`, 136
   `match?`, 136, 191
   `music`, 136
   `measure`, 127–30, 136
`measures` slot. *See* `phrase object` slots
Mellish, Chris, 44, 154
melodic pattern matching, 97, 98, 99, 102
melody, 20, 28, 31, 33, 35, 37, 65–67, 74, 86, 115, 210
Mendelssohn, Felix, 16, 18
   String Quartet, op. 44, no. 2, 16
   Elijah, 18
Metamuse, 36
metaobject protocol, 131
`meter` slot. *See* `phrase object` slots
`*meter*`. *See* SARA variables
methods, 139
Meyer, Leonard, 14, 20, 79
micro augmented transition network (MATN), 175–77, 181, 194, 197, 201, 204, 205, 210
MIDI, 24, 26, 57, 58, 59, 118, 214, 217, 223, 234–35
middleground, 65–67. *See also* Schenker, Heinrich
Miller, Molly M., 25
`mode` slot. *See* `phrase object` slots
`modifier-phrase`. *See* `create-phrase` functions
`mono-function-list` slot. *See* `lexicon object` slots
mono-measure, 137
Morovec, Hans, 246, 248
Mozart, W. A., 12, 14, 25, 28, 37, 40, 81–82, 99, 104, 118, 223, 232, 236, 238, 248
   *ars combinatoria* and, 7
   ATN and, 177
   computer analysis of the style of, 28–29, 40, 46, 104, 118, 232
   Don Giovanni, 224
   Fantasia in C minor, K. 475, 205, 209
   Magic Flute, 14, 224
   *Musikalisches Würfelspiel* and, 7, 38
   Piano Sonata K. 279, 92, 94, 162–163
   Piano Sonata K. 281, 61–63, 92
   Piano Sonata K. 282, 61–63
   Piano Sonata K. 283, 29, 31, 32, 38–39, 94, 105
   Piano Sonata K. 284, 162–63
   Piano Sonata K. 309, 92, 94, 162–163
   Piano Sonata K. 310, 94
   Piano Sonata K. 311, 100
   Piano Sonata K. 330, 29, 31, 32–33, 38–39, 92, 105
   Piano Sonata K. 332, 56, 100
   Piano Sonata K. 333, 92
   Piano Sonata K. 457, 15, 20–21
   Piano Sonata K. 533, 94
   Piano Sonata K. 545, 18, 56, 92, 94, 172–73
   Piano Sonata K. 547a, 105
   String Quartet K. 80, 182–83
   String Quartet K. 155, 180–81, 184
   String Quartet K. 465, 16
   Symphony no. 40, 65–66
multiple inheritance, 131, 132
`music` slot. *See* `measure object` slots
*Musikalisches Würfelspiel*, 2–12, 26, 38, 43, 53, 127, 162, 237, 246, 248
   C. P. E. Bach and, 3–7
   Antonio Callegari and, 8
   E. F. Delange and, 8
   Francesco Galeazzi and, 10, 11
   Joseph Haydn and, 7, 9–10, 38
   Pierre Hoegi and, 8
   Johann Philipp Kirnberger and, 2–3, 4, 7, 11, 12
   Heinrich Christoph Koch and, 10
   Wolfgang Amadeus Mozart and, 7, 38
   Pasquale Ricci and, 8
   Joseph Riepel and, 10

Maximilian Stadler and, 8
my-position. *See* SARA functions

## N

natural language processing, 19, 25, 28, 40, 42–45, 154; ATN and,
Newman, William S., 11, 12
NLP. *See* natural language processing
nonfinite languages, 43–45
nonlinear transition networks, 162, 164
nonlinear recombinant music, 162, 164, 165
noun-phrase-object. *See* create-phrase functions
noun-phrase-subject. *See* create-phrase functions
*number-present*. *See* EMI variables

## O

object orientation (OOPS), vii, 25, 123–31, 168
Ockeghem, Johannes, 17
  Malheur, 17
ornaments, 60, 88. *See also* embellishments
Oulipo, 246

## P

*p-augmentation*. *See* EMI variables
*p-diminution*. *See* EMI variables
*p-fragmentation*. *See* EMI variables
*p-interpolation*. *See* EMI variables
*p-inversion*. *See* EMI variables
*p-order*. *See* EMI variables
Palestrina, Giovanni, 25
Palo Alto Research Center (PARC), 123, 124
parsing, 45, 152, 154
*pattern-size*. *See* SARA variables
*pattern-size*. *See* EMI variables

performance practice, ; integrated with composition, ; quality of music and,
phrase, 127–28, 131, 134, 135, 136, 140, 141, 143, 154
phrase object slots
  creator, 134, 136
  matching-line-number, 190
  measures, 136, 140
  meter, 136
  mode, 136
  tempo, 136
Plantinga, Leon, 12
polymorphic functions, 130
Pope, Stephen Travis, 125
postcept slots, 134
precept slots, 134
preparation, 30. *See also* SPEAC
prepositional-phrase. *See* create-phrase functions
Printz, Wolfgang, 1
  *Phrynis Mytilenaeus oder der Satyrischer Componist*, 2
Prokofiev, Sergei, 238–42
Purcell, Henry,
  Dido and Aeneas, 19

## Q

Queneau, Raymond, 246

## R

Rachmaninoff, Sergei,
  Before My Window, 109, 115
  pattern matching and, 109–18
  Second Suite, op. 17, 109, 111–14, 117
ragas, 121
Rameau, Jean-Philippe, 65
rank-the-matches. *See* SARA functions
Ratner, Leonard, 1, 2, 6–7, 11
real variation, 85, 86, 93
recombinancy, 1, 11, 14, 19, 20, 23–25, 26, 28, 33, 40, 48, 57, 61, 112, 113, 118, 121, 123, 124–25, 137, 144, 151, 162, 184, 185, 213, 217
*recombinancy*. *See* SARA variables
recursive transition networks, 43–44, 151, 152, 154, 162–71

reflexive pattern matching, 218–232
remove-last-chord. *See* SARA functions
reset. *See* create-phrase functions
rhythm, 61, 220, 234
  EMI and, 54, 91, 93, 204, 220
  SARA and, 54, 64, 72, 96, 97, 103
*rhythm*. *See* SARA variables
rhythm?. *See* SARA variables
Ricci, Pasquale, 8
Riepel, Joseph, 10, 11
Roads, Curtis, 23
Rodet, Xavier, 125
Rowe, Robert, 23, 35
RTN. *See* recursive transition networks

## S

Saint-Saens, Camille, 17
  Le rouet d'Omphale, 17
SARA, 19, 23, 25, 26, 35–38, 40, 45, 53–78, 79, 83, 85, 90, 96, 102–3, 104, 109, 118–21, 125, 127, 128, 131, 133–38, 140, 144, 151, 155, 162, 175, 183–86, 189, 190, 191, 193, 197, 198, 199–201, 210, 211, 213, 214, 215, 238, 239
SARA variables
  *amount-off*, 102, 103, 104
  *analysis-lexicon*, 71, 72, 73
  *cadence-match*, 194
  *history*, 194, 215
  *intervals-off*, 102, 103, 104
  *layer-tuner*, 193
  *meter*, 193
  *pattern-size*, 96, 97, 99, 102, 103, 104
  *recombinany*, 199
  *rhythm*, 91, 96
  rhythm?, 103
  *threshold*, 99, 102, 103, 104, 119
SARA functions
  add-the-matches, 119
  analyze, 71–73
  challenge-the-matches, 119, 120

compose, 193, 194
create, 192–93
create-work, 192–93
find-closest, 184
get-function, 71, 72, 73
insert-music, 189, 190
interchange-channels, 194
layer-analysis, 185
make-best-choice, 184, 185, 191, 196
match-the-database-music, 119
match-the-databases, 119
my-position, 184
rank-the-matches, 119
remove-last-chord, 194
schenker-plot, 73, 185, 186
simple-compose, 194–95, 196
splice-cadence-channels, 194
top-level-matcher, 118, 119
translate-to-events, 118–19
translate-ur, 73, 186
translate-urlinie, 73, 185, 186
weight-notes, 71, 72, 73
Schenker, Heinrich, 30, 65, 67, 69, 73, 155
schenker-plot. See SARA functions
Schoenberg, Arnold, 67
  Phantasy for Violin with Piano Accompaniment, 67
Schubert, Franz, 17
  Symphony no. 4, 17
Schumann, Robert, 16, 74, 76–77
  Kinderszenen, 74, 76–77
  String Quartet, op. 41, no. 2, 16
Scriabin, Alexander, 89
second-order pattern matcher, 99, 101
Selfridge-Field, Eleanor, 237
semiotics, 23
  thematic borrowing and, 15, 19
setf. See LISP functions
Shakespeare, William, 154–57
SHRDLU, 42
signature dictionary, 119, 218, 219
  SARA and, 119

signatures, 1, 11, 23, 37, 48, 81–82, 101, 194, 197, 217, 243
  ATN and, 174–75
  Bach, J. S., 25
  Beethoven, Ludwig van, 88, 201
  Chopin, Frederic, 88
  clarifying databases and, 104
  controllers and, 36, 89–90, 93, 103, 104, 118,
  EMI algorithm and, 11, 25, 26, 36, 37, 40, 48, 54, 79, 90, 102, 103, 109, 112, 113, 115, 118, 120, 121, 123, 151, 175, 218, 219, 220, 224, 243
  hybrid, 220, 222–24, 228, 232
  Joplin, Scott, 201
  Mozart, W. A., 25, 46, 81–82, 91–94
  multi-measure, 141
  objects and, 109, 119, 123, 151
  pattern-matching for, 36, 79, 91, 102, 108–9, 120, 121, 151, 168, 198, 218, 245
  Prokofiev, Sergei, 239
  Rachmaninoff, Sergei, 109, 113, 115
  recombinancy and, 26, 40, 123, 187, 191, 210
  reflexive pattern matcher and, 224
  rhythm, 54, 96
  SARA and, 54, 96
  Schumann, Robert, 74–77
  Varèse, Edgard, 220, 223
  Simon, Herbert, 34–35
simple-compose. See SARA functions
Slawson, Wayne, 25
slots, 131–38, 141
SPEAC, 57, 76,
  ATN and, 26, 109, 136, 141, 171, 175, 177, 183–87
  definition of, 30
  hierarchy and, 69
  music and, 26, 125
  musical function and, 31, 32, 73–74, 162, 175, 177, 184
  pattern matching and, 26, 64–65, 99, 109, 136,
  SARA and, 54, 64–65, 68, 73–74, 136–37

splice-cadence-channels. See SARA functions
Stadler, Maximilian, 8
statement, 30. See also SPEAC
statistical analysis, 33, 36, 218–19
  EMI and, 218–19
Steele, Guy, viii
Stein, Gertrude, 42
stochastic probability generators, 23
Stravinsky, Igor, 25, 245
  Petrouchka, 67
structural analysis, 27–33, 53–78
subclasses, 128, 131
Sumner, Richard K., 34–35
superclasses, 128, 131

T
Taubert, Karl Heinz, 7
Tchaikovsky, Peter Ilyich, 19
  Symphony no. 6, 19
tempo slot. See phrase object slots
texture, 184, 220, 245
  clarifying databases and, 61, 62, 214
  contouring, 224
  controllers and, 99
  counterpoint and, 211, 213
  SARA and, 213
  style and, 54
*threshold*. See EMI variables
*threshold*. See SARA variables
Thurstone Letter Series Completion Test, 35
timbre, 25, 54, 200, 220, 224, 234
  channels and, 24, 224
  pattern matching and, 83, 121, 220, 223, 228
  samplers and, 59
  SARA and, 55
tonal variation, 85, 86, 90, 91, 200
top-level-matcher. See SARA functions
transformational grammar, 44, 151–54, 157, 171, 174
transition networks, 40–44, 151–52, 170–72
  augmented (ATN), 40–48, 151–87

finite state (FSTN), 40–45, 151, 152, 154, 162, 164, 165, 169, 171, 193, 197
  linear, 162, 164
  non-linear, 162, 164
  recursive (RTN), 43–44, 151, 152, 154, 162–171
`translate-to-events`. *See* SARA functions
`translate-ur`. *See* SARA functions
`translate-urlinie`. *See* SARA functions
`triple-function-list slot`. *See* `lexicon object slots`
`triple-measure`, 141
Twain, Mark, 154–57

**U**
UNIX, 34, 35
*Urlinie*, 66, 69, 74, 185, 187. *See also* Schenker, Heinrich
*Ursatz*, 69. *See also* Schenker, Heinrich

**V**
Varèse, Edgard, 220–23
  Hyperprism, 220–23
`*variants*`. *See* EMI variables
Vaughan-Williams, Ralph, 18
  Pilgrim's Progress, 18
Vercoe, Barry, 234
Verdi, Giuseppe, 18
  Aida, 18
voice-leading, 36, 48, 76, 175–77, 243, 245

Bach, J. S. and, 166–69
SARA and, 201

**W**
Watson, Mark, 154
weight-notes. *See* SARA functions
Weizenbaum, Joseph, 41
White, Jon L., 130
Widmer, Gerhard, 232
Winograd, Terry, 23, 42
Winsor, Phil, 23
Woods, William, 44, 151

**X**
Xenakis, Iannis, 23